THAI LITERARY TRADITIONS

Edited by

Manas Chitakasem

Produced by

Institute of Thai Studies,
Chulalongkorn University

Chulalongkorn University Press
1995

200.-

Thai literary traditions/edited by Manas Chitakasem

1. Ancients and moderns, Quarrel of
2. Literature, Comparative
3. Thai literature
4. Folk literature, Thai

895.91

ISBN 974-631-175-1

CUP. 425

First Printing : 1995

1,000 Copies

Distributed by the Chulalongkorn University Book Center,
Phyathai Road, Bangkok 10330 , Thailand
Tel. 2183980, 2187000 Fax.2554441

Published by the Chulalongkorn University Printing House
Tel. 2153612, 2153626

Foreword

Thai Literary Traditions is the outcome of the Fifth International Conference on Thai Studies held at the School of Oriental and African Studies, University of London, in July 1992. At the Conference, Thai Literature formed a separate panel where more than twenty papers were presented by scholars from all over the world. It was a convivial gathering and an exchange of ideas and knowledge of a truly international body of experts and scholars working on Thai literature. Fourteen of those papers are represented here in this volume.

The original theme, *Thai Literary Traditions: Classical and Regional Literature of Thailand*, was broadly conceived in order to engage the interest of international scholars who were doing research on a variety of aspects of Thai literature. The panel was also convened to ensure the participation of established scholars from Thailand who pioneered the study of Thai regional and local literatures which had long been neglected and was so little known in the West.

Most of the original papers have been considerably revised and reworked, taking into account subsequent research and the discussions that took place during and after their presentation at the Conference. The success of the "Thai Literature Panel" was due largely to the quality of the discussions contributed by all participants including those whose papers are not represented in this volume. We wish to express our gratitude and appreciation to them all for providing stimulating papers and for their participation. We are especially grateful to our guest discussants, Professor Harald Hundius of Passau University, Dr. David Smyth of SOAS, University of London and Dr. Henry Ginsburg of the British Library, for providing valuable criticism and sharing with us their knowledge of Thai literature.

Many people have assisted in the editorial process as well as in the production of this volume; thanks to them all, especially Rachel Harrison, Peter Koret, Prakong Nimmanahaeminda, Pranee Kullavanich, Jack Corman, River Books and Chulalongkorn University Press.

Manas Chitakasem
February, 1995

Nitaya Masavisut, P.E.N. International Thailand Centre, Bangkok.

Manas Chitakasem, School of Oriental and African Studies, London.

Soren Ivarsson, Nordic Institute of Asian Studies, Copenhagen.

Rachel Harrison, School of Oriental and African Studies, London.

Ruenruthai Sujjapun, Ramkhamhaeng University, Bangkok.

Suvanna Kriengkraipetch, Chulalongkorn University, Bangkok.

Suchitra Chongstitvatana, Chulalongkorn University, Bangkok.

Thomas John Hudak, Arizona State University, Tempe, Arizona.

Cholada Ruengruglikit, Chulalongkorn University, Bangkok.

Priyawat Kuanpoonpol, Harvard University, Cambridge, MA.

Prakong Nimmanahaeminda, Chulalongkorn University, Bangkok.

Suthiwong Pongpaiboon, Institute of Southern Thai Studies, Songkhla.

Dhawat Poonotoke, Ramkhamhaeng University, Bangkok.

Peter Koret, School of Oriental and African Studies, London.

CONTENTS

CONTENTS

KINDLING LITERARY FLAME : THEN AND NOW

Nitaya Masavisut

Earlier this year a seminar on "Literary creation: Past, Present and Future" was held at Thailand's Cultural Centre to celebrate National Artists' Day and to honour Khamsing Srinawk, the 1992 National Artist in literature. The seminar was organized by the Office of National Culture Commission. More than a hundred writers were present. Among them were two National Artists in literature and five recipients of Southeast Asian Write Award. Publishers, editors and literary critics also came in full force. The program started with poetic rendition by Naowarat Phongphaibun, a S.E.A. Write poet, paying homage to the National Artist. Naowarat's moving rendition was followed by a panel discussion on the theme of the seminar. The panelists included two national artists, Acin Pancaphan and Khamsing Srinawk; S.E.A Write Awardees, Atsiri Thammachot and Wanit Carungkit-anan; a well known contemporary writer, Camlo'ng Fangchonlacit, and Niransuk Buncan, a short story writer and editor for *Siam Rat Weekly* magazine. To add variety and colour to the panel a literary scholar and critic, Dr. Kusuma Raksamani, was chosen as the moderator.

The afternoon session was a lecture on "Ways and Means to Promote and Transmit Literary arts to the New Generation" by Suchat Sawatsi, the veteran writer and editor of several literary magazines. The lecture was followed by a lively and long discussion led by "Phailin Rungrat,"[1] a writer and well known critic.

There are several points to be pondered over this unusual literary gathering. Firstly, it was initiated and organized by a government agency. Secondly, all parties concerned in the process of creating and producing literary works, namely writers, publishers, editors as well as literary critics participated in this seminar. It is interesting to note that this gathering not only attracted writers of different schools and generations, but different groups of regional writers, such as writers from the South, Northeast and

---

[1] Pen name of Chamaipho'n Saengkracang.

North, also showed keen interest in the subject and became active participants.

Can it be said that both the government agency and people in the literary circles share the same concern? Perhaps they feel that our literary flame is dimming and it would take concerted efforts on everyone's part to rekindle the flame and make it glow. So the government agency provided the stage and writers were invited to play their parts.

The performance was lively and the atmosphere congenial. Writers freely voiced their opinions and aired their grievances. However, there was a pessimistic undertone that ran throughout the entire seminar. Many writers felt that literary works produced nowadays have been dictated by commercial and consumer demand, and therefore are of rather low quality. The national artist, Khamsing Srinawk, on the other hand, was more concerned about readership and the change in literary medium. He even quoted Dr. Chetana Nagavajra, a highly respected literary scholar and critic as saying, "the novels in Thailand are dead and gone. They are no longer written to be read but to be seen. Perhaps writers have to adapt themselves to this new phenomenon of "visual tradition", and find some other ways to convey their messages to the audience.

In spite of certain pessimistic notes the seminar ended with a high hope that with joint efforts our literary flame can be rekindled and take on a new glow.

KINDLING THE LITERARY FLAME: THEN AND NOW

Actually an attempt to keep the literary flame glowing has always been with us since King Ramkamhaeng's invention of the Thai alphabet. Thai monarchs from Sukhothai, Ayutthaya down to Rattanakosin period have been able to keep the fire burning and pass it on from one generation to another. Their means and motives may be different from those of modern times, but the end results should be the same.

THEN: UNDER THE ABSOLUTE MONARCHS

During Ayutthaya period in the 17th century A.D. King Narai gave his court poet, Si, a ring as a reward for the poem he had newly composed for the king. On his way home through the palace gate he was stopped by the gate-keeper who must have spotted the ring on Si's finger. Out of curiosity the gate-keeper asked:

> Wherefore did you get this ring?
> Lord of the earth, our King , granted it.
> What did you do, prithee, to please him thus?
> A poem for him I composed to deserve this prize.
>
> (Pariyat Thammathada 1967: 45)

Another anecdote was when Si accompanied King Narai on a hunt in the wood. He composed some lines which so pleased His Majesty that he was given the title "Si Prat " on the spot. On his return to the palace he was asked by a prince as to where and how such great honour was bestowed upon him. Si Prat told the prince that the title was given to him because he composed some lines that pleased His Majesty while on a hunt in the wood. Si Prat was immediately ridiculed that the title did not befit him, since his complexion was so dark and dull. The conversation ended with an instantaneous repartee from Si Prat:

> Outside I may be dark and dull,
> But inside I am made of gold.
>
> (Pariyat Thammathada 1967: 32)

Several interesting points can be observed from these two incidents. Apparently it was customary for a court poet to compose for the king, and whenever his composition pleased His Majesty he would be granted a "literary prize." The prize could be anything from a title to a ring. Presumably the king was the sole judge, and the "literary prize" was a personal gift from him. Some of the courtiers may have witnessed the presentation of the "literary prize", and the court poet could easily become the target of "professional jealousy." Except for the gate-keeper, no one outside the court circle was involved. Such was the literary atmosphere when the monarch was patron of the arts. Although it may seem different from what we are familiar with nowadays, it cannot be denied that the basic fuels to keep the literary fire burning were there.

Like their predecessor, King Narai, The Rattanakosin monarchs before the change from absolute to constitutional monarchy were directly involved in artistic creativity. Their courts were often used as arenas for courtiers to display their poetic talents.

King Rama I of Rattanakosin period (1782-1809) firmly believed that literature was the real mark of a country's civilization. Having completed the task of building the new capital city he then turned to literature. In order to salvage the literary masterpieces believed to have been destroyed during the fall of Ayutthaya in 1767 A.D., King Rama I called an assembly of poets which consisted of courtiers and members of the royal family and entrusted them with the task of revising and rewriting the damaged manuscripts. With the exception of the King's own compositions such as *Inao, Dalang* and *Unarut,* the corpus of literary masterpieces written during this reign can be attributed to the collective efforts of a "council of poets" with the king himself as "Chairman". They include the great masterpieces such as the poetic dance-drama *Ramakian* (Ramayana), *Wetsando'n Chadok (Vessantara Jataka),* and the translated works in prose such as *Sam Kok* (Romance of the Three Kingdoms), *Saihan* and *Rachathirat .*

The second king of Rattanakosin, Rama II (1809-1824), seemed to follow his father's footstep in his attempt to restore and conserve the literature of the Ayutthaya period. Some old tales and folk dramas had been rewritten. King Rama II himself rendered new versions of folk dramas *(bot lakho'n no'k)* such as *Sangtho'ng, Krai Tho'ng, Khawi* and *Mani Phichai* for court performances, while Suntho'n Phu, his favourite court poet, retold old tales in his newly invented poetic form.

With the exception of the King's own masterpiece, *Inao,* other literary works of considerable length were composed by a "council of court poets". Each of them would be assigned a section to work on. Preliminary reading of the work was held in court in front of the whole congregation of poets and courtiers. Presiding over the event was none other than the King himself. After the literary presentation the "floor" was open to "comments" and "suggestions". Correction and improvement of the works would be done right then and there. Here it looks as though "literary criticism" was involved in the process of "literary creation". However, this means of literary creation may have produced such great work as *Khun Chang Khun Phaen ,* but it could also create animosity among the "masters" who would feel slighted if their works were publicly criticized.

In order to keep the literary flame glowing King Rama III (1824-1851) took another step forward. In the process of restoring Wat Pho he had commissioned his court poets to select and rewrite traditional compositions, particularly didactic verses, and had them inscribed on the stone panels and columns of the temple. Many of these have served as "standard manuals of prosody" (Chetana 1994: 21-22) for poets of later generations. In addition to literary works on the stone inscription, the third reign also produced a great number of literary masterpieces. Among them were Prince Paramanuchit's *Pathomasompothikatha* and *Lilit Taleng Phai*, Suntho'n Phu's *Nirat* and his narrative poem, *Pra Aphai Mani*, Mo'm Rachothai's *Nirat Lo'ndo'n* and Pra Maha Montri's *Radenlandai*. The last two can be considered as new phenomena since one is probably the first "exotic nirat" to be written and the other is the first poetic composition ever written that dared to parody the masterpiece of a great king.

The literary flame under the royal patronage seems to be perpetually glowing. Literary masterpieces such as *Ramakian, Inao, Khun Chang Khun Phaen, Maha Wetsando'n Chadok, Pra Aphai Mani, Sam Kok* and *Rachathirat* are all products of the first three reigns of the Rattanakosin period when the monarchs were personally involved with literary creativities. However, certain dark areas can be observed in spite of this luminous atmosphere.

In view of the literary activities of the first three reigns of the Rattanakosin period it can be concluded that literary masterpieces of this period were mostly composed by royal commands and by "council of court poets". Critical reading of the compositions was done orally either by the King himself or by members of the council, and can be considered as part of the writing process. Literary activities were very limited since producers and consumers were the same group of people. They were either members of the royal family or courtiers who worked for the King. With the exception of Rama III 's inscriptions at Wat Pho and Suntho'n Phu' s *Phra Aphai Mani*, people outside court circle had very little or no access at all to the great masterpieces. Outstanding poets became the King's favourites and were given rewards of different kinds. Like Si Prat who was given a title and a ring by King Narai for his poetic composition, Suntho'n Phu, as Rama II's favourite, was titled "Khun Suntho'n Wohan ", and was granted a house and a small piece of land. It is also interesting to note that both Si Prat and Suntho'n Phu had been punished by their patrons because of their "misconducts". Si Prat was exiled while Suntho'n Phu was imprisoned, but they were both recalled to the royal courts when their patrons needed help with the new compositions. In this case Suntho'n Phu was fortunate enough to be set free, but with Si Prat it was too late. He was executed by his "enemy" before his patron could rescue him.

The next four reigns before the revolution of 1932 saw many changes in literary activities. The period has been considered the dawn of Modern Thai literature, since it was then that new literary genres and new types of drama were introduced or adapted from the West, that prose emerged as a dominant means for creative expression and literary journals and magazines gradually replaced the court as centres of literary creativities. It should not be too far wrong to assume that these changes had been brought on by our contact with the West, since with the West came printing technology, new literary genres, public education, and Western educated elite. All these factors were essential to the development of Modern Thai literature. Some played a very important role in the creation and dissemination of literary works while others were responsible for the propagation of readership. Although literary creativities during this period were still under royal patronage, they were no longer composed by "royal command." (with the exception perhaps of a new version of Ramakian which Rama V had commissioned the "council of poets" to compose by using different poetic form for the mural paintings at the temple of the Emerald Buddha.) Literary arena had gradually been shifted from the court to literary journals, literary clubs and associations. Since the introduction of printing technology by the American missionaries during Rama III's reign, newspapers, literary journals, periodicals and printed books have played a very important part in literary promotion. During Rama IV's reign (1851-1868) literary classics such as *Sam Kok, Rachathirat, Pra Aphai Mani, Khun Chang Khun Phaen* and Mom Rachothai's *Nirat Lo'ndo'n* were published. Some were serialized and sold by chapter. These publications gave people outside court circle an access to literary masterpieces.

Rama V (1868-1910) took a step forward in the direction of literary promotion. In order to encourage literary creativities he founded Wachirayan Library which served as a literary society. The library issued a monthly literary journal called *Wachirayan Wiset* to provide new literary venues for members of the royal family and the intellectual elite. "With the King himself as President of the society it is quite understandable why everyone wanted to write for this journal "(Phra Wo'rawetphisit 1991: 157). Contributors included the King himself, the Crown Prince and other members of the Royal Family. The Western educated elite were also active participants of this journal. *Wachirayan Wiset* proved to be the seat for literary innovation and creation. It was here that a new literary genre, the short story, was introduced. The most controversial one was *Sanuk Nu'k* by Prince Pichitprichako'n which created an uproar among readers who had never before been exposed to this kind of writing and took it as an insult to religious institution.

Following the lead of *Wachirayan Wiset* many more journals were issued. The two most significant ones were *Lak Witthaya* and *Thawi Panya*. As its name proclaimed *Lak Witthaya* "stole" knowledge from the West. Its purpose was "to encourage translations and adaptations of good foreign stories to help develop a new genre for modern Thai readers who no longer took interest in the traditional Thai romances "(Mattani 1988: 21). Consequently, the first translated novel in Thai *Khwam Phayabat* (The Vengeance) was published in this journal. Many literary scholars believe that this translated novel gave rise to the first novel in Thai *Khwam Mai Phayabat* (The Non-Vengeance), believed to have been written by Luang Wilatpariwat to counteract Phraya Surinthraracha's *Khwam Phayabat*. While *Lak Witthaya* aimed at "stealing knowledge" *Thawi Panya's* objective was to "increase intellect" presumably of it's readers. Literary works published in this journal included adaptations and translations of foreign tales and different types of prose fiction. These journals not only provided literary forums for writers to try their hands at the new literary genres, but they also had their arenas opened for dialogues between writers and their audience. This phenomenon definitely helped paving the way for literary criticism. It appeared as though the court as centre of literary creativities had, to a certain extent, been replaced by literary journals and periodicals. But the publishers, the editorial staff, and active contributors of these journals were none other than the "court people" themselves. They were either members of the royal family or the educated elite, most notably was Crown Prince Vajiravudh. This select group were mostly Western educated and had been the main force behind the change in literary creativities of this period. Through them new literary genres, namely the short story, the novel and the spoken drama were introduced. Admittedly, it was also under their influence that literary prose writing found its way into the Thai literary soil.

In addition to his attempt to promote the publication of literary journals, Rama V also founded The Royal Academy of Arts and Antiquities. The objectives of this Academy were to promote the writing of literature, education, history, and archeology. Members consisted of the royalty, scholars, and civil servants. With regard to literature, the Academy was to select out–standing literary works to be commended and impressed with the royal seal. The works eligible for commendation could either be the old classics or the newly written ones. With the Academy's approval these commendable works would subsequently be published. However, there was no evidence of any newly written work being published by the Academy. Only three "classics" were recognized and published with the imprint of the royal seal.

Like prose fiction new types of drama were also created by members of the royal family. They started out as being court entertainments but later found their ways into public and private theatres outside the palace.

It is interesting to note that while the royalty and the intellectual elite were preoccupied with "new literature", small entrepreneurs outside the palace made a fortune out of publishing popular folk tales retold in verse form. People still enjoyed the "abduct the daughter and kill father-in-law" story line. Besides, these stories were published in series and sold at a very low prize. Everyone wanted to try their hands at writing these popular stories since they sold well. Even some monks had this kind of work to their credit. However, with the increase in literacy and with the reading public becoming more sophisticated, the "melodramas" in verse eventually disappeared from the literary scene.

With Rama VI (1910-1925) literary activities were brought back to the court where the King led his close associates, writers, poets and dramatists in literary creation. As patron of the arts and literature he generously rewarded his favourites and talented courtiers with titles, properties and invaluable gifts. These rewards may have, to a certain extent, served as incentives for his courtiers to engage in artistic and literary creation. Also during this reign the impact of public education became more evident. More people could read and write. Producers of literary works and consumers had never before been so compatible. It is therefore not surprising that many literary scholars consider this reign "the golden age" for literature.

Beside his own literary creation it is believed that Rama VI's most significant contribution to the world of Thai literature was his establishment of the Royal Academy of Literature in 1914. Realizing that there had been a significant increase in the number of both writers and readers of literary works,and being aware that writers never paid much attention to neither the content nor the language used, Rama VI felt that it was his responsibility to salvage the situation by trying to promote literary writings of high quality. To follow his father's footstep he passed an Act to set up The Royal Academy of Literature. The Academy's main objectives were to promote contemporary creative writing, preserve traditional Thai literature,and set the standard for the writing of the Thai language. According to the Act a well written book had to be ethical and apolitical " so as not to create nuisance to His Majesty's government "(Prungsri 1981: 649). Also, the Thai language used had to be correct and real. Any imitation of a foreign language would not be accepted by the Academy. The works submitted had to be in the five categories namely poetry, Thai drama (in verse), spoken drama, tale, and essay. They could either be old classics or newly written ones. The selection of outstanding works were made by the Academy's committee members. The works selected would be given the Academy's certificates, only the exceptional ones were granted Wachirayan's medals (Prungsri 1981: 651). The Academy lasted only until the end of Rama's VI's reign. During the eleven years of its existence the Academy had selected ten masterpieces, one for each category, to be commended for the prestigious certificates and the Wachirayan's medals. Since then the ten masterpieces commended by the Royal Academy of Literature have been taken for prototypes of Thai Literature.

That was probably the first time that literary promotion became institutionalized and made official under the Royal patronage.

BEFORE THE REVOLUTION OF 1932: A TRANSITION

Even before the change from absolute to constitutional monarchy there was a steady flow of literary activities from the court to literary associations and institutions, literary journals, newspapers, and magazines, and finally to the general public. Although politically and economically the country was going through a difficult time, literature managed to survive and grow. It is true that Rama VII (1925 -1935) was heavily burdened with the country's social, political, and economic problems, and could not afford to hold court for literary activities nor initiate any "academy" that offered literary prizes. But it was during his reign that the Compulsory Education Act which was proclaimed by Rama VI had its real effect. The pleasure of reading and writing was no longer confined to the privileged groups. Common people also had their share of the "intellectual property" formerly owned by the elite. Different groups of writers issued their own magazines "to support the writing of prose and poetry, to be a trial ground for both experienced and inexperienced writers, and to promote readership among general public "(Nitaya and Kwandee, 1985: 10). With the exception of the "Literary Society" established by the Royal Institute it seems that these magazines took over the role of the royal patron in promoting literary creativity. The two most influential among them were *Thai Khasem* (1924) and *Suphapburut* (1929), which serialized the "real Thai novels"written by distinguished writers such as

Do'kmaisot, Si Burapha, Prince Akatdamkoeng, and Malai Chuphinit. Book reviews and literary columns also appeared in these magazines and daily newspapers. Their impact was quite evident when Prince Akatdamkoeng's novel, *Lakho'n Haeng Chiwit* (The Theatre of Life), was sold out shortly after the review of this book appeared in one of the daily newspapers. It seems that this literary phenomenon rightly paved the way for what was to come after the revolution in 1932.

NOW: DURING THE DEMOCRATIC ERA

Nineteen thirty two marks the dawn of Thailand's "democratic era". Political power had been transfered from the royalty into the hands of the military and civilians. "The court and the aristocrats no longer played an active role as patrons of the arts and literature. The centre of intellectual and creative activities had shifted to the educated middle class" (Mattani 1988: 35). It is rather ironical, however, that during the past sixty years of this so-called "democratic era" literary activities had frequently been suppressed, and a great number of writers, publishers and newspapermen had been arrested and imprisoned. All through the years, there had been a constant political tug-of-war between the military and the civilian leadership which often resulted in the dissolution of parliament, the enactment of martial law and the subsequent press censorship. Also during this period the country was threatened by communist insurgency and the Anticommunist Act was invoked intermittently by the Government. Every time the Act was enacted writers, publishers, and newspapermen would be among the people who were arrested. The most infamous one is the Anticommunist Act of 1952 which arrested writers, newspapermen, young military officers and politicians who were members of the so called "peace movement." They were accused of cooperating with the Communist Party of Thailand in trying to overthrow Phibun's "democratic government." During Sarit's military regime (1957-1963), the government also used communists threat as a pretext to impose press censorship. A number of newspapers were ordered closed, writers and publishers were arrested and jailed without trial. The most recent suppression of this kind was in 1976, when the arm forces under the leadership of Admiral Sangat Chalo'yu seized power after the October 6 violence "in order to restore stability and law and order to the kingdom" (Morell and Chai-anan 1981: 275). A civilian who happened to be an arch anticommunist was appointed Prime Minister, the suppression was, therefore, carried on in full force. Writings with any flickering towards the "left" were banned and destroyed. University syllabi and school text books were censored. It was another dark period for literary creativity in the democratic era.

It looks as though the democratic government under marshal law or elected parliament is no substitute for royalty as far as literary promotion is concerned. Phibun is probably the only leader of the democratic government who made an attempt to promote the writing of literature. But it is rather obvious that his motive was purely political. Being aware of "power of the pen," he tried to use language and literature as a means to achieve his notorious nationalistic policy. In 1942 he established the Council of National Culture and founded a "Literary Society" whose members included several noted literary scholars such as Prince Wan Waithayakorn, Phraya Anuman Rajadhon and Luang Wichitwathakan. The Prime Minister himself was President of the Society. The objectives of this "Literary Society" were to promote the creation and dissemination of Thai language and literature. The society issued a literary journal, *Wannakhadi San*, which published literary works and articles written by members of the society.

However, Phibun's nationalistic policy which greatly effected literary creativity was his national reform of the Thai language. "Words and letters deriving from Sanskrit, Pali, and Khmer, with intricate spelling and lettering were simplified and reduced to rudimentary forms" (Mattani 1988: 40). Pronouns which indicate relationship and social status customarily used in the Thai language were discarded. Only the basic ones such as "I", "you", "she", "he", "they" were kept. In addition, many rules and regulations were imposed upon literary writings. One of the rules for fiction writing was that the story line must be kept "clean." A married man was not allowed to even think of another woman who was not his wife, let alone committing adultery. Consequently, many writers stopped writing. Some resorted to the use of literary conceits while others began to write novels with exotic setting. Phibun's nationalistic policy clearly shows that his government was aware of the power and the potentials of language and literature. However, his attempt to promote the writing of literary works by imposing absurd rules and regulations upon writers and their writings proved to be more of a hindrance than a promotion. After Phibun's failed attempt to have control over the use of the Thai language and the creation of literature, no other regime during the democratic era had directly been involved with literary creativity. Without the royal patrons and with the government acting more like a foe than a friend

11

writers and people in literary circle had to fend for themselves. To keep the literary fire burning different kinds of fuel had been used.

In spite of the periodic suppression and the imprisonment of a few writers and newspapermen, the period between the revolution of 1932 and Sarit Thanarat's coup d'etat in 1957 saw many new developments in literary activities. Writers, newspapermen and intellectual elite continued to carry on their literary mission which had been initiated during the short period before the coup. During this time a considerable number of newspapers and magazines were founded, and served as main venues for literary creation. Among the notable ones were *Daily Mail Wan Can* which serialized K. Surangkhanang's *Ying Khon Chua* (The Prostitute), *Thai Mai, Pracha Chat,* and *Suphapburut-Prachamit.* It is interesting to note that many of these newspapers and magazines were initiated by writers themselves. Si Burapha, for example, formed a group of writer-friends to set up a magazine, *Pracha Chat,* with Prince Wan Waithayako'n, the renowned literary scholar, as its financier. Literary works published in this magazine include Si Burapha's two novels, *Songkhram Chiwit* (The War of Life) and *Khang Lang Phap* (Behind the Painted Picture), Malai Chuphinit's *Chai Chatri* (The Real Man), and Yakho'p's masterpiece, *Phuchana Sip Thit* (Conquerer of Ten Realms). Not long after the demise of *Pracha Chat* when political climate was more congenial Si Burapha and his writer- friends founded another magazine, *Suphapburut-Prachamit,* which proved to be another important venue for literary creation.

Although economically the country was going through a difficult time, writers found the atmosphere after World War II more congenial to creative writing than the previous decade when censorship and political suppression dominated literary scene. During this time newspapers and magazines flourished, and many writers made their debut in the literary world. While *Piyamit* published Suwat Wo'radilok's, K. Surangkhanang's, and P. Inthapalit's works, *Bangkok* magazine provided the the the stage for Seni Saowaphong, Prayat S. Nakhanat, and Pramun Unhathup. The works of other novelists such as Ing-on, Utsana Ploengtham, Seni Butsapaket were also introduced for the first time in various magazines. However, a new phenomenon which emerged as a strong competitor to these magazines was the publication of serialized "best sellers" in small book form. With their heart-rending, heart-throbbing, and humourous story lines, these "best sellers" seem to dominate the reading market for quite some time during the post war period (Trisilp 1980: 277).

As magazines and newspapers came out in great quantity, many writers felt the threat of the capitalists looming over their creativities. To ensure that literary works rested in responsible hands, a group of writers and intellectual elite led by Sot Kuramarohit decided to form the "Artists' Empire." Artists of all fields and newspapermen were invited to join this "Empire." Their main objective was to counter the capitalist-publishers by publishing literary works of high quality. They also had three commendable magazines, namely *Ekkachon, Suan Akso'n,* and *Sinlapin* to their credit. Through these magazines many noted novels were published, one of which was Sot Kuramarohit's best known work, *Pakking Nakho'n Haeng Khwamlang* (Peking, the City of Memories).

Another significant development in literary activity is the forming of *Chomrom Nakpraphan* (Writers'Club) in 1950. Influenced by socialist thoughts and writings that were widespread at the time, a number of writers became more aware and more conscious of their roles as potential agents for social change. Supported by a well known publisher, Aree Leevera, and managed by a group of active writers, the club served as a venue for writers to meet and exchange their ideas about arts and literature. The topics for discussion included the purpose and meaning of literature, literature and society, and the role and responsibilities of writers. This same group of writers were also active contributors of three influential magazines namely *Niko'n Wan Athit, Pituphum,* and *Akso'nsan.* Their articles echoed the spirit and the concern of the "Writers' Club". This development naturally gave rise to a new trend of literary creation. It actually triggered off the "literature of social justice "movement. Si Burapha's *Con Kwa Rao Ca Phop Kan Ik* (Till We Meet Again), Seni Saowapong's *Khwam Rak Kho'ng Walya* (Valya's love), and poems by Nai Phi, Plu'ang Wannasi, Jit Phoumisak, and Ujjeni represent the early outcome of this movement. Unfortunately, the literary activities of the "Writers' Club" had to come to an abrupt end when the government staged the "peace movement" arrest in 1952 (Trisilp 1980: 300).

In 1946, even before the "Writers' Club" came into existence, a number of literary scholars felt the need to have a forum for people in the literary circle to meet and exchange ideas about literature. Consequently, a literary club called *Wong Wannakhadi* (Literary Circle) was formed. Founding members included well known scholars such as M.R. Sumonchat and Thanpuying Somroj Swadikul, Cu'a Satawethin and Chaluai Kancanakhom. In addition to holding regular meetings at different places, the "Literary Circle" also published a literary journal called *Wong Wannakhadi.* Although it was short lived the journal was well received and widely read among literary people. The journal's strength lies in its regular publication of literary critiques written by noted literary scholars (Suwanna 1989: 100).

Upon Prince Prem Burachatra's suggestion, members of the "Literary Circle" made a move to establish a full fledge literary club which later became a member of International P.E.N. and was taken under the royal patronage of the present King. Since its establishment in 1959, with Phraya Anuman Rajadhon as its first President and Khun Nilawan Pinthong as Secretary General, International P.E.N., Thailand Centre has played an active role in promoting Thai language and literature both at home and abroad. The centre also shares and adhere to the International P.E.N.'s belief in freedom of expressions for writers, and "stands for the principle of unhampere transmission of thought within each nation and between all nations."

The period between Sarit's coup d'etat in 1957 and the student and popular uprising which toppled the military government of Thanom in 1973 saw many interesting developments in literary activities. Many writers especially the progressive ones found the six years under Sarit's dictatorial regime the darkest for their creativities. During this time the Anticommunist Act was reinforced, and with Article 17 of the "Interim Constitution," Sarit virtually had absolute control over the country.

However, literary activities did not really come to a complete standstill during this "dark age." Weekly magazines such as *Satri San, Piyamit,* and *Fa Mu'ang Thai* continued to publish "apolitical" novels and short stories with a social message. But literary atmosphere did not really come alive again until after Sarit's death in 1963. Although still under the military regime of Thanom, writers did not find the atmosphere as oppressive. Perhaps after six years of suppression they had learned to use the "art of implication (Wilson 1972: 245) in their writings.

The most interesting development during this pre-October 14, 1973 incident was the awakening and the involvement of university students and young graduates in literary activities. Perhaps literary creativity was the only outlet for them to air their grievances and dissatisfaction with the social and political climate at the time. Numerous groups and clubs were formed to provide the "youngs" and the "actives" arenas to meet and exchange ideas. The two most influential ones were *Chomrom Pracan Siao* (The Crescent Moon) and *Num Nao Sao Suai* (The Young and the Beautiful). These two groups put out in paperback edition collections of short stories, poems, plays, and articles

14

written by their young members (Sujit: 1971). Influenced by existentialist thoughts and modern literary techniques, these writers had successfully produced a number of outstanding literary pieces with a difference. Among them were the now renowned literary figures such as Nikhom Raiyawa, Withayako'n Chiangkun, Suchat Sawatsi, Sathian Canthimatho'n, Naowarat Pongpaibun, Surachai Canthimatho'n, Anut Aphaphirom, Sujit Wongtes, Phaibun Wongtes, and Khanchai Bunpan.

In addition to this "seekers of truth" movement there were other developments which bore significant contributions to the literary promotion of this period.

While weekly magazines such as *Piyamit, Satri San, Fa Mu'ang Thai,* and *Chao Krung* provided arenas for veteran and potential writers to try their hands at writing short stories, novels and poems, journals such as *Sangkhomsart Parithat* (Social Science Review), *Sayam Rat Weekly Review, Thammasat University journal, P.E.N Journal, Chulalongkorn University's Wannasin, Sathirakoses-Nagapradipa Foundation's Pacarayasara,* had their forums opened for literary reviews and critiques. These forums encouraged the dialogues between writers, readers, and literary critics which should have to a certain extent created some impact on literary creation.

During this short period international organizations, government agencies, foundations, and certain individuals also had their share in promoting the literary climate. They published contemporary masterpieces and literary criticism, issued literary journals and magazines, and established literary prizes.

In 1968 Southeast Asia Treaty Organization (SEATO) initiated literary prizes to promote literary activities among member countries. Annual literary awards were given to the best writers of fiction, prose, and poetry of each country. In Thailand two government agencies namely, the Department of International Organization of The Ministry of Foreign Affairs and the National Education Council of the Prime Minister's Office, were responsible for the selection of award winners Literary scholars, university professors, and established writers were recruited to form the juries. During the four years of its existence Thailand SEATO literary awards were given to poets, novelists and essayists, most notably were the three women novelists, Khritsana Asoksin, Suwanni Sukhontha, and Botan. The first two novelists were already accomplished writers by the time they received the awards. As for Botan, her prize winning novel *Cotmai Cak Mu'ang Thai* (Letters from Thailand) immediately placed her on literary stage alongside of Kritsana Asoksin, and Suwanni Sukhontha.

The SEATO literary award was replaced by that of ASEAN in 1977. The two government agencies involved were ASEAN Department of the Ministry of Foreign Affairs and the National Education Council. This time each country had to select a winner to enter the ASEAN international contest. The late Nimit Phumithawo'n's novel's, *Soitho'ng*, was selected to represent Thailand, but did not win the prize. It was defeated by *The Pilgrim*, a novel written by an Indonesian writer, Ivan Simatupung. This literary prize lasted only one year. No one seems to know the reason for its demise.

Another literary promotion endorsed by the government was initiated by UNESCO in connection with the "International Book Year 1972". The Ministry of Education had been entrusted with this task. Every year since its initiation in 1972, the Ministry has organized an annual book awards for outstanding works in poetry, fiction, non-fiction, and children literature (Nuancan 1986: 58). Unfortunately, reading public have not been very enthusiastic about this award. The prize winning works have been criticized as not being outstanding enough. It is rather doubtful whether this government sponsored award would have any real impact on literary creation as awhole. In 1972 the Bangkok Bank initiated an annual literary prize known as the *Wannakam Thai Bualuang* (Lotus Literary Award). In the beginning this award took a rather conservative approach. It was given to two categories of writing, prose and poetry. The works submitted had to be newly written. In trying to preserve traditional literary convention, the awards for poetry were given to poetic compositions which best adhered to traditional poetic prosody in addition to other literary merits. It was not until recently when the Bangkok Bank Foundation took over this responsibility that the organizers of the "Lotus Literary Award" decided to take other literary genres such as the novel and the short story into their consideration. Because of the conservative nature of the award coupled with poor publicity this literary award did not receive much response from the reading public, let alone literary critics.

The prestigious Foundation, Sathirakoses-Nagapradipa, was also established during this period, with Sulak Sivaraksa as chairman of the administrative committee. Its main objective was to promote and disseminate outstanding contemporary Thai poetry. In 1972 the Foundation selected Angkhan Kalayanapong as the recipient of the award for the best contemporary Thai poet. In 1978 the Foundation published a book entitled *Three Thai*

Poets to be presented at the ASEAN poetry festival in Indonesia (Sulak 1978). It is a collection of poems written by Angkhan Kalayanapong, Naowarat Pongpaibun, and Withayako'n Chiangkun. The income derived from the sale of *Three Thai Poets* was spent "on charitable works mostly to help artists and writers to survive with dignity, in order to pursue their creative talents meaningfully"(Sulak 1986: 9).

Another non-profit organization which played quite an active role in literary promotion in the "pre October 14" era was the Thai Chapter of International P.E.N. Its approach was rather conservative compared to that of the progressive groups, but its contribution cannot easily be overlooked. In addition to organizing monthly literary gathering among members and people in the literary circle, Thai P.E.N Centre also issued biannually literary journals whose articles have been widely used as reliable references. Also in order to provide literary people and general reading public with valuable literary publications, the Centre published works such as Dr. Wit Sivasariyanond's *Wannakhadi Lae Wannakhadi Wican* (Literature and Literary Criticism), Kulap Manlikamat' *Khati Chao Ban* (Thai Folklore), and Sathit Semanin's *Wisasa*, which is a collection of articles on the history of Thai newspapers. Another publication of note is *Thai Short Stories* which is a selection of contemporary Thai short stories translated into English.

Certain individuals in their capacity as editors and publishers also played very important part in literary promotion. Acin Pancapan, a forerunner of paperback publication who founded *Fa Mu'ang Thai* (Thai Sky), declared that he wanted to open a new literary horizon for "those who love to write"(*Sinlapin Haeng Chat* : 1991: 29). During the twenty years of its existence *Fa Muang Thai* had become a literary arena for both veteran and young writers. Among them were San Thewarak, Sot Kuramarohit, P. Netrangsi, Nimit Pumithawo'n, Khampun Bunthawi, Yok Burapha, Khanchai Bunpan, and Sujit Wongtes. Most of these "young writers" are at present among prominent figures in the Thai literary scene.

Khun Nilawan Pinthong, a Magsaysay Awardee for public service, who has been at the helm of *Satri San* since its establishment forty six years ago has also been very instrumental in the promotion of contemporary literature. It was at this weekly magazine that well known woman writers such as Kritsana Asoksin, Suwanni Sukhontha, Si Fa, and Botan made their debut. These four writers have been winners of different literary awards. Kritsana Asoksin in particular was winner of SEATO and S.E.A.Write literary award, and in 1988 was named "National Artist " in literature.

As a publisher and the first editor of Social Science Review Sulak Sivaraksa has made a great contribution to the Thai literary circle. Beside providing a stage for writers, scholars, literary or otherwise, to freely exchange their views, Sulak was also responsible for the publication of contemporary masterpieces of two most distinguished literary artists. In his capacity as editor, he published Angkhan Kalayanapong's poems in the inaugural issue of Social Science Review. It was probably the first time that Angkhan's poetry was introduced to the reading public. Angkhan's profound concept of man, nature, and the universe coupled with his unconventional use of poetic diction created quite an uproar among the reading public as well as literary scholars. As publisher of Suksit Sayam Printing Company Sulak published another four volumes of Angkhan's poetry, all of which have won national and international acclaims for the poet. Sulak's other literary contribution is his publication of Lao Khamho'm 's[2] collection of short stories *Fa Bo' Kan* (The Sky Is Not In The Way) which had to go underground during Sarit's dictatorial regime. Again, the book took the reading public by storm. It has been translated into six foreign languages, and has won for its author the prestigious title of "National Artist" in literature.

FROM OCTOBER TO OCTOBER

The three years between the popular and student uprising of October 1973 and the coup d'etat following the violence of October 6, 1976, has rightly been referred to as the period of "exuberant democracy." It was the time when censorship was lifted and free speech and protests were the order of the day. Ironically, with the exception of Angkhan Kalayanapong's *Sip Si Tula* (October 14), Naowarat Phongphaibun's *Phiang Khwam Khlu'an Wai* (Mere Movement), Khanchai Bunpan's *Ruang Mu'an Bai Mai Ruang Nai Ru'du Laeng* (Like Leaves Falling In The Dry Season). Sujit Wongtes's *Wat Bot* (Wat BoteTemple), and Jang Sae Tang's *Wanni Tok Taek* (Today Fallen and Shattered) which were all poems written on the October 14 event, a great number of literary works produced during this period did not show any mark of originality or literary excellence. They merely imitated the styles, parroted the metaphors, and quoted the predictions of their post-war predecessors.

But as far as literary promotion and dissemination is concerned, the atmosphere has never before been so active. Although rather one sided, the

---

[2] Pen name of Khamsing Srinawk.

attempt to kindle the literary fire is very strong.

During this very short period the "literature of social consciousness" or "literature for life" movement staged a come-back and practically dominated the literary scene. Traditional literature was rejected and popular novels were branded *Nam Nao* (stagnant water). Literature worth reading had to touch on social conditions and advocate social change. The writing of young writers such as Wat Walayangkul, Wisa Khanthap, Rawi Domphracan, Si Daoru'ang, and Sathapo'n Sisatcang were among the favourites. However, the movement's valuable contribution is the reprinting of literary works of the post-war era. Novels, poems and short stories of noted authors such as Seni Saowaphong, Si Burapha, Jit Phoumisak, Lao Khamho'm, and Nai Phi which had disappeared from the bookstands for sixteen years were again available in paperback editions. The reprint of these literary works were particularly popular among university students and the new generation of intellectual elite.

Another valuable publication that came out during this period is the collection of contemporary short stories in four volumes, compiled and edited by Suchat Sawatsi who was the editor of *Sangkhomsat Parithat* (Social Science Review) at the time. In his foreword Suchat stated that the short stories selected for the four volumes were written between 1964 and 1975, and the title given to each volume clearly reflected its theme. The first volume *Laeng Khen* (Hardship) deals with life in the country while *Thanon Sai Thi Nam Pai Su Khwamtai* (The Road That Leads to Death), and *Kham Khan Rap* (The Answers), deal with city life and life at the university respectively. This publication has proved to be a very valuable source for literary study. (Suchat 1975a, 1975b, 1976a, 1976b).

In addition to reprinting old masterpieces and compiling contemporary works, other literary activities include the organizing of seminars, round- table discussions, and other forms of gathering to discuss about the trends and directions of contemporary literature. These gatherings were jointly organized by university professors and "activist" students. Literary scholarship was also encouraged. Studies on different aspects of Thai literature by university professors and literary scholars were collected and published by literary clubs of different universities. Candidates for a master's and a doctorate degrees in Thai literature were involved in scholarly research on Thai literature. Many literary magazines were also produced by university students. The most controversial one was *Akso'nsat Phican* (Literary Critique) which was started by a group of students with Chonthira Sattayawatthana, a well known literature professor, at the helm (Morell and Chai-Anan 1981: 301).

FREE AT LAST: 1977 TO PRESENT

After one year of severe suppression under the civilian government of Thanin Kraiwichian, writers, literary scholars, university professors and students breathed the air of relative freedom when General Kriangsak Chomanan took over the rein as the new Prime minister in 1977. He expressed a program of moderation and a policy of reconciliation, ended Bangkok curfew, and allowed more open expression of views in the press and on university campuses (though by no means endorsing freedom of speech)" (Morell and Chai-Anan 1981: 278). Between 1978 and 1979 an amnesty was granted to students, intellectuals and others who have gone to the hills after the October, 1976 event. A great number of the "lost sheep" had come back to the fold. Many of them have become prominent figures in today's literary circle.

The last two decades has witnessed a considerable development in the writing of prose fiction and poetry. Naowarat Phongphaibun's, Atsiri Thammachot's, Chart Kobjitti's, Nikhom Raiyawa's, Mala Khamchan's, Jiranan Phitpricha's, and Saksiri Misomsu'p's literary works could very well illustrate this point. Although many of them wrote about the events of October 1973 and 1976, their short stories and poems were not of propagandistic nature. They had been through terrible experiences, but their thoughts and feelings had been reflected upon "in tranquility". With original styles and literary techniques, they had been able to create works of great literary value. Naowarat Phongphaibun's *Phiang Khwan Khlu'anwai* (Mere Movement), Atsiri Thammachot's *Khuntho'ng Cao Ca Klap Mu'a Fa Sang* (Khuntho'ng, You Will Return at Dawn), and Jiranan Phitpricha's *Bai Mai Thi Hai Pai* (The Lost Leaf) can serve as the case in point. Some of these writers went well beyond social concern. In their novels, *Kham Phiphaksa* (The Judgement) and *Takuat Kap Khop Phu* (The Alligator and the Rotten Bough), Chart Kobjitti and Nikhom Raiyawa touched on the "universal themes." Chart's novel deals with the fate of an individual who has been victimized by the "judgement" of his own society, while Nikhom 's symbolic work is about man's search for the ultimate source of evil.

Two of the most recent works of note which have won S.E.A. Write Literary Award in 1991 and 1992 can also demonstrate the new and interesting development of contemporary writings. Mala Khamchan's novel *Chao Can Pom Ho'm, Nirat Phrathat In Khwaen* (The Fragrant Haired Princess Chand:

A Pilgrimage to Phrathat In Khwaen) has been criticized for not being a "real"novel. It is felt by some that his language is too lyrical for prose fiction and that the work is too short to be a novel. In other words the award winning novel of Mala Khamchan does not meet the conventional requirements of a novel. Naturally, the novel does not receive much response from the reading public, but has been hailed by literary scholars as one the of great contemporary masterpieces. Saksiri Misomsu'p's collection of short poems, *Mu' Nan Si Khao* (That White Hand) has also been criticized for not being a collection of "real" poems since his work does not follow standard prosody. But stronger attack comes from religious fanatics who believe that the work may contaminate young people's mind and can be detrimental to religious institution. What are the factors that bring about the change and development in these contemporary writings? Which are the fuels that help kindling the literary fire? Perhaps there is no simple answer to such question. An examination of the literary atmosphere as a whole may shed light on this complicated issue.

In 1978, two years after the *Social Science Review* came to an end, its former editor, Suchat Sawatsi, and the owner of Duangkamon Publishing Company, Suk Sungsawang, founded the first real literary magazine, *Lok Nangsu'* (Book World). The magazine featured "brain storming square;" interviews with writers, translators, critics and editors; literary reviews and critiques of Thai and foreign literature. For several years it served as a "literary crossroad "for writers, critics, and literary scholars to come and exchange their views. It has also been a valuable source of literary scholarship. Following in *Lok Nangsu''s* footstep was *Thanon Nangsu'* (Book Path), a smaller scale literary magazine with Suchat Sawatsi as the honourary editor. Although *Thanon Nangsu'* did not last very long and did not create as great an impact as did *Lok Nangsu'* its contribution to the literary world cannot be ignored.

After the demise of *Thanon Nangsu'* and *Lok Nangsu'*, Wilat Maniwat, a veteran writer and journalist, attempted to set up another literary magazine called *No'n Nangsu'* (Bookworms). However, it came to an end after the publication of the third issue. Then towards the end of 1992 *Writer Magazine* emerged as the newest literary magazine for "readers, writers, and young people of today." It was founded by a group of young writers with veteran writers and editors such as Lao Khamho'm, Rong Wongsawan, and Suchat Sawatsi as members of the advisory board. The basic structure of this magazine echoes that of *Lok Nangsu'* but the tone is more aggressive and reflects negative attitude towards literary establishments, particularly towards the granting of literary prizes such as The S.E.A. Write Literary Award.

In addition to literary magazines, many daily newspapers, weekly and monthly magazines such as *Siam Rat Weekly Review, Matichon Weekly, Sarakhadi Feature Magazine, Sakun Thai, Satri San, Phu Catkan,* and *Bangkok Post* (until 1991) set aside special columns for literary news, book reviews, and literary critiques. The best known one is probably *Siam Rat Weekly Review* which devotes four columns to literary subjects. The two columns, *Pakka Khon Nok* (Quill Pen) *and Sing Sanamluang's Bon Sonthana* have been instrumental in providing "battle ground" for readers, writers and literary scholars to engage in literary "warfare." The fight becomes even more exciting after winners of literary awards, especially those of the S.E.A.Write's, have been announced.

During the course of the seminar held at the Office of Culture Comission, a question was raised as to whether the granting of literary prizes has enhanced literary creation. Most writers felt that literary prizes might have enhanced the literary atmosphere, but they could not have been the source of inspiration for literary creation. Nevertheless, the granting of literary prizes has always been on the literary scene throughout the entire history of Thai literature.

During the last two decades a number of literary prizes have been established in addition to the ongoing ones. Among them were Thai P.E.N. Literary Award for poetry and the short story; Rawi Domphracan Literary Prize for poetry and the novel; The S.E.A. Write Literary Award, and Cho' Karaket Award.

Established in 1977 when Noranit Setabutr was President, the P.E.N Literary Award 's objective is to "promote and encourage the writing of Thai literary works, particularly the writing of short story and short poem (Witthayako'n 1979: 5)." The project has been carried on annually until now. Among those who have been awarded the P.E.N Literary Prize are now renowned writers such as Prapatso'n Sewikun, Si Daoru'ang, Wat Wanlayang-kun, Anchan, Phaithun Thanya, and Jiranan Phitpricha.

Rawi Domphracan is the literary prize established by the Rawi Dom-phracan Fund in memory of the late Rawi Domphracan, a former student activist whose poem *Wake Up Free Man* became an inspiration to students during the uprising of 1973. The prize has been given annually to newly written novel and poem. As Naowarat Phongphaibun has pointed out in his interview with *Writer Magazine,* that the award has its drawback in that it is given to the work written particularly for the prize, "it is not natural and cannot be considered a creative work of art (Naowarat 1992: 28)."

Initiated by the editor of *Cho' Karaket Magazine*, Suchat Sawatsi, the *Cho' Karaket* Literary Prize is given to writers of short stories whose works have been selected and published in *Cho' Karaket Magazine*. In the introduction of *Cho' Karaket 13* its editor, Suchat Sawatsi, declares that his publication is a magazine whose objective is to provide a venue for writers to try their hands at writing short fiction (Suchat 1993: 15). It should not by any means be considered as a collection of short stories. This is a new literary dimension. Now writers can have their own literary stage to play on.They no longer have to be part of the 'chorus line' (Chusak 1993: 192).

The most controversial literary prize to date is the Southeast Asian Write Award. Established in 1979, the award was initiated by the management of the Oriental Hotel upon the suggestion of Prince Prem Purachatra. Sponsers include Thai International, Ithal Thai Group, Bangkok Bank, Jim Thompson Foundation, and Riche Monde (Bangkok) Ltd. The main objective is to promote contemporary writers both at home and among the neighbouring Asian countries. In Thailand Thai P.E.N. Centre and the Writers' Association have been responsible for the selection of the works to be awarded annually (Noranit 1988). During the past fourteen years five novels, five collections of short poems, and four collections of short stories have been selected and awarded the literary prizes. Among them are Khampun Bunthawi's *Luk Isan* (Son of the Northeast), Naowarat Phongphaibun's *Phiang Khwamkhu'anwai* (Mere Movement), Atsiri Thammachot's *Khuntho'ng Cao Ca Klap Mu'a Fa Sang* (Khuntho'ng, You Will Return at Dawn), Angkhan Kalayanaphong's *Panithan Kawi* (The Poet's Pledge), and Chart Kobjitti's *Kham Phiphaksa* (The Judgement).

Two other literary activities of note are the Government's National Artists Project and the newly established Mom Luang Bunlua Thepyasuwan Fund's Literary Critique Prize.

Launched by the Office of the National Culture Commission, the Ministry of Education in 1985, the National Artists Project 's main objective is to recognize and honour artists in three different fields namely literature, visual arts, and performing arts. Each year artists have been selected and honoured with the tittle "National Artists." A plague of honour and a golden insignia pin are presented to each national artist on National Artists Day by Her Royal Highness Princess Maha Chakri Sirindhorn as representative of His Majesty The King. Since its initiation nine writers and one poet have been honoured with this prestigious title. The National Artists Project is rather different from other literary prizes in that it recognizes the artists' life long accomplishments; and in order to enable the artists to continue working with relative ease, financial assistance and medical care have also been provided for them.

In an attempt to promote contemporary Thai literature, members of the executive committee of the M.L. Bunlua Thepyasuwan Fund feel that the writing of literary critique needs to be encouraged. Since M.L. Bunlua herself is a pioneer in this field, a prize for literary critique initiated by the M.L Bunlua Thepyasuwan Fund is most appropriate. The project was launched for the first time in 1991 and two young literary critics with great potential have been chosen for the prize. Although it is quite evident that during the last two decades literary prizes have played a very significant role in enhancing the literary atmosphere, it cannot be easily concluded that they have been responsible for the development of contemporary Thai literary writings. However, some literary scholars believe that literary prize such as the S.E.A.Write Award has definitely created an impact on contemporary writings. They are quite certain that this particular literary prize has set a new trend and direction for contemporary writings. Unfortunately, most writers do not seem to agree with the literary scholars' assumption. The awardees themselves feel honoured, but they do not think the award will have any impact on their literary creation in the future. Some writers such as Camlo'ng Fangchonlacit goes as far as to say that the only impact the S.E.A.Write Award has on literary writings is that it increases the sale of the works by twenty fold. It is just a windfall for the award winner, and nothing else (Camlo'ng 1992: 43). However, it cannot be denied that literary prize such the S.E.A. Write Award has managed to sift a considerable number of gold nuggets from pebbles and sands, and expose them to the reading public and critics. As to whether or not they are real gold has always been the popular topic for debate among the reading public, literary critics and among writers themselves.

It appears that since 1976 there have been all kinds of fuels to keep the literary fire burning. Then why was there a common concern among literary people at the recent gathering organized by the Office of National Culture Commission, that the literary flame may be dimming and that there was a need to rekindle the fire.

The cause for their concern may lie in the threat of commercialism and consumerism. Since 1977, one year after the October 1976 political upheaval, there has been a steady increase in the publication of weekly and monthly magazines which cater to different groups of readers. They are usually categorized by gender, age, profession, and social status. These popular magazines, regardless of their specialty, serialize novels and publish short stories and poems of popular writers. Some writers have their novels concurrently serialized in five magazines. Consequently, the number of novels produced during this period have increased in great quantity. As for quality, it is too much to expect from the "mass produced" novels.

From the publishers and editors' point of view it is also difficult to control the quality of literary writings since magazines cannot survive without sponsors, and sponsors have to lend their ears to the demand of the consumers who are mostly literary illiterate. It seems like a vicious circle that can never be solved.

Another threat to the literary flame is the "visual tradition" which has been brought on by modern technology. As Khamsing Srinawk rightly fears, people are now glued to the new literary medium that they no longer read. "The novels in Thailand are dead and gone. They are no longer written to be read but to be seen" said Dr. Chetana Nagavajara. But there is a brighter side to this phenomenon. Having watched T.V. dramas based on popular novels, many viewers who may or may not have read the novels before turn to the authentic text. Most of the time it is a matter of curiosity. Those who have not read the novels before turn to read them because they want to get ahead of what they have watched on television. The serialized T.V. scripts which appear in daily newspapers cannot sufficiently satisfy their curiosity. As for those who have read the novels before and notice the distortion in the T.V. version of the novel, it is exciting for them to go back to the novels and find the discrepancies between the two versions. There are also those sentimentalists who, after having watched T.V. dramas, go back to read the novels for old time's sake. At any rate the readership of the novels that have been made into T.V. dramas has markedly increased, and the book-renting business flourishes. Perhaps the new literary medium that may seem like a threat can be turned to our advantage after all.

Finally, it can be concluded that in spite of many obstacles and several drawbacks the attempt to promote contemporary literature has not been in vain. The literary flame is still glowing. The age that has produced the poetic works of Angkhan Kalayanaphong and Naowarat Phongphaibun; the novels of Khamphun Bunthawi, Mala Khamchan and Nikhom Raiyawa; the short stories of Lao Khamho'm and Atsiri Thammachot has every reason to be proud of its own literature. However, an age can only produce a certain number of masterpieces. Can lesser ones serve as well? Khamsing Srinawk, the National Artist in Literature, once said that "the literary world is like a forest where all kinds of trees thrive and grow. Different trees serve different functions. They should all be accepted as long as they are complete and whole." Perhaps, it takes all the trees in the forest to keep the literary flame aglow.

REFERENCES

Chetana Nagavajara,
 1994 "Literature in Thai Life: Reflections of a Native", *South East Asia Research* 2: 1: 12-52.

Chusak Patharakunvanich,
 1974 "Kan To' Do'k: Looking Back in Search of the Past", *Sarakhadi Feature Magazine* 9: 97

Mattani Mojdara Rutnin
 1988 *Modern Thai Literature: The Process of Modernization and the Transformation of Values,* Bangkok: Thammasat University Press.

Morell, David and Chai-anan Samudavanija,
 1981 *Political Conflict in Thailand: Reform, Reaction and Revolution,* Massachusetts: Oelgeschlager, Bunn & Hair.

Naowarat Phongphaibun
 1992 Interview, *Writer Magazine* 1: 1: 28

Noranit Setabutr,

    1988   *Sip Pi Si Rai : Kham Hai Kan Ru'ang Wannakam Sangsan Yot Yiam Haeng Asian Pi 2522-2531* (10 Years of S.E.A. WRITE: Statement on the Southeast Asian WRITE Awards 1979-1988) Bangkok: Sarn Mual Chon.

Nuancan Ratanapo'n et al.,

    1986   *Literary Awards in Thailand 1907-1986*, Bangkok: O.S. Printing House.

Pariyat Thammathada (Phae Talalak), Phraya

    1967   Tamnan Siprat . In Pho' Na Pramuanmak (ed.) *Kamsuan Siprat Nirat Narin*, Bangkok: Phrae Phitthaya, pp. 22-62.

Prungsri Vallibhodama,

    1981   *Wanakhadi Samoso'n: Saranukrom Prabat Somdet Phra Mongkutklao Chao Yu Hua* (Encyclopedia of King Rama VI), Bangkok: Chareonwit Karn Pim.

Suchat Sawatsi, ed.,

    1975a *Laengkhen (Hardship):* Bangkok: Duang kamol.

    1975b *Thanon Sai Thi Nam Pai Su Khwamtai* (The Road That Leads to Death). Bangkok: Duangkamol

    1976a *Mu'an Yang Mai Khoei* (As If It Never Was), Bangkok: Duangkamol.

    1976b *Kham Khan Rap* (The Answers), Bangkok: Duangkamol.

    1993   Kan To' Do'k, *Cho' Karaket 13,* Bangkok: Thammasan.

Sujit Wongtes, et al.,

    1971   *Num Nao Sao Suai Lae Phracan Siao* (The Young and The Beautiful and The Crescent Moon), Bangkok: Praphansarn.

Sulak Sivaraksa (ed.)

1978   *Three Thai Poets*, Sathirakoses-Nagapradipa Foundation,
Bangkok.

1986   *Angkarn Kalyanapong: A Contemporary Siamese Poet*,
Sathirakoses-Nagapradipa Foundation, Bangkok: Rungsang
Kanphim.

Suvanna Kriangkraipetch and Suchitra Chongsatitvatana (eds.)

1989   *Tho' Mai Nai Sai Nam: So'ng Ro'i Pi Wannakhadi Wican
Thai*   (Weaving Silk in the Stream: the Bicentennial of
Literary Criticism in Thailand), Bangkok: Samakkhisan.

Trisilp Boonkajorn,

1980   *The Novels and Thai Society (1932-1957)*, Bangkok: Sangsan.

Wilson Edmund,

1972   "Marxism and Literature", *20th Century Literary Criticism*,
David Lodge, (ed.), London: Longman.

Witthayako'n Chiangkun, ed.,

1979   *Outstanding Poems and Short Stories 1978, International
P.E.N. Thailand Center*, Bangkok: Sanguan Karn Pim.

Wo'rawetphisit, Phra

1991   *Wannakhadi Thai* (Thai Literature), Bangkok:
Chulalongkorn University Press.

NATION BUILDING AND THAI LITERARY DISCOURSE:
THE LEGACY OF PHIBUN AND LUANG WICHIT

Manas Chitakasem

> My present position is that of an Army Commander making war. So I see the
> editor as a commander also but he commands *Wananakhadi San*- the voice of Thai
> literature. *Wannakhadi San* will be our mouth, like a sharp weapon, which will
> bring an ultimate victory to our Nation. All works of literature will construct for
> us a Literary Victory Monument. A grand finale will be a review parade passing
> this monument - like adding the euphonic syllables to the end of a poem. The
> only difference is that, for this instance, as we march we cheer "Hurrah, Thai
> literature!" (Phibun 1942: 2).

When Phibun became Prime Minister in 1938 he initiated a Nationalistic
programme popularly known as the *nayobai sang chat* (nation-building policy),
which aimed to arouse consciousness of selfhood among the citizenry. The
policy attached the greatest importance to the manifestation of culture which
was to have a profound effect on all aspects of Thai life. The ruling elite
sought to inspire and instil into the people the spirit of nationalism, pride,
greatness, prosperity and equality with the West. The term *chat* (Nation) was
given a new meaning and the State was given a new specific character. The
name of the country was changed from Siam to Thailand in 1939. According to
Chai-anan, it was during this period of the creation of State identity that an
official version of culture and cultural norms was superimposed on popular
culture and subcultures (Chai-anan 1989). During the time of the absolute
monarchy, Siamese Kings prided themselves as rulers of a diversified kingdom
consisting of Thai, Shan, Lao, Mo'n, Northern, Northeastern, Southern, and
Muslim peoples. Now this diversity was to be united into one entity known as
'the Thais' in the name of 'National Unity' for which the term *samakkhi chai*
(United Victory) was duly created. All this was to be carried out with the
blessing of the great majority, grandly termed *maha chon* (the public/the

majority).[1] Phibun said in his broadcast address to the nation on the National Day of June, 1939 that education and patriotism alone were not complete qualities in themselves and that they had to be complemented by national traditions, of which the government would notify the public from time to time, under the name of *rattha niyom* (State Conventions/Prescriptions)- the unwritten law of the State (Wan Waithayakon 1991: 32, Thongchai 1988: 412), or Cultural Mandates (Thamsook 1978: 32). In reality, however, *rattha niyom* was a mechanism used by the State to impose its policies on the people. It was a mechanism manipulated by those who held the power of the State, a power which was above the constitution and could be used to control the public whenever the ruling authority deemed it necessary. Altogether, twelve *rattha niyom* were issued within the course of three years, from 1939 to 1942. [2] In order to legitimize its action, the government contended that *rattha niyom* had similar characteristics to those of *phra ratcha niyom* (Royal custom and convention), which belonged to the *ancien regime* . The difference is that *phra ratcha niyom* constituted the opinion of the king alone, while *rattha niyom* constituted the opinion of the State, formed in conformity with public opinion (*maha chon*) as a national tradition. That is to say that now, with the advent of the constitutional regime, the Government naturally had to take the lead formerly taken by the king himself (Wan Waithayakon 1991: 33).

The source of inspiration behind the *rattha niyom* was Wichit who was appointed president of the committee to advise on *rattha niyom* which he himself had helped to draft. Wichit was known to be the architect of much of Phibun's cultural policy which became the official version of national culture and national identity. He was a self-made man, highly ambitious and hard working. Coming from a humble background he was sent to Bangkok to study in a temple school where he learned Pali language in the monastery before joining the Ministry of Foreign Affairs. He worked as a clerk writing official documents for his superiors while studying law at the same time as a

---

[1] The term was coined for the regime by Prince Wan.

[2] These concerned (1) changing the name of the country from Siam to Thailand; (2) the country's security; (3) discouraging the use of the terms Northern Thais, Southern Thais, Northeastern Thais, and Islamic Thais in favour of 'the Thais'; (4) showing respect and loyalty to the Thai flag, national anthem and royal anthem; (5) encouraging the use of Thai produce; (6) the approval by the army of the Thai national and royal anthems (7) the Thais are to build their Nation; (8) the new wording of the royal anthem; (9) the duty to uphold the Thai language; (10) the wearing of suitable dress; (11) daily works for the Thais; (12) the treatment of children, the aged and the sick.

part-time student. He soon worked his way up and was sent to Paris to serve as an assistant-secretary to the Ambassador. There, he was later promoted to the position of secretary to the Ambassador. His appointment abroad enabled Wichit to learn diplomatic skills from moving among diplomatic circles while continuing to study law and foreign languages in Europe (Pra-o'nrat 1985: 23-58 and Jiraporn 1992: 174-182).

His career in the diplomatic service led finally to the position of assistant director-general of Department of Political Affairs in 1932. He left the government service soon after the 1932 revolution and took up a new career as a writer for a newspaper as well as creating his own magazine *Duang Prathip* (The Torch). He read widely and wrote prolifically. His writings showed nationalist leanings as early as 1928 when his book *Maha Burut* (Great Men) appeared. Wichit expressed great admiration for men like Mussolini, Hitler, Napoleon, Okubo etc. It was, in fact, Okubo, a Japanese who impressed Wichit with the idea that in order to compete with the West it was necessary to study and learn the way of the West so that the country could adapt accordingly (Wichit 1980: 67). In his lecture on *Khwamrak* (Love) in 1930, he contended that love for one's nation required an absolute sacrifice including one's own life (Wichit 1930: 70). However, it was not until he returned to government service in 1934 as Director General of the newly created Department of Fine Arts that he was seriously involved with the plotting of nationalism with the new regime which had ultimately left a lasting effect on the attitude, values, and, indeed, all forms of social, cultural, and political behaviour of the Thai people. Wichit's unreserved approval of the Bushido resulted in the doctrine being transformed into a national code of valour *(wiratham)* which was proclaimed by the government in 1944 when World War II was at its crucial stage. Wichit's writing on 'Bushido' appeared in his magazine *Duang Prathip* in April 1933 (Wichit 1933: 3). To Wichit, Bushido was the 'soul of Japan' and it was the practice of the Bushido doctrine by the people of Japan that lifted that country to the level of civilization equal to that of the West (Wichit 1933: 3). Wichit later wrote :

> Japan became the most civilized nation in Asia because of Bushido ideology which I have had the opportunity to study thoroughly. I have had the good fortune to have met Professor Nitobe, the author of the book on Bushido, when he was living in Switzerland. It has been my dream for more than ten years

now that I want to establish the Bushido doctrine in Thailand and make it applicable to the Thai situation (Wichit 1933: 6).

By this time, Wichit had become a professed nationalist. He invented the term *latthi chuchat* for 'nationalism' as he waited for the opportunity to put it into practice in Thailand. It should be noted that before the 1932 revolution staged by the Coup Group *(khana rat)*, Wichit, as a diplomat in Paris, had known and sympathised with some of the students who were now leading Coup promoters. After the revolution, he was disappointed at not being nominated to the Assembly. He was also unhappy with the decision of the new regime to close down a newspaper with which he was closely associated. This was probably the reason why he resigned from government service (Stow 1991: 35). As an ambitious man Wichit wanted the opportunity to do great, powerful things. So, in Janauary 1933, he joined a group calling itself *khana chat* (Nationalists) which applied to the government for official registration as a political party (Stow 1991: 35).[3] When the application was turned down by the government, Wichit responded with his writing on the subject of 'Nationalism' *(latthi chu chat)* advocating the need for the adoption of such a doctrine in Thailand:

> The reason why my associates and I have physically and mentally devoted much of our energy to establishing the Nationalist Party is due to our main objective to create an ideology in Thailand. We must fully understand the importance of *chat* (Nation) and the way in which those who love the Nation *(rak chat)* and want to glorify the Nation *(chu chat)*, should behave (Wichit 1933: 5).

This article, *Latthi Chu chat*, is one of the most revealing documents written by Wichit. It helps to explain the author's mentality and understand his psychopolitical will, beliefs, attitudes and obsessions which, by 1939, had been translated into many of the policies and actions to be embraced by the first Phibun government. [4]

---

[3] Members comprised mainly civilian officials and military officers, most of whom had lost influence or career prospects since the end of the absolute monarchy.

[4] I am grateful to Kusuma Prasertsud, who is doing research on Luang Wichit's "Drama and Propaganda" at SOAS, for lending me her copies of Luang Wichit's writings used in this paper.

Unlike King Vajiravudh's programme of Nationalism where the King's plays and other literary contributions essentially only spread among the elite community, the Phibun-Wichit's programmes to create National Culture penetrated far and wide. Through the network of national media under the newly created Department of Public Propaganda /Information new messages and concepts reached the masses in a way unprecedented in Thai history. This period has been referred to as the "golden age" of radio broadcasting (Charnvit 1993: 16). Anyone who could read or had a radio would be aware of what the government wanted of its citizenry. Like Vajiravudh, Wichit employed drama as a tool for propaganda. His plays were largely written with simple plots and stories drawing mostly from historical events which are seductive to patriotism. Heroes and heroines were made to exemplify messages intended for the audience relying on passionate language and songs to arouse patriotic feelings. These songs were drummed through the national radio network every day, again and again, to liberate the public through hearing them. Wichit produced ten plays of this type between 1936 to 1940.

The concept of *chat*, Nationhood, Nationalism, and Identity *(ekkalak)* are inter-related and much scholarly research on the subject has recently been published (Cf. Batson 1974, Charnvit 1974, Thak 1978, Thamsook 1978, Thongchai 1988, Nakharin 1989, Chai-anan 1991, Reynolds 1991). Whereas scholars agreed that the period of Phibun's nation-building (or State-building according to Chai-anan) is crucial to the study of Thailand, published works on this particular period have, up to this point in time, been the concern of historians and political scientists. It is the purpose of this paper, therefore, to attempt to examine a literary journal, *Wannakhadi San*, which was issued and directly sponsored by the State during the first Phibun government in order to try to understand the literary discourse engaged under the atmosphere of that political climate and the impact such a discourse has or might have on Thai literature.

The literary journal *Wannakhadi San* was the product of the National Cultural Development Act, promulgated in 1940 as a part of the Government's plan to foster and promote national progress. Culture is defined in that Act as showing flourishing development, good order, harmonious progress of the nation and good public morals. Thais now have the duty to comply with 'national culture' and to foster and promote national progress by preserving what was good in the 'traditional culture' and co-operating in improving such culture in consonance with the times (Wan Waithayakon 1991: 34). The

Institute of National Culture was set up two years later. It had the status of a public body under the Presidency of the Council and was divided into five bureaux, one of which was the 'Bureau of Literary Culture'. A literary revival had, therefore, been set in motion.

Essentially, in the Thai literary context, language and literature are synonymous as one cannot do without the other. While the orthography was given a new identity,[5] a monthly literary journal was published with Prince Wan as Editor under the auspices of the Literature Association of Thailand (*Wannakhadi Samakhom Haeng Prathet Thai*) with Phibun, the Prime Minister, acting not only as President but also as founder of the Association. A working committee on the Promotion of Thai Language Culture was also set up at the same time, again with Phibun as President. Its main aim was to foster and promote language and literary writings (*nangsu' Thai*). Members of the committee were drawn from prominent members of the society, most of whom were already well-established in their respective professions. Many of these members were also regular contributors to the journal.

These names formed a very impressive list comprising academic giants and internationally known scholars such as Yong Anuman Rajadhon, Worawet Siwasariyanon, Plu'ang Na Nakho'n, Montri Tramot, Sanga Kanchanakhaphan and Tri Saraprasert etc.. These names were enough to ensure the legitimacy and high standing of the Association and the Journal.

The choice of Prince Wan as editor was a significant one. Before working as one of Phibun's close political allies and advisors the Prince was Phya Phahol's personal advisor with vast experience. He had the reputation of having one of the most astute political brains in Siam. Prince Wan used to control the newspaper *Prachachat* which had come to be regarded as the main exponent of government views. Moreover, the Prince was also known as a great scholar trained in the West. His knowledge in the field of language and literature coupled with journalistic experience were unsurpassed. But, most important of all, Prince Wan was a man of integrity highly respected by young writers and journalists on all sides of the political spectrum including the young Siburapaha, who used to work for the Prince's newspaper.[6] To have

---

[5] The orthography was simplified by the elimination of 13 consonants and 5 vowels.

[6] Sulak, for example, who would write negatively about Phibun and Wichit and virtually everyone associated with their policy, had a great deal of praise for prince Wan and Phya Anuman. According to Sulak, without these two great scholars working within this regime, the Thai language would have been dead. Between them they helped in compiling

such a man as editor would silence many liberal-minded journalists and writers who might otherwise voice dissatisfaction with the regime. Indeed, Prince Wan was the greatest asset for *Wannakhadi San*. The appointment of Prince Wan as editor must have attracted other prominent scholars to join the journal.

Many scholars and academicians regarded the journal as a legitimate platform to expound their knowledge of Thai language and literature. Such works can be seen in the scholarly contributions of Anuman Rajdhon, Worawet Siwasariyanon, and Plu'ang Na Nakho'n who published their works in the journal regularly. Some contributors combined the opportunity of expounding knowledge with flirtation with the leader and used their writings to support and promote official policy. Some were outright propagandists who used poetry as a tool to openly propagate *rattha niyom* and *wiratham*. Many of the verses produced by these authors were meant to be nothing more than 'let's follow the leader' verses. Short verses of this nature formed a regular feature on many pages of the journal, eulogizing not only the Leader but also his wife and Wichit. They were written on a scale comparable to the conventional panegeric poetry composed by court poets in the old days.

In examining the content of works published in *Wannakhadi San*, it is important to remember that the journal had been given a mission which it aimed to accomplish. As we have seen from the quotation at the beginning of this paper, Phibun saw the Journal's editor as the commander of an army at war. The written words, published in the journal, were compared with the weapons, which, in this context, were fighting the war of culture, and the victory of this war would become monumental i.e. the symbol of glory. Each contributor was the Nation-cum-Phibun's private soldier, joining hands in making the creation of the 'Thai State' *(chat Thai)* a cultural victory *(watthana chai)*.

Phibun, as President of the "Literature Association", regarded himself as the Supreme Commander. In launching the first issue of *Wannakhadi San*, he declared that "the soul of Thai literature had been revitalized" and he was filled with a surge of excitement and enthusiasm (Phibun 1942: 1). Such an exalted state of feeling had only happened to him three times before in his life - when he learned that Thailand had finally won back the territory lost to France; when he heard the National anthem played over the radio to the cheer

---

dictionaries, encyclopedia, and coining Thai words to satisfy the demands of the growing nation. See Sulak sivaraksa "The Crisis of Siamese Identity" in Reynolds 1991.

of the Thai people at the signing ceremony in Battambang; and when the Thai army won the war at Chiangtung (Phibun 1942: 3-4). Phibun concluded his writing by saying that he was "full of joy" *(plap plu'm)* in seeing Thai literature rooted firmly on Thai soil. Thai language and literature would spread and prosper together with the expansion of a great and prosperous 'nation'. Finally, readers of the journal were reminded that "the nation's progress, civilization and influence" depended on the success of the Thai language and literature i.e. the nation's cultural victory (Phibun 1942: 4-5).

In reply, Prince Wan, as the journal's editor, wrote that the journal accepted that the Prime Minister had relied fully on the success of the 'Language and Literary Programme' in lifting Thailand to the status of a powerful nation (Wan Waithayakon 1942: 7). The Prince invited members of the Association to write articles for the journal and urged them to sacrifice their time, energy, intelligence and knowledge for the sake of the new found *chat*. The 'literature' acceptable for publication in the journal was clearly defined to cover the following areas.

1) Linguistics, including principles of language, words, meaning (semantics), grammar, and construction of words *(akkhara withi)*.

2) Literature which included:

a) Poetry or writing in verse such as *khlong, chan, kap,* and *klo'n* in any subject and

b) Prose which could be in many forms such as an essay, short story, proverb, and even translation from foreign languages regardless of content provided they were accepted as 'good writing'.

3) Related subjects such as history, geography, fine arts, music etc.

4) Literary criticism which could include principles of criticism, literary history, and critical review of literary works. (Wan Waithayakon 1942: 9-10)

But why was it so essential for language and literature to be used for such a purpose? Phibun's line of thinking was that the 'soul of the Nation' manifested itself in culture (Nakharin 1989: 259). The knowledge of good literature was good for the mind and using good language was good for manners and behaviour. To instil such knowledge in the public was part of the idea of human revolution perceived by the leadership. Wichit gave a long speech in November, 1939 on this subject stressing the urgent need to liberate the minds of the people. If the revolution was to survive, he said, people must be made to change their behaviour along the line prescribed by the authority.

According to Wichit, the human mind and behaviour *(laksana nitsai cai manut)* had to be changed from an undesirable state to a desirable one.

> In changing the form of Government, the system of economy or any other things, if we do not change human minds and behaviour then our effort becomes a complete waste. To stage a revolution without human revolution is a half-baked revolution and one ends up digging one's own grave (Wichit 1939: 322).

Wichit himself took the lead in writing 'propaganda' messages on the pages of the journal. His contribution to the journal was written in the *klo'n paed* verse form under the title *Khwamsuk Kho'ng Chan* (My Happiness). Wichit's happiness was neither wealth nor honour. Neither did it concern any form of entertainment such as plays and films nor did it involve women and drinking. It was none of those things:

สุขของฉันอยู่ที่งานหล่อเลี้ยงจิต	My happiness is in work that nourishes my mind.
สุขของฉันอยู่ที่คิดสมบัติบ้า	My happiness is to think about something profound.
คิดทำโน่นทำนี้ทุกเวลา	I think of doing this and that all the time.
เมื่อเห็นงานก้าวหน้าก็สุขใจ	I am happy when I see progress in this work of mine.

(Wichit 1942: 30)

No' Saranupraphan used nature to promote his leader in verse. Human beings were compared with a tree, the symbol of oneness and unity. It comprised roots, a trunk and many branches, flowers, fruits, and leaves. The leader of the Nation was like the tap root while other main roots formed the government. The trunk and branches represented the government officials and leaves, fruits and flowers were the people. Everyone should adhere to *samakkhi chai* (united victory). The poem concluded:

เมื่อผู้นำคือรากแก้วนำแถวหน้า	When the Leader, our 'tap root', leads the way
เหล่าประชาราสตร์ตามมาหาคร้ามไม่	The people follow without fear
เกินตามท่านจนบันลุวัธนชัย	Walk behind the leader to cultural victory
คือที่หมายของชาติไทย ชโย เทอน	That is our destination. Hurray!

(No' Saranupraphan 1942: 39)

According to Wichit, the lack of commitment to working hard was a deeply rooted Thai characteristic. Thais did not work hard enough (Wichit 1939: 324) and therefore this habit had to be changed. The law concerning the 'kitchen garden' *(suan khrua)* was no joke. On the contrary, it was an important action required by the need for 'human revolution'. The 'kitchen garden' law was not simply aimed to help supplement the family's income but the ultimate aim was to instil the work ethic in the people (Wichit 1939: 323).

Some Thai literary classics were regarded undesirable, especially those works borrowed from India. In this instance, the Ramakian was singled out. The hero Rama, according to Wichit, was a weak, indecisive and ineffectual character. As commander of the army, Rama was dependent on Phiphek. Indeed, Rama could not be regarded as a good human example and yet, Wichit complained, Rama, like many other heroes in Thai literature, was loved and respected for becoming good by doing nothing. It was Pali literature, however, that Wichit favoured especially the Buddhistic tales related to cannonical as well as non-cannonical texts (Wichit 1939: 328-9).

Nearly half of the contributors for the Journal devoted their efforts towards the promotion of the government's cultural policy in creating the new state identity and directing the process of nation-building. Certain authors, especially Prasoet Sapsuntho'n, Cho' Suntho'nphiphit and No' Saranupraphan, etc. took charge in writing regularly on specific subjects and themes to stimulate patriotism, order and unity. The message was always clear: things "we" Thais should and should not do and how "we" Thais should behave and think. Issues raised were often those related to the *rattha niyom* and other government policies currently issued by the ruling power.[7] Wichit's Bushido code of conduct, *wiratham,* for example, was put into verse for the Journal by Co' Suwannathat (1943b: 16-29) and was propounded again three months later by Camlong Kasikaphan (1943: 6-12). No' Saranupraphan gave a detailed account of his composition of the lyrics of the new National Anthem. The author highlighted his effort by relating that he had to spend three days of intense mind-storming and deep contemplation to pack all essential elements necessary for the shaping of the new Thai characteristic traits into the anthem. These were, Thai nationhood; Thainess; preservation of independence; unity and fraternity; ethic and civic duty of the Thais; bravery and readiness to sacrifice one's lives for the country; the Thais are peace-loving but always

---

[7] Most of these writings were presented in the form of short poems with explicit or obvious titles such as *"sang chat"* (building the nation) (Cho' Suntho'nphiphit 1942: 25-26); *"samret yu thi tham"* (success depends on action) (So' Satakurama 1943: 3-4); *"koet pen Thai"* (born to be Thai) (Prasoet Sapsuntho'n 1942: 54); *"chat - satsana"* (nation - religion) (Co' Suwannathat 1943: 46-50) etc.

ready to fight when provoked; nation-building, and the nourishing of nationalism (No' Saranupraphan 1943a: 32-54).

Contributions on the language and literature in the journal were by established scholars including Anuman Rajadhon, Dhanit Yupho, Montri Tramot, Worawet Siwasariyanon and Plu'ang Na Nakho'n. Although their works were undeniably scholarly and informative, their reasons for writing them were strictly within the context of "nation-building".

Dhanit Yupho, writing on "Thai Literature" made a serious effort to construct a Thai literary history. His article was dedicated to Phibun as the founder of the Literature Association of Thailand. The history of Thai literature began with Wichit's nationalistic version of Thai history, giving an account of the time when people belonging to the Thai race were driven South by the Chinese. They were dispersed and finally settled in Indo-China, Burma, Laos, Tonkin, Cambodia, and Assam. The most important group among these, however, were

> The group of people who were able to set up an independent state and govern themselves by the people of their own race with a strong democratic form of government under the present Thai constitution (Dhanit 1942: 106).

This piece of Thai literary historiography followed the official line of state identity building. After all, it was during this period that the Thais were told the origins of their race. This episode of historical imaginaire had been intensely created, constructed, and articulated through songs, plays and novels relating to the Kingdom of Nanchao.

Dhanit's literary history started by informing the readers that Thai literature was a great ancient literature handed down from their ancesters for generations. The author cited de la Loubere for attesting that 'Thais were natural poets'. The narrative moved on to give an account of the Thai's first piece of literature -the Ramkhamhaeng Inscription, the great literary work which had been studied by Wichit. By quoting Wichit, the narrative went on to say that Ramkhamhaeng was the first Great King of the Thais, who not only freed the Thai race from foreign domination but also built up Thailand into a strong nation. Then the more direct political message followed:

> We were new comers so we had to follow the way of the people who lived there before us. We had accepted so much of Mon and Khmer civilization that we were

assimilated into becoming Mon and Khmer. When we were set free from the Khmer by the great King we stopped using the Khmer language and brought our own language back into full use. ....At the beginning, when we were first set free from the Khmer, changing ourselves back into true Thais again became our priority, including things such as our dress and language. We had to invent essential things such as the alphabet and national literature as a matter of urgency. We also needed our own moral code in order to advise the people (Dhanit 1942: 105-133).

A series of articles on "History of Thai Poets" by Worawet Siwasariyanon is also most informative as well as interesting. His reason for writing the 'history of Thai poets' was ascribed to his strong sense of duty as a Thai who must take part in the creation and the making of "Thainess" all for the benefit of the "Nation"(phu'a prayot kho'ng chat). Like Dhanit, Worawet constructed the history of Sukhothai as a great, expansive and prosperous Thai Kingdom where King Ramkhamhaeng the Great, the first poet in his repertoire, created Thai orthography and the famous stone inscription. Worawet's interpretation of history here reflected the trends of thought and the mood and mode of thinking of his time. Thus not only did King Ramkhamhaeng ruled over an expansive Kingdom, he also had a good relationship with great powers such as China which he visited twice. The King showed strength at war, supported Buddhism, and created his own language identity by replacing the Kho'm writing system with the newly created Thai alphabet. Worawet stressed here that King Ramkhamhaeng the Great had freed the Thais from foreign domination. He was a brave, intelligent, and just King (wira rat, thiara rat, thamma rat) (Worawet 1942: 86), and by means of comparison, these qualities were evident in Phibun--the new leader. The composition of Suphasit Phra Ruang (Maxims of King Ruang) was also attributed to King Ramkhamhaeng. According to Worawet, Suphasit Phra Ruang comprised genuine Thai teaching i.e. free from Pali and Sanskrit influences and they were written down by the King because King Ramkhamhaeng realized that:

Thai people had just become free people and therefore had to rebuild themselves. In building the 'nation' during that period of history the King as the leader had to take the lead and thus he issued the banyat niyom i.e. the suphasit phra ruang, in the same way that we have our rattha niyom (State Prescriptions) today (Wo'rawet 1942: 90).

The most interesting personality of Wannakhadi San was probably the editor himself. He was much admired and respected by Phibun and members of the ruling power but was sometimes accused of being a 'turn-coat' for collaborating with Phibun (Sulak 1991: 51). His acceptance of the editorship of the Journal had clearly given the leadership and the *rattha niyom* some legitimacy. Moreover, his constant praise and admiration for Phibun coupled with statements of endorsement of the regime's policies made his position more untenable. Unlike Prince Wan, Phya Anuman Rajadhon, who served as the Vice-President of the Literature Association, stuck firmly to his task as a scholar. He contributed regularly to the Journal on the subjects of Thai language and culture and had never openly shown any sign of flattery with Phibun, at least not in writing. His regular contributions were mostly on the subjects of both linguistic and literary interest, such as *Khwam Khli Khlai Kho'ng Kham Thai* (the moderation of Thai words), *Pha Khao Ma* (the loin cloth) and *Khru'ang Prathip Nai Wannakhadi Thai* (Lamp torch in Thai Literature).

Prince Wan's main contribution to the field of language and literature in the Journal was on etymology, philology, and literary criticism. The introduction of Western literary knowledge to the readers of the journal can be seen as the editor's programme of selective modernization in which only good, practical, and useful Western literary concepts were adopted. Western knowledge on literary theories such as Aristotle's *'Poetics'*, Arnold Bennet's *'Literary Taste'*, Abercrombie's *'Literary Criticism'*, and I.A. Richards *'Principles of Literary Criticism'* were introduced, simplified and explained by the editor under various titles such as *Kot Ken Nirutti Witthaya* (theory of etymology), *wannakhadi wiphak* (literary criticism) (Wan Waithayako'n 1943: 75-87, 1944: 65-75) etc. Later Pin Malakun and his wife, Dutsadi, added to the modernizing process by publishing the introduction to and the translation of the opera version of Goethe's Faust, which they believed to be the "highest form of literary and artistic culture of Western civilization" (Pin 1944: 24-30 and Dutsadi 1944: 31-38).

It is worth noting, however, that inspite of Prince Wan's effort to modernize and redefine 'literature' none of the contributors seemed to pay any attention to contemporary literature. The type of literature being dealt with in *Wannakhadi San* appeared to be those of conventional literature drawing on the knowledge expounded by scholars of the Siamese court. All contributors on literature, Dhanit, Worawet and Plu'ang conformed to classical literary conventions, and their views, attitudes, and conception on Thai literature belonged to those of Prince Damrong's School. Their views on Thai literary history showed a close link with the past. It was how the past was used in their exposition of traditional literature for nation-building ideology and the responsibility which was placed before them that made them different. In order to carry out their mission successfully Thai literary scholars had to undertake the task of reconstructing, reasserting as well as repositioning classical literature to serve the new interest.

In 1942, Worawet was Head of the Thai Department at Chulalongkorn University and had already published poems and articles on Thai literature before joining the Journal. He was a great scholar of Thai literature and a teacher who was much loved and respected. He was a recognized expert on Thai literature and many foreign researchers often sought him out for his knowledge of Thai literature (Supho'n 1960: 1-25). Plu'ang was taught Thai literature by Worawet at Chula. He in turn became famous as a Thai literature specialist for his book *Parithat Haeng Wannakhadi Thai* (Review on Thai Literature), a two-volume-book which was published in 1937. The review of Plu'ang's book by Prince Chula was printed in many newspapers including *Sayam Niko'n, Sikrung, Thai Mai,* and *Prachachat* which gave the author the good publicity he needed. He started writing on Thai literature for the *Ekkachon* magazine from 1942 which later formed the third volume of his "Review on Thai Literature" (So' Phlaino'i 1984).

Apart from the nationalistic messages contained in their writings, Worawet and Plu'ang's contributions to the *Wannakhadi San* Journal were substantial. Their writings were the inspirational force that brought credibility and respectability to the Journal. Worawet's articles on History of Thai Poets and Poetry Composition *(Kan Kawi)* appeared in nearly every issue of the Journal. His narrative was clear, instructive, and packed with useful information on Thai poets and their works. His approach to Thai literary history represented the solid old school of Thai literature whereby the different periods of Thai literary history followed a strict division of Thai history using the names of the Capitals of the old Kingdoms. Plu'ang, however, restricted his writings to versification, starting from *Klo'n, Kap,* and *Chan* respectively drawing his knowledge mostly from the work of Luang Thammaphimon (Thu'k) on versification.

Versification and poetry did, however, represent the link with the greatest of Thai literary past and were used aggressively by the Journal. All forms of verse were experimented with by nearly every writer. Phibun's wife was praised for her ability to compose in *Khlong, Klo'n,* and even in *Chan* which she wrote usually to uplift the spirit of the soldiers and the virtues of the supporting roles of Thai women (No' Saranupraphan 1943b). Cham Tho'ng-khamwan, an expert on Thai and Khmer languages from Chulalongkorn University, put the names of the new set of the Thai alphabet into rhymes making it easy to remember and adding to it a nationalistic flavour. Poetry competitions were organized monthly by the Association which later published the winning poems in the Journal and granted membership to the winners. A list of proverbs and old sayings were set for competitors to choose for their composition. The aim was to encourage Thai people to preserve their proverbs, learn them correctly, and hold dear to their hearts for self-benefit and national-identification. By July, 1943, one year after the establishment of the Association, the Committee initiated a new practice - new members were asked to recite the acceptance of their membership in verse, either in *Kap*, *Klo'n*, *Khlong*, or *Chan*, when badges were presented to them by Phibun at a public gathering. The biggest and most ambitious project for poetry competion was also organized to co-incide with the celebration of the 10th anniversary of democracy. The topic *"Sip Pi Haeng Watthana Chai"* (10 years of cultural victory) was the subject for poetry competition and, in order to insure the sacredess of this event, contestants were required to use the most prestigeous *Chan* verse form. The aim, this time, was to promote Thai "Language Culture" (*watthanatham thang phasa*).

Prince Wan, the editor, took the lead in initiating the debate on the prestigeous *Chan* metre which soon gathered momentum. Contributors to the knowledge of the *Chan* included Luang Bunyamanop (better known as Saeng Tho'ng), Plu'ang Na Nakho'n and Sawet Piamphongsan. The revival of the *Chan* was finally endorsed and authorized by Phibun who recognised the symbol of civilization that was attached to it and the prestige it brought to the nation (Phibun 1943: 93-94). Saeng Tho'ng published his translation from English, the *Nakhri Kham Chan* in order to popularize the use of the metre. Finally, in order to bring the point home for the readers, the Journal published a comedy play entitled *Sukkha Nattakam Wannakhadi Thai* (A Comedy on Thai Literature) where the characters hummed the *Chan* recitation as their daily routine at home (Cho' Suntho'nphiphit 1943). Even a *Nirat* poem, *Nirat Chanthaburi*, was written in the *Chan* verse form. Finally, in order to enhance the prestige of *Wannakhadi San* , the editor agreed that the serialization of a more modern classic, *Inlarat Khamchan* , would form one of the regular features of the Journal.

It is clear that scholars of Thai literature had effectively identified themselves with what they conceived to be the greatness of their literary past by looking to classical literary convention as the model. Texts which were available on Thai literature owed much to Prince Damrong, founder of the National Library. With the assistance of the French and German scholars, Coedes and Frankfurter, manuscripts were sorted and classified, and many were published in the Vajirayan Journal and later in book form with introductions by Prince Damrong. Altogether, nearly 200 prefaces and introductions were written by the Prince and a set of systems on Thai literary classification, genres, were laid down for future generations. The discourse of Thai studies as a whole was carried out very effectively during the time of the absolute monarchy and a well-known body of Siamese knowledge had been solidly constructed by such great scholars as King Chulalongkorn, Prince Damrong, and Phya Anuman Rajadhon etc. These works had become the source of Siamese knowledge of a high scholarly standard upon which new scholars like Plu'ang and Worawet could depend and build. Like other forms of Thai culture, court literature still formed the basis, indeed, the core of knowledge of Thai literature.

Moreover, the *rattha niyom* policy had also made it difficult, if not impossible, to mention any regional literature in the *Wannakhadi San,* let alone to discuss or publish it. Many of the new elements articulated and enforced by the new culture, such as new names, dress, new year date, music and dance forms etc. caught on to become part of a new national culture and was embraced as the culture of the bureaucrats. However, regional art forms such as *Phleng Cho'i, Mo' Lam, Nora,* and *So' Mu'ang* as well as regional literary forms became unimportant, being regarded as popular, subcultures from then onwards.

The 12th volume of the 1st year of the Journal was entirely devoted to Phibun's birthday celebration. All regular contributors and members of the Journal were united in writing poems to glorify the leader. Prince Wan, for instance, wrote *Phibula Sirawat* (Bowing to Phibun) in the *Chan* metre. No' Saranupraphan went even further and wrote *Phibun Bucha* (in Worship of Phibun) in the *Klo'n* verse form.

In the following year, the Journal repeated the same act of reverence and devoted its 12th volume of the 2nd year to Phibun's birthday. A new name, Somrot Sawatdikun wrote *Sip Si Karakada* (July 14, which was Phibun's birth date) to glorify Phibun and to wish him happiness on his birthday. Such

a poem defies translation and is reproduced here in its original form in order
to illustrate the scale of flirtation exemplified by one of Phibun's admirers.

อรุนรุ่งหล้าฟ้าเบิก   สุภเรกล์กรกศาสิบสี่
อมรินท์ปิ่นฟ้าอารี   ประทานเทพมนีแก่ไทย
เปนจินการัตนจรัศแสง   เรืองแรงรัศมีสิไล
ส่องรัตรี่นวัยนชัย   ชื่นใจแก่ชาวประชา
ขอรัตนรุ้งร่วงควงนี้   จงคงสักก็สรีสง่า
นึกไกไกัดังจินดา   เทิดไทยคู่ฟ้าชาตรี

(Somrot 1944: 23)

Somrot emerged as a young literary star by becoming the double winner of
poetry competitions organized by the Literature Association of Thailand. Not
only were her prize-winning poems published in the Journal but she was also
invited to become a member of the Association. Association membership was a
great honour and only well-established persons were accepted and given a
membership badge. Prominent members of high society, well-known scholars
and experts in the fields of language and literature were sought out or
nominated and, if suitable, accepted by the Association's Committee. Names of
new members were printed on the last page of the Journal. Some members,
such as Prince Damrong and Prince Naris, were invited to join the Association
because they added prestige and respectability to the Association.

Somrot's contribution to Thai literary studies, *Khwam La-iat Nai Kan
Phitcarana Nangsu' Thai* (A close and careful reading of a Thai Literary Text)
appeared in the 4th volume of the second year of the Journal. Her work was
important and will be taken as a case study here for two reasons.

1. It represented the courage, confidence, and a sense of pride of a
young and successful scholar nourished under the new imagined society
created by the new regime. It will be assumed here that she was a product of
this new ideology.

2. It attracted the attention of Atsani Phonlacan, better known as Nai
Phi who was himself a scholar of Sanskrit literature and a well-known poet as
well as a literary critic, who opposed the ideology of imagined nation-building
created by the regime.

Essentially, Somrot claimed that Thai artistic creation was one of the
best in the world, so good that it was beyond any comparison. She was in
disagreement with those who dared to say that Thai art forms were inferior to

45

those of the West. According to Somrot, the problem was that few Thais understood Thai arts because their knowledge of them was shallow and superficial; they, therefore, praised Western arts as being better than their own. She went on to say that the Thai artistic standard was so high that it was not an easy thing to understand let alone to appreciate. It was not created for laymen and only those who seek knowledge and were really interested in arts would be able to see its aesthetic virtues. This was why ordinary people often overlooked Thai arts which they often devalued it below the values of arts of 'other people' (Somrot 1943: 42).

Somrot then turned to literature. She asserted that it was difficult to read good literary work and appreciate its aesthetic beauty, especially when the reader lacked knowledge and thoroughness. This had caused people to find it hard to understand our national literature (*wannakhadi kho'ng chat*). It made people feel discouraged and they were unable to see its special virtues. She therefore wished to set a standard by illustrating how one could read a *Nirat* poem by Phraya Trang. Some difficult *khlong* stanzas were then selected to show that by depending on one's knowledge of Thai history, and, in some places, knowledge of geography, one would be able to read the poems with full understanding. The aesthetic knowledge was also expressed by comparing certain stanzas of the *Nirat* (by now she had proved when and by whom it was written) with *Khlong Kamsuan Siprat* of the Ayutthaya period making the judgement that some of Phraya Trang's poetry was as beautiful *(Phairo')* as the *Kamsuan Siprat* and pointing out that one of Phraya Trang's *Khlong* stanza was even more beautiful than that of *Kamsuan Siprat*. She finally praised Phraya Trang as a great Thai poet who had written a great poem (Somrot 1943: 44-63).

Two months later Atsani Phonlacan reacted in his reply article entitled *Lam Nam No'i Ik Khrang Nu'ng (Lam Nam No'i* Once More) which was also published by *Wannakhadi San*. Aisani pointed out that he had published a similar study some months ago. He also singled out Somrot's misunderstandings and misinterpretations of some of the vocabulary using the Sanskrit theory of aesthetics as the basis to disprove Somrot's judgement on the beauty of some of her examples in the article (Atsani 1943: 76-84).

If one reads between the lines, Atsani's main complaint was simply that Somrot seemed to think that she was the only expert who held the keys to all the truths on Thai literature - like a missionary preaching a religion. He clearly disapproved of Somrot's exegetical approach to the exposition of Thai literary knowledge.[8]

Both Phibun and Wichit might have been dead for a long time but the nation-building imaginaire they created has not died with them. The intense programme for 'Nation-Building' they created had effectively established hegemony of state power over civil society which had extended, strengthened and legitimized the power and authority of the state-controlled 'Cultural Instutition' to which Thai language and literature belonged. The Literature Association and the *Wannakhadi San* might have been broken up when Phibun lost his Premiership but their discourse remains and the effects have been pervasive and long lasting.

Great scholars such as Phya Anuman, Worawet, and Plu'ang, had between them produced many scholarly works on Thai literature. Phya Anuman wrote authoritatively on Thai language, culture, customs, and literature. His volumes on Thai literature *(muat wannakhadi)* were his lectures given at Chulalongkorn University where he was a guest professor. Khun Phra Worawet, as he is now remembered, was at the same Institution, teaching Thai literature to students in the Faculty of Arts, many of whom became teachers of Thai literature themselves. Plu'ang Na Kakho'n's book *Prawat Wannakhadi Thai Samrap Naksu'ksa* (A History of Thai Literature for Students) is still one of the best, now in its eighth edition, together with numerous writings on Thai literature both in book form and as articles which appeared in journals. By working for one of the biggest publishers in the country, he also helped to publish many literary works by younger scholars and academics.

Other members of the Literature Association who had been nourished under the umbrella of *Wannakhadi San* later became prominent. These were members of the bureaucracy, writers, teachers, scholars, and poets who joined the Association either because they were well established in their fields or through winning a poetry competition. Some of the significant names include Pin Malakul who later became Minister of Education; Cu'a Satawethin, who wrote so many books on Thai literature for both adults and children; Wit

---

[8] Atsani's reaction to this type of writing by many contributors to the Wannakhadi San Journal was to become much more comprehensive. Collections of his articles written under the pen name (Si Intharayut) have been published in two books entitled *Kho' Khit Cak Wannakhadi* and *Sinlapakan Haeng Kap Klo'n*. These articles began to ask some interesting questions along Marxist lines. They aroused social consciousness, questioned the validity of Classical literature, a matter which came to a head after the student uprising in October 1973.

Siwasariyanon, the son of Worawet, who authored one of the most authoritative books on literary criticism in Thai; Kamchai Tho'ng Lo' the author of books on Thai language and literature and a Royal instructor for Thai language.

These were influential men who had many students and followers and commanded great respect. Some were great scholars who enjoyed complete authority in their respective fields and who, in some ways, had been part of the management of Thai literature and part of Thai literary discourse at a crucial moment in Thai history. So much involved were they that they developed a sense of ownership and could become not only protective but also defensive on matters relating to the language and literature and even on anything Thai. They had been at the forefront of the creation of Thainess itself. Together they had achieved great success in shaping and directing the attitudes and values concerning Thai literature.

The attitude of Somrot mentioned above is a streotypical one. It helps to understand the squabbles and debates concerning Thai literature which took place soon after the 1973 'student uprising'.

Writings on Thai literature by prominent authorities such as Kulap Mallikamat, Satcapo'n Singhaphalin, Ru'ang-Urai Kusalasai, Pha-Op Posakritsana, Thapani Nakho'nthap, Supho'n Bunnak etc, to name just a few, and not to mention school textbooks produced, sponsored, or endorsed by the Ministry of Education, reflect the scale of success of Thai literary discourse during the Phibun-Wichit's nation-building period. It is always admirable for instance, to see the reverence paid to the classical texts by Chanthit when he worked on Thai literary classics such as *Yuan Phai, Phra Lo', Khlong Kamsuan Siprat* and *Khlong Thawathotsamat;* or to read Supho'n's interpretation of *Phra Lo'* and *Khun Chang Khun Phaen* in her series entitled *'Sombat Kawi'.* (The Poet's treasure).

When Chonthira applied Western psychological theory to analyse Thai literary characters in her M.A. thesis (Chonthira 1970), Supho'n reacted sharply and emotionally. Western psychologists, according to Supho'n, were those who had "lost faith in their parents' religion" and without faith they had to look for something to hold on to. Freud and Jung had no faith in religion and were socially rejected foreigners who invented unworthy theories to satisfy their egos (Supho'n 1973: 13-15). After all, Thai literary characters could not possibly be subjected to those awful Western psychological complexes (Supho'n 1973:19-20). A true Thai like Supho'n who loved 'Thai Heritage' (*sombat kho'ng chat Thai*) certainly could not allow that to happen and so had the duty to speak out (Supho'n 1973: 20).

A more scholarly debate on the study of Thai literature can be seen from the review article by Sumali criticizing an article entitled *Watthanatham ·Kradumphi Kap Wannakam Ton Rattanakosin* (Bourgeois Culture and Early Bangkok Literature) by Nidhi Aewsrivongse (Sumali 1982: 113-125).[9] Here Nidhi's scholarly and insightful multi-disciplinary attempt to show relationship between literature and socio-economic history, which should be valuable in understanding Thai literary development and transformation, was simply brushed aside and ignored. Instead of being an asset to Thai scholarship, Nidhi's stature was reduced to a mere someone who "did not study and research the history and characteristics of Thai literary works thoroughly enough" and therefore much of his evidence was "outdated, incorrect, as well as lacking in rationality and plausibility" (Sumali 1982: 113). Nidhi was also guilty of trying to bend his facts in order to suit his theoretical framework which was not only foreign (Western) but also class-conscious (Sumali 1982: 114).

A professor of Philosophy once accused Nidhi of trying to cause division and incite conflict. Making reference to the favourite school literary classic, *Samakkhiphet Khamchan*, which has been constantly used by Thai authorities to instil unity, he wrote:

> This line of thinking would create political conflict between those who agree with the idea and those who do not. This is the same method that Watsakara Phram used to trick King Litchawi (Pricha 1989: 307).[10]

Phibun's nation-building ideology had effectively and deeply instilled the imaginary concept of *chat* and *Thainess* in its members. To them *chat* and *Thainess* meant harmony. Conflict, differences, or even diversity, became taboo - the undesirable elements of society. Differences implied division which was undesirable, while harmony meant unity and was hence desirable. Sumali objected to Nidhi's idea of division and conflict when analysing Thai society as *watthanatham munnai* (court culture/culture of the ruling class) and *watthana-*

---

[9] Nidhi responded to Sumali's criticism in the following issue of the same journal. See Nidhi 1983: 406-411.

[10] This was Pricha's reaction to Nidhi's article entitled *"Phasa Thai Mattrathan kap Kanmu'ang"*. See Nidhi 1989: 11-37.

tham phrai (country culture/culture of the commoner) or to talk about *wannakam munnai* (court literature) and *wannakam phrai* (literature of the commoner). In the *chat Thai* society where, every member is supposed to live in harmony, there could only be *wannakam Thai* (Thai literature) and *watthana-tham Thai* (Thai culture).

Thais have been led to imagine that in such a conflict-free community so long as everyone does his duty then there would be harmony in that community. Whenever there is a breakdown in the system, it is either because someone carries out an un-Thai activity or there is a lack of unity. As we have seen, the 'foreign' or 'un-Thai' element has been one of the factors that provoked Somrot, Supho'n, and Sumali to voice their objection and launch their attack. Such a mentality fits perfectly into the framework which Thongchai called the "Negative Identification" i.e. the "we/us" versus "they/the others" criteria (Thongchai 1988: 3-9).[11] When it comes to the matter of 'Thainess' or 'Being Thai' it is a novelty for Thais to blame the 'foreign elements' for anything they consider evil or threatening to their selfhood and 'national security'. In this context, Supho'n, Somrot, and Sumali stand as a living testimony to Phibun's success in creating a new nation as a thing called *chat Thai* which has been loyally served by *wannakhadi Thai*.

Phibun and Luang Wichit can safely claim their *watthana chai* (Cultural Victory) especially among members of the bureaucratic elite, the majority of whom still feel that the essence of Thainess and Thai identity has been well preserved and that it is their duty to protect and defend what they believe to be their heritage.

REFERENCES

Anuman Rajadhon, Phraya
    1988a *Ngan Niphon Chut Sombun Kho'ng Sattracan Phraya Anuman*
        Rajadhon, Muat Wannakhadi Lem thi So'ng Ru'ang Khwanru Kiao
        Kap Wannakhadi Lae Thep Niyai Songkhro, Bangkok.

---

11 See also Nidhi 1991: 146-148.

1988b *Ngan Niphon Chut Sombun Kho'ng Sattracan Phraya Anuman*
       Rajadhon, Muat Wannakhadi Lem Thi Sam Ruang Kan Su'ksa
       Wannakhadi Ngae Wannasin,. Bangkok.

Atsani Phonlacan
  1943 "Lam Nam No'i Ik Khrang Nu'ng". *Wannakhadi San* 2: 6: 76-84.

Chai-anan Samudavanija
  1991 "State-Identity creation, State-Building and civil society". In
        Craig Reynolds (ed.) *National Identity and Its defenders, Thailand*
        1939-1989. Monash Papers on Southeast Asia No.25. Aristoc
        Press Pty. Ltd. Victoria, Australia.

Charnvit Kasetsiri
  1993 "Latthi Chat Niyom - Latthi Thahan: Ratthaban Co'mphon
        Po' Phibun Songkhram 2481 - 2487". In *Ekkasan Prako'p*
        Kansammana Ru'ang Co'mphon Po' Phibun Songkhram
        Kap Kanmu'ang Thai Samai Mai (Papers presented at a
        seminar on "Phibun and Modern Thai Politics"). Faculty of
        Liberal Arts, Thammasat University. pp. 1-33.

Chonthira Sattayawatthana
  1970 "Kan Nam Wannakhadi Wican Phaen Mai Baep Tawantok Ma
        Chai Kap Wannakhadi Thai". MA Thesis, Chulalongkorn
        University.

Cho' Suntho'nphiphit
  1942 "Sang Chat". *Wannakhadi San* 1: 10: 25-26.

  1943 " Bot Lakho'n Sukkha Nattakam Ru'ang Rot Wannakhadi".
        Wannakhadi San 1: 11: 55-72.

Co' Kasikaphan
  1943 "Wiratham Haeng Chat Thai". *Wannakhadi San* 2: 6: 6-21.

Co' Suwannathat
  1943a "Chat - Satsana". *Wannakhadi San* 1: 6: 46-50.

1943b "Wiratham Kham Chan". *Wannakhadi San* 2: 3: 16-29.

Dhanit Yupho
1942 "Wannakhadi Thai". *Wannakhadi San* 1: 1: 105-133.

Dutsadee Malakul (trans.)
1944 "Faust Ong thi Ha (Chak 2)". *Wannakhadi San* 3: 1: 31-38.

Fine Arts Department
1978 *Sarup Phon Kan Sammana Wannakhadi Thai*, Bangkok.

Jiraporn Witayasakpan
1992 "Nationalism and the Transformation of Aesthetic Concepts:
Theatre in Thailand during the Phibun Period". Ph.D
Dissertation, Cornell University.

Nakharin Simektrairat
1989 "Rabop Niyom Co'mphon Po' Phibunsongkhram: Kan Ko'
Rup Kho'ng Naeo Khwam Khit Lae Khwam Mai Thang Kan
Mu'ang". *Ratthasat* 14:3 - 15:1,228-274.

Nidhi Aewsrivongse
1982 "Watthanatham Kradumphi Kap Wannakam Ton
Ratanakosin".*Warasan Thammasat* 11:1, 71-87.

1983 "Cotmai Thu'ng Bannathikan". *Aksonsat, Mahawitthayalai
Sinlapako'n* 6: 1-2: 407-411.

1989 "Phasa Thai Matrathan Kap Kanmu'ang". *Phasa Lae Nangsu'* 17:
2: 11-37.

1991 "Chat Thai Lae Mu'ang Thai Nai Baep Rian Prathom Su'ksa".
Sinlapa Watthanatham 12: 10: 142-164.

No' Saranupraphan, Phan Ek
1942 "Manutsachat Kap Pru'ksachat". *Wannakhadi San* 1: 1: 38-39.

1943a "Nu'a Ro'ng Phleng Chat 82". *Wannakhadi San* 1: 11: 32-54.

1943b "Than Phuying Kap Wannakhadi". *Wannakhadi San* 2: 3: 34-40.

Phibun, Field Marshal
1942 "Aphinanthanakan Dae Wannakhadi San". *Wannakhadi San* 1: 1: 1-6.

1943 "Khunkha Wannakhadi". *Wannakhadi San* 1: 12: 1-3.

Pin Malakul, Mom Luang
1944 "Faust: Khamnam". *Wannakhadi San* 3: 1: 24-30.

Pra-o'nrat Buranamat
1985 *Luang Wichit Wathakan Kap Bot Lakho'n Prawattisat.* Bangkok: Thammasat University Press.

Pricha Changkhwanyu'n
1989 "Mattrathan Thang Watanatham Kap Kantham Hai Keot Ngu'an Thang Kanmu'ang". *Ratthasat* 14: 3 - 15: 1. 275-310.

Reynolds, Craig J. (ed.)
1991 *Nationalism and its defenders: Thailand, 1939-1989,* Monash Papers on Southeast Asia -No.25. Victoria, Australia: Aristoc Press Pty. Ltd.

Si Intharayut
1975a *Sinlapakan Haeng Kap Klo'n.* Bangkok: Thap Na Ram.

1975b *Kho Khit Cak Wannakhadi.* Bangkok: Sun Klang Nakrian Haeng Prathet Thai.

So' Phlai No'i
1984 *Chiwit Lae Ngan Nai Tamra Na Mu'ang Tai,* Bangkok: Ruam San.

So' Satakurama
1943   "Samret Yu Thi Tham". *Wannakhadi San* 2: 4: 3-4.

Somrot, Sawatdikun Na Ayutthaya
1943   "Khwam La-iat Nai Kan Pitcarana Nangsu' Thai". *Wannakhadi San* 2: 4: 41-63.

1944   "Sip Si Karakada". *Wannakhadi San* 2: 12: 23.

Stow, Judith A.
1991   *Siam becomes Thailand: A Story of Intrigue.* Honolulu: University of Hawaii Press.

Sumali Wirawong
1982   "Kho' Khit Nu'angcak Bot Khwam Ru'ang 'Watthanatham Kadumphi Kap Wannakam Ton Ratanakosin' Kho'ng Nithi Iaosiwong". *Aksonsat Mahawitthayalai Sinlapakon* 5: 2 : 113-125.

Supho'n Bunnak
1960   "Sangkhep Prawat Kho'ng Phra Wo'rawet Phisit". In Wo'rawet Phisit, *Worawet Niphon,* Cremation Volume. Bangkok: Siwapho'n, pp. 1-25.

1973   "Kan Yatyiat Pom Wiparit Ru'ang Phet Hai Kae Wannakhadi Thai". *Phasa Lae Nangsu* ' 8: 9-40.

1978a   "Phra Lo'". In *Sarup Phon Kan Sammana Wannakhadi Thai,* Bangkok: Fine Arts Departement, 228-250.

1978b   "Mo'radok Thai". In *Sarup Phon Kan Sammana Wannakhadi Thai,* Bangkok: Fine Arts Department, 342-365.

Thamsook Numnonda
1978   "Pibulsongkram's Thai Nation-Building Programme During the Japanese Military Presence". 1941-1945. *Journal of Southeast Asian Studies* 9: 2: 234-247.

Thongchai Winichakul
1988   "Siam Mapped: A History of the Geo-body of Siam". Ph.D
        Thesis, University of Sydney.

Wan Waithayakon, Prince
1942   "Bot Bannathikan", *Wannakhadi San* 1: 1: 7-17.

1943   "Kot Ken Nirutti Witthaya". *Wannakhadi San* 1: 10: 75-87.

1944   "Wannakhadi Wiphak". *Wannakhadi San* 2: 9: 65-75.

1991   *The Centennial of His Royal Highness Prince Wan
        Waithayakon Krommun Narathip Bongsprabandh.*
        Bangkok: Office of the National Culture Commission.

Wichitwathakan, Luang
1928   *Mahaburut,* Bangkok.

1933a   "Bushido". *Duang Prathip* 2: 28: 3.

1933b   "Latthi Chu Chat". *Duang Prathip* 2: 36: 5-6, 10-30.

1939   "Manutsa Patiwat". In *Pathakatha Lae Kham Banyai,* Bangkok
        311-345.

1942   "Khwamsuk Kho'ng Chan". *Wannakhadi San* 1: 1: 26-31.

Worawet phisit, Phra
1942   "Prawat Kawi Thai". *Wannakhadi San* 1: 1: 78-104.

1960   *Wo'rawet Niphon,* Cremation Volume, Bangkok: Siwapho'n.

THE STUDY OF *TRAIPHUM PHRA RUANG* : SOME CONSIDERATIONS

Søren Ivarsson

INTRODUCTION

Depicted as the first independent kingdom of importance in Thailand, the Sukhothai kingdom has occupied an unique position in Thai historical studies for a long time. Personified by King Ramkhamhaeng and King Lithai, this period has become a metaphor for the original Thai culture and the foundation upon which modern Thailand is based.

This is an interpretation which can be traced back to a period when Siam was under pressure from the European colonial powers in the area and when the origins of the new national state, which was under formation, was searched in history. Previously the Bangkok Kingdom had perceived itself as a continuation of the Ayutthaya Kingdom, sacked by the Burmese in 1767. But by use of stone inscriptions from the Sukhothai period that were discovered during the 19th century, it became possible to trace connections back to a kingdom that already in the 13th century possessed a territory almost equivalent to present-day Thailand, possessed its own alphabet, and appeared as a harmonious society with a prosperous Thai culture. The later generally accepted sketch of Thai history as proceeding along a geographical and temporal axis consisting of Sukhothai, Ayutthaya, and finally the Bangkok Kingdom, is an outcome of this construction.

The cosmological text *Traiphum Phra Ruang* appears as an important element in the writing of the history of the Sukhothai Kingdom. *Traiphum Phra Ruang* was written in Thai and it has traditionally been assumed that it was written in 1345 by King Lithai, before he became king. According to this dating of the text, *Traiphum Phra Ruang* not only becomes the oldest cosmological text written in Thailand but also becomes the first book written in Thai. Together with the so-called Ramkhamhaeng inscription, *Traiphum Phra Ruang* has become the epitome of the traditional Thai values that the Sukhothai Kingdom is associated with.

Not only for Sukhothai history, but also for the history of Thailand more generally, *Traiphum Phra Ruang* has been assigned a paramount importance. Thus, in many historical studies, the text is perceived as an important source to an understanding of the organization of the state and social relations up through the history of Thailand, and to the people's perception of these institutions. *Traiphum Phra Ruang* is also believed to have exerted a major influence within a cultural and artistic universe. Thus the cosmological elements and symbols found in the text are believed to have manifested a significant influence on later cultural and artistic traditions in Thailand.

However, the oldest copy of *Traiphum Phra Ruang* that exists today only dates from 1778 and it is not without problems to place the original text in the Sukhothai period. In fact, the dating of the text already caused problems when *Traiphum Phra Ruang* was first published as a book in 1912 (Damrong 1912). The dating of the text is entirely based on internal criteria, and later, in 1974, Michael Vickery seriously criticized the foundation on which the dating of the text was based (Vickery 1974, see also Vickery: 1991). Whether one agrees or disagrees with the points raised by Vickery, it is thought-provoking that this criticism more or less has been ignored; not only in the studies dealing with *Traiphum Phra Ruang*, but also in the introductory paragraphs found in recent editions of the text. This problem was also ignored at a major seminar entirely devoted to the study of *Traiphum Phra Ruang*, that took place in 1983 (Prungsri: 1984). Only in 1990 did Piriya Krairiksh follow in the footsteps of Michael Vickery and challenged the autencity of the *Traiphum Phra Ruang* (Piriya 1990).

I believe that the reason why the puzzling problems surrounding the dating of the text have been ignored for such long a time, is to be found in the potent symbolism associated with the text. This symbolism blocked for any serious questioning of the dating of *Traiphum Phra Ruang*. The symbolism wrapped around *Traiphum Phra Ruang* and the neglect of the problems related to the dating of this text are consequently two closely interwoven topics.

Bearing this in mind the following account directs attention towards the literature related to *Traiphum Phra Ruang*. Throughout this presentation the aim is to outline the potent symbolism that surrounds this text and to indicate how this cosmological treatise can be viewed as an ideological battlefield for contesting ideologies. It will be outlined how

Traiphum Phra Ruang is perceived as a metaphor for Thailand's golden age, and as an important symbol for Thailand's cultural heritage and national identity. And it will be outlined how this text is perceived as part of the ideological bastion that through the years has served the ruling class and justified an unequal class society. This presentation will be related to political developments in Thailand from the 1970s. In this period not only a new meaning, from a historical perspective, was associated with *Traiphum Phra Ruang*, but the text also served as an entry for an understanding of political developments in modern Thailand. Consequently, the presentation will illustrate different currents in the academic and political life of modern Thailand. But first some remarks on the transmission of the text and the problems concerned with the dating of the text.

THE TRANSMISSION OF *TRAIPHUM PHRA RUANG*

According to information found in the manuscript, the oldest complete copy of the text dates back to 1778, when it was copied by the monk Maha Chuay (Damrong 1912: 308). From the same period exists a copy prepared by the monk Maha Can in 1787 (Reynolds 1982: 38). Both texts are in the Thai language written with Khmer letters. Beside these copies there exists only a fragment of what maybe is a copy of *Traiphum Phra Ruang*, possible dating from the end of the Ayutthaya period (Phitoon 1984: 2). Thus there exists a timespan of about 400 years between the supposed time of writing in the Sukhothai period and the time where the oldest copy we know of was copied. In the literature focusing on *Traiphum Phra Ruang* the transmission of the text is normally not a subject elaborated upon, but a standard explanation for this vacuum is that older copies must have been destroyed when the Burmese sacked the old capital of Ayutthaya in 1767 (see for example Reynolds 1982: 37 & Suphani 1971: 45).

But if we try to trace the history of the text through other sources this proves very difficult. In the inscriptions from the Sukhothai period there are found no references to the text. Nor have I come across references to later written chronicles in which there is referred to a cosmological treatise composed by Lithai. Furthermore there are no references to the text in other cosmological texts written later than the time *Traiphum Phra Ruang* supposedly was written, such as *Cakkavaladipani* or the illustrated *Traiphum*-manuscript produced in 1776. It is true, though, that in the last mentioned manuscript we find the information, that the King wished an examination of the "from old time handed over *Traiphum*-manuscript" (in Wenk 1965: 14). But much indicates that this is a reference to an illustrated *Traiphum*-manuscript from the Ayutthaya period and not a reference to *Traiphum Phra Ruang* (Wenk 1965: 18-19). Finally Lithai's text is not found in the list of works that *Trailokavinitchai-Katha* is based upon (in Jones 1851: 538).

Thus the origins and the later transmission of the text is uncertain and the two copies produced in the end of the 18th century are the only extant testimonies of the existence of *Traiphum Phra Ruang* over the centuries. Therefore a determination of the author of and the time for the composition of *Traiphum Phra Ruang* depends on the information about this found in the extant copies. If we look closer at this information, it is found that neither an identification of the author nor the time the text was written is straightforward.

PHRA RUANG: THE FIXING OF THE TEXT IN TIME AND SPACE

Damrong Rajanuphab figures as one of the pioneers in modern Thai historical writing. Not only with his own historical writings but also by being in charge of the publication of numerous historical documents, Damrong has contributed to the study of Thailand's history in a very important way. It was also Damrong who took the initiative to publish the first printed edition of *Traiphum Phra Ruang*, which was distributed at a cremation in 1912. At that time the text only existed as a manuscript in the National Library in Bangkok. An important feature of this publication is that Damrong did not use *Traiphumi-Katha* (or *Tephumi-Katha*), which is the name found several places in the manuscript, as the title of the publication. Instead he chose the title *Traiphum Phra Ruang*, which is the title the text has later been associated with.

While *katha* is a term designating "treatise" or "discourse", *Phra Ruang* is a term associated with the kings of the Sukhothai Kingdom and can be found in various chronicles written later than the Sukhothai period (for example in *Jinakalamali* and *Northern Annals*)[1]. During the reign of King Vajiravudh (1910-1925) a promotion of Thai culture and history took place. Historical figures that led to a union or re-union of the Thai people

---

[1] See Damrong 1914: 81-82 and Vickery 1978: 194-195 for different accounts of the origin of the term *Phra Ruang*.

were transformed into metaphors of the exemplary relationship that ought to exist between the monarch and the population. Especially was *Phra Ruang* a recurring character in the writings of King Vajiravudh, who used it with reference either to Intharathit (who established Sukhothai as an independent kingdom) or to Ramkhamhaeng (who radically expanded the territory of the kingdom) (see Vella 1978: Chapter 8). In plays, travel accounts and poems the legendary *Phra Ruang* was brought back to life as an eternal symbol for Thailand's golden age and for the unity and independence of the Thai nation. A symbolism further developed when a naval vessel, purchased after a national fund-raising campaign, was named *Phra Ruang* (Vella 1978: 95-101). By linking the cosmological treatise with this powerful symbol, Damrong not only increased the authority of the manuscript; he also separated this text from other cosmological texts (*Traiphum* texts) and located it in time and space as a creation of the Sukhothai period. In this way Damrong in an important way marked later generations' view of this manuscript.

Damrong associated the manuscript with the Ruang dynasty because he identified the author as Phraya Lithai, the fifth monarch of the Sukhothai dynasty (Damrong 1912: 1). Damrong does not inform us explicitly about the basis for this identification. But, as mentioned above, it has to be based on the information about the author and the time of composition found in the text. Information of this kind can be found in three sections: in the exordium, in the colophon, and in the "words of praise" (*khatha namatsakan*). If we look closer at this information it turns out that these sections of the manuscript display differences with respect to the genealogies, regal titles, and months for the time of writing (Damrong 1912: 9, 357). Damrong did not inform the reader about these ambiguities in his introductory remarks, but simply identified the author as King Lithai (Damrong 1912: 1).

As far as a more exact dating of the text is concerned, two dates are found in the exordium and colophon that could be expected would help in this dating; that is, that the text was composed in the "Year of the Cock, Year 23" when the author "had reigned 6 years in Si Satchanalai" (Damrong 1912: 9 & 357). As for the "Year 23" this is a year it is impossible to reconcile with the eras found in the inscriptions from the Sukhothai period (Damrong 1912: 4, see also Vickery 1974: 279-280). Therefore Damrong was unable to use this information as an entry to a dating of the text. As for "had reigned 6 years" this was an information left unused by Damrong.

Therefore Damrong was unable to date the text more precisely, but although he found that the manuscript included linguistic elements that it would be anachronistic to place in the Sukhothai period, still for him there was no doubt, that the original text dated from this part of Thailand's history. Thus in Damrong's introductory remark, we find the following argument, that is brought forward in many studies on *Traiphum Phra Ruang*, to support the age and authencity of the text:

> When we read this text, we will discover that it is a very old text. Thus it
> contains many words that are incomprehensible for us and we only have come
> across in the inscriptions from the Sukhothai period. Therefore it is likely
> that the original edition of *Traiphum Phra Ruang* was written in this period.
> But in connection with the transmission of the text it has been copied (*khat*
> *lo'k*) innumerable times. In this way deviations from the original edition has
> crept in (*wipalat khlatkhlu'an*) and in some instances the style of writing
> (*samnuan*) has been changed (*datplaeng*). But none-the-less, the language
> (*wohan*) indicates that we are confronted with a text that, except for the
> known inscriptions, is older than any other text written in Thai (Damrong
> 1912: 1-2).

Therefore, according to Damrong, we are here confronted with nothing less than a copy of the first book composed in Thai at some unspecified point of time by King Lithai.

That the text was composed when the author had "reigned six years in Sri Sachanalai" later became the principal element leading to the traditional dating of *Traiphum Phra Ruang*. In 1917 George Coedès published an article in which he combined this information with information about the reign of King Lithai found in two of the inscriptions from Wat Pa Mamuang, leading to the year 1345 as the year the text was composed (Coedès 1917: 8-9). In his reading of the Khmer inscription from Wat Pa Mamuang, Coedès rejected the traditional reading of this inscription. Accordingly 1345 as the year for the composition of *Traiphum Phra Ruang* was not readily welcomed among many Thai historians. The historian Prasert na Nagara, for example, mentions that in 1944 he had also advocated 1345 as the date of the composition of *Traiphum Phra Ruang*, an interpretation regarded as utterly controversial and led to a reprimand from a senior historian (Prasert 1966: 43-44). After this censure Prasert was more circumspect, but later he went in the offensive in a crusade against what he saw as a rigid interpretation of Thai history. In the same manner as Coedès he rejected the traditional reading of the Khmer inscription and fixed the year for the composition of *Traiphum Phra Ruang* as 1345 (Prasert 1966: 45).

Earlier we have seen how Damrong initially was unable to solve the riddle surrounding the inexplicable "Year 23". But later Damrong pointed out that this year might refer to an era institutionalised by King Lithai (Damrong 1914: 94). Here Damrong refers to two of the inscriptions from the Sukhothai period in which it is mentioned that Lithai had corrected an irregularity in the calender. Moreover, according to the *Northern Annals*, *Phra Ruang* introduced a new era. Damrong therefore sees "Year 23" as a testimony for that it might be Lithai who introduced this era (Damrong 1914: 94). In the inscriptions from the Sukhothai period, we have no knowledge of such an era, but in the literary work *Nang Nopphamat*, which purports to be written in the Sukhothai period, an era attributed to *Phra Ruang* is found. In the above-mentioned article Prasert shows how "Year of the Cock, Year 23" fits into the era found in *Nang Nopphamat* (Prasert 1966: 46). But is this linking together of an era found in *Nang Nopphamat* and a year found in *Traiphum Phra Ruang* indicative of an era institutionalised in the Sukhothai period? For although *Nang Nopphamat* describes the Sukhothai period and it purports to be written in this period, there is much that indicates that it actually was written in the early Bangkok period (see Nidhi 1979). Therefore *Nang Nopphamat* rather represents a later period's interpretation of Sukhothai history and is of no value as a source to Sukhothai history. This might be the reason why this interpretation of "Year 23" not is put forward in the *Epigraphic and Historical Studies* that Prasert produced together with A.B. Griswold (see for example the comment in Griswold & Prasert 1973: 71-72).

This is exactly the point raised by Michael Vickery in his criticism against the foundation on which the dating of *Traiphum Phra Ruang* is based (Vickery 1974). Since *Nang Nopphamat* has been found to be a text composed considerably later than the Sukhothai period, Vickery maintains that the chronology found in this text reflects a much later period's interpretation of Sukhothai chronology. And when the same chronology is found in *Traiphum Phra Ruang*, then the main argument of Vickery is:

... that the date in the exordium and colophon, whatever the age of the text as a whole, is due to an Ayuthaya period copyist at a time when true knowledge of Sukhothai chronology had been lost (Vickery 1974: 283).

Vickery also points out that the regal title *cao phraya*, found in the colophon, indicates that the colophon is written later than in the reign of King Lithai (Vickery 1974: 277). In addition Vickery offers an explanation of how the confused genealogy found in the colophon, can be based on a later misunderstanding of inscriptions from the Sukhothai period. Also in this connection, the main line in Vickery's argument is that this part of the text must have been composed later than the Sukhothai period (Vickery 1974: 276-278). All in all, Vickery argues that neither the exordium nor the colophon can be used as a key for a dating of the text itself. Instead he asks for a detailed study of the language of the text as the only method to place it in a specific period.[2]

Whether one agree or disagree with the conclusions regarding the dating of *Traiphum Phra Ruang* presented by Vickery, I believe that Vickery was right in demanding a critical evaluation of *Traiphum Phra Ruang*'s place in time and space. Therefore it could be expected that his contribution would have formed the point of departure for such a discourse.

In 1974 a new edition of *Traiphum Phra Ruang* was authorised by the Department of Fine Arts (the Phitoon edition) (Phitoon 1974). This edition later formed the basis for the *Modern Edition* (Traiphumikatha 1985) and it is included in the reprint series of classic Thai literature (*Wannakam* 1985). In this manner the Phitoon edition seems to have

---

[2] Later Frank and Mani Reynolds brought forward the "words of praise" found in *Traiphum Phra Ruang*, in which the author is said to be King Lithai, as evidence for the placing of the text in the Sukhothai period (Frank & Mani Reynolds 1982: 354). But it seems very dubious to use this part of the manuscript as an entry to a dating of the text, since the meaning of the text in this part of the manuscript is very unclear (see for example the comment by Sathianphong Wannapok in Prungsri 1984: 94-95).

replaced the Damrong edition as the new standard version of the text. In that connection it could be expected that a discussion of the criticism put forward by Vickery would have been included in this edition. Although Phitoon does not explicitly refer to Vickery's article, part of his introduction can be read as an indirect reply. According to Phitoon, for example, the manuscript forms a whole written by one single person (Phitoon 1984: 1). But this "wholeness" of the manuscript is more treated as an uncontested truth than as a statement that has to be verified. Finally Phitoon mentions that the time for the composition of the text has yet to be established for sure (Phitoon 1984: 9). But in this connection nothing new is presented by Phitoon. Just like Prasert and Vickery, he emphasizes the apparent parallel that exists between the year found in the colophon/exordium in *Traiphum Phra Ruang* and the era found in *Nang Nopphamat*. But whereas Vickery saw this connection as a point of departure to contest the authencity of these parts of the text, Phitoon has no reservations what-so-ever. According to him "Year 23" simply refers to a new era (*cunlasakkarat mai*) established by *Phra Ruang* (Phitoon 1984: 11-13). Therefore, in relation to the dating of *Traiphum Phra Ruang*, nothing new is presented by Phitoon. On the contrary the text is kept in an iron grip that blocks all new interpretations.

Nor was the dating of the text discussed at a 1983 seminar entirely devoted to the study of *Traiphum Phra Ruang*. In this connection, though, the presentation by the historian Dhida Saraya is worth mentioning, because it expresses some important considerations regarding the study of the ideological function of the Buddhist cosmology in Thailand (Prungsri 1984: 89-94).[3] According to Dhida the Buddhist cosmology has to be regarded as an important element in the socialization process in Thai society. But as far as where *Traiphum Phra Ruang* fits into the study of this process, Dhida breaks away from the general accentuation of *Traiphum Phra Ruang* that took place at the seminar. Thus she emphasizes that *Traiphum Phra Ruang* is only one out of many accounts of the Buddhist cosmology found in Thailand, and she calls for a more varied study of the Buddhist cosmology in Thailand based on other sources than *Traiphum Phra Ruang*. Therefore she accentuates the need to separate *Traiphum Phra Ruang* as a text (*pen tamrap*) from the *Traiphum*-cosmology as a system of ideas (*pen khwamkhit*) (Prungsri 1984: 89). In this way *Traiphum Phra*

---

[3] See Dhida 1984 for a more detailed presentation of the same ideas.

Ruang is dislodged as the absolute centre for the study of the cosmological tradition and its dispersal in Thailand, and the holiness that surrounds *Traiphum Phra Ruang* is shaken. But in no way have these considerations left their mark on the official summary of the seminar (Prungsri 1984: 243-244).

Moreover, the traditional dating of the text is reproduced without comments in the *Modern Edition* published in 1985 (*Traiphumikatha* 1985). If we scrutinize the exordium and colophon as they are presented in this edition, it is found that without any further comment the text in these parts of the manuscript have been altered to smooth out ambiguities, although they do not completely disappear; the regal titles, for example, have been altered to fit the titles found in the Sukhothai inscriptions believed to be contemporary with *Traiphum Phra Ruang* (*Traiphumikatha* 1985: 13 & 243). In this way a smokescreen covers up some of the problems concerned with the dating of the text and the uneven edges of the odd pieces in the jigsaw are polished so they fit together and form an almost homogenous picture. Not until 1990 was this standstill broken in a provocative way by the Thai art historian Piriya Krairiksh.

PIRIYA KRAIRIKSH - THE CHALLENGE FROM A NEW UNIVERSE OF KNOWLEDGE

Piriya Krairiksh is one of the main architects behind the challenge of the Ramkhamhaeng inscription's authenticity. Instead of being composed by King Ramkhamhaeng, this *"Magna Carta"* of the Thai nation becomes a product of King Mongkut (Piriya 1989). On the basis of this assumption Piriya later continued his frontal attack on Thailand's history when he wanted to show that *Traiphum Phra Ruang* was also composed by King Mongkut (Piriya 1990). With this as the leading motive Piriya lay down the general outline of a radically different universe where new and different links are drawn between *Traiphum Phra Ruang*, on the one hand, and the inscriptions of the Sukhothai period and later Thai literature on the other hand.

Besides his interpretation, Piriya's contribution is significant since he bases his argumentation on the kind of analysis of the language which Vickery had asked for. With reference to certain words and phrases, for example, Piriya shows that a close relationship exists between the Ramkhamhaeng inscription and *Traiphum Phra Ruang* (Piriya 1990: 222-

224). At first sight there is nothing special about this, since these two texts, according to the traditional view, are closely connected in time and space. But in Piriya's presentation this becomes a dangerous cocktail for, according to him, this indicates that both texts are written by the same person namely King Mongkut (Piriya 1990: 224). Moreover Piriya indicates that many of the words *Traiphum Phra Ruang* and the Ramkhamhaeng inscription have in common are either lacking in the inscriptions composed by Lithai or they are used with another meaning than normally found in the Sukhothai inscriptions but with a meaning close to the one used in early Bangkok literature (Piriya 1990: 222). Finally Piriya also maintains that *Traiphum Phra Ruang* contains themes that it would be anachronistic to place in the Sukhothai period (Piriya 1990: 230-231).

However, with reference to other words and phrases, Piriya points out that the Ramkhamhaeng inscription, *Traiphum Phra Ruang*, and the inscriptions attributed to Lithai, display similarities (Piriya 1990: 224-225). But within Piriya's universe this just indicates:

> that the author of the Ramkhamhaeng inscription and *Traiphum Phra Ruang* most likely has read Lithai's inscriptions and borrowed passages from these when the two other texts were composed (Piriya 1990: 225).

In this way Piriya presents a new universe of knowledge where differences and similarities in language become pieces in an elaborate jigsaw puzzle, where *Traiphum Phra Ruang*, instead of being Thailand's first book, becomes a literary work from the first half of the 19th century. Consequently Piriya attempts to break with the generally accepted view of the link between *Traiphum Phra Ruang* and classic Thai literature. Instead of being the horn of plenty, from which subsequent literature has drawn inspiration and themes, *Traiphum Phra Ruang* is turned into a text written in the 19th century in accordance with earlier and contemporary literary traditions.

Damrong had already pointed out that the edition of *Traiphum Phra Ruang* he published in 1912 was marked by the period in which it was copied (Damrong 1912: 1-2). Therefore there is actually nothing new in Piriya's point that in *Traiphum Phra Ruang* we can find traces of the early Bangkok period. But what makes Piriya's presentation striking is that he regards *Traiphum Phra Ruang* as a text composed (and not copied) by King

Mongkut in this period. But I find Piriya's presentation too coloured by his attempts to show that King Mongkut is the author. All information seems to be selected and adjusted to this end. Although Piriya brings a new perspective to the study of *Traiphum Phra Ruang*, I see this article as being more of a provocative than clarifying nature and the discussion concerning the dating of *Traiphum Phra Ruang* still unsettled. But I welcome Piriya's text as a much needed provocation in the non-existing debate and tacit acceptance of *Traiphum Phra Ruang*'s authenticity. In the following section the symbolism surrounding *Traiphum Phra Ruang* will be outlined in order to get an insight into why this debate never has taken place.

TRAIPHUM PHRA RUANG AND AN OPPRESSIVE STATE IDEOLOGY - PRESENT AND PAST

Following the upheaval in 1973, Thailand experienced a turbulent period in which the radical literature of the past was "re-discovered" and new analyses of Thailand's history and classical literature were initiated. In that connection the trinity consisting of nation-king-religion was subject to critical studies in which the nationalistic and royalist mythology was challenged. In that context *Traiphum Phra Ruang* played a special role because of the justification of royal power and social injustice that can be found in this text. Something that caused "groups of leftist modernists" to demand that books like *Traiphum Phra Ruang* be burned because of their "deluding nature" (Rajavaramuni 1983b: 56).

Symptomatic of this new view on *Traiphum Phra Ruang* is the analysis presented by Chonthira Kladyu, who taught Thai literature at the Chulalongkorn University in the beginning of the 1970s. Already as a student she drew attention to herself with an controversial analysis of a Thai literary classic (*Khun chang khun phaen*) based on Freudian theories (Morell & Chai-anan 1981: 301). This new and different approach to the Thai literary heritage Chonthira later followed up, and among the texts analyzed by her we find *Traiphum Phra Ruang* (Chonthira 1974).

By placing the text in a geopolitical context Chonthira - who does not question the dating of the text - wants to show that *Traiphum Phra Ruang* has to be regarded as a key political document that served an important political function in the Sukhothai period. Thus Chonthira finds that the text reflects how King Lithai used Buddhism as a political tool to centralise and consolidate the power of the monarch, both in relation to the local population and in relation to neighbouring states (Chonthira 1974: 111-118). *Traiphum Phra Ruang* thus becomes the work of a clever statesman, and Chonthira thereby paints a picture of Lithai's reign that differs radically from earlier accounts, where Lithai mainly was presented as a monarch whose exclusive concern with religious chores contributed to the downfall of the Sukhothai Kingdom (see Andaya 1978).

But Chonthira not only viewed *Traiphum Phra Ruang* and Lithai's reign from a new point of view. She also used the text as a key to understand the exceptional position of the monarchy in modern Thailand, and thereby she tries to shed new light on recent political developments in Thailand. Thus Chonthira points out that the religious justification of the monarchy found in *Traiphum Phra Ruang* on the long run has formed the basis for the political ideology found in Thailand (Chonthira 1974: 118). And it is here Chonthira finds the reason why the monarchy has remained one of the pillars of the Thai society, despite the political upheavals Thailand had experienced in modern time (Chonthira 1974: 119-120).

This approach to *Traiphum Phra Ruang* was met with criticism from many different sides. Chonthira herself mentions the "literary lawsuit" that the older literati threatened her with (Chonthira 1974: 112). Another critic, though more sympathetic towards the analysis, finds that Chonthira exaggerates the importance of *Traiphum Phra Ruang* as the foundation for and carrier of the political ideology (Withayakorn 1975). Thus he is of the opinion that the culture and ideology of a society always will be the product of its economic structure. As such, even without a text like *Traiphum Phra Ruang* the specified political ideology would have existed and been transmitted (Withayakorn 1975: 167). But at the same time, the analysis presented by Chonthira became an inspiration for other studies that tried to break with this very orthodox marxist and mechanistic understanding of the ideological superstructure that we find expressed in the above-mentioned review.

One who follows in Chonthira's footsteps in this way is Charoenkiat Thanasukthaworn in a study that focuses on the ideological dimension of Buddhism throughout Thailand's history (Charoenkiat 1977). In his presentation Charoenkiat indicates how the ruling class has manipulated Buddhism to their own advantage and, in this context, finds that *Traiphum Phra Ruang* is of great importance because of the linking between status and religious merit expressed in this text. Thus he sees

Traiphum Phra Ruang as an expression of the ruling class's calculated attempt to promote its own social status and to secure the stability of society through the propagation of Buddhism (Charoenkiat 1977: 117ff.).

Despite this argument Charoenkiat finds it erroneous to juxtapose Buddhism with an oppressive state ideology. Thus he draws a dividing line between doctrinal Buddhism and popular Buddhism (religious praxis). Whereas he portray doctrinal Buddhism as a healthy philosophy that aims at activating people so they can influence their own existence, his criticism is directed towards popular Buddhism which the ruling class has manipulated. In this way Charoenkiat tries to show the ideological plurality of Buddhism and show that Buddhist doctrine contains an ideology that can form the basis for resistance against social injustice.

Just as Charoenkiat was inspired by Chonthira's analysis of *Traiphum Phra Ruang*, Chonthira's thoughts are also an important ingredient in a study by Kancana Kaewthep (Kancana 1982). This article dates from a period when the Thai left wing was in a phase of ideological readjustment. After the brutal killing of students at Thammasat University and the removal of the civil government in October 1976, many of the students took shelter in the jungle where they joined the Communist Party of Thailand (CPT). Discontented with what they saw as an undemocratic leadership in the Party and tempted by the amnesty offered by the Government, many of these former students left CPT and returned disillusioned to a life in the cities after 1979 (see for example Santi 1981 & Thirayuth 1985). This created a situation where many from the Thai left wing felt a need for a critical re-evaluation of the Marxist theories they earlier had subscribed to.

In this context the above-mentioned article by Kancana is the first in a series of articles in which she discusses the continued relevance of Marxism for academic and political life in Thailand (see Hong 1991). It was especially the role of ideology - the production, reproduction and institutionalisation of ideology - that Kancana wanted to explain. Kancana emphasized that orthodox Marxism prescribes an analysis of ideology that is far too mechanistic and simplistic as it only treats the ideological dominance of the ruling class as an established fact without offering a satisfying answer as to how this dominance is created (Kancana 1982: 28). In this endeavour to establish a more sophisticated analysis of the ideological superstructure, Kancana became an important exponent of new Marxist theories to intellectual circles in Thailand.

In the above-mentioned article Kancana focuses on the "fear" (*khwam-klua*) she believes is widespread in modern Thai society. Kancana argues that this fear, which is indoctrinated in Thai children, is instrumental in creating law-abiding citizens who submit to the desires of the ruling class (Kancana 1982: 42). In this way Kancana maintains that "fear" have been manipulated by the ruling class in the class struggle, and in this connection she locates *Traiphum Phra Ruang* as a central component in the ideological bastion of the ruling class. From a historical point of view Kancana relates *Traiphum Phra Ruang* with the justification of an unequal class society in the Sukhothai period (Kancana 1982: 35-36). On the long view she combines the ideology found in the text, and the different shapes it has been reproduced in, as the basis for the construction of this fear in Thai society (Kancana 1982: 44-45). Because of this analysis, Kancana labels *Traiphum Phra Ruang* as "The Book of Fear" (*tamnan-khwamklua*) (Kancana 1982: 44).

A similar attempt to modify orthodox Marxist analyses of the Thai social order is found in a study by Lae Dilokvidhyarat which also focuses on the production and reproduction of ideology (Lae 1982). This study offers a historical perspective, and through an analysis of how the monarchy has manipulated the ideological superstructure through out the history, Lae seeks to explain the persistence of the monarchy in Thailand. In this connection *Traiphum Phra Ruang* is specifically linked with the justification of an emerging unequal class society in the Sukhothai period (Lae 1982: 16 & 78-79). It has been pointed out that one of the reasons for the Thai student movement's lack of success in the 1970s was their lack of understanding for the political potential in modern Thai society of premodern symbols like the monarchy, in modern Thai society (Hong 1991: 105). If this is the case, then Lae's study indicates a break with this position. Thus, by investigating premodern ideology, Lae's study is indeed such an attempt to understand the resilience of the premodern symbols that are part of the political ideology of modern Thailand.

There is no doubt that we can find a political ideology or political understanding expressed in *Traiphum Phra Ruang*. But if we look at how the above-mentioned studies have made use of the text as a source to the history of the Sukhothai Kingdom, we are confronted with a major problem. Here not only do I have in mind problems related to the dating of the text, which none of the studies addresses. But also I find it highly problematic if a political or religious ideology expressed in a text like *Traiphum Phra Ruang* is automatically taken as evidence for how the society functioned, when such an analysis is based only on this text. This is a weakness connected with many of the above-mentioned articles, and as such they appear very mechanistic. Charoenkiat, for example, points out:

> ... we may cite some other passages in this book [*Traiphum Phra Ruang*] to prove that King Li Thai had used it to promote the status and power of the King and other members of the ruling class (Charoenkiat 1977: 119).

An awareness of this problem is reflected in an article by Sombat Chanthornwong in which *Traiphum Phra Ruang* is only used as a source to the history of ideas and consequently is perceived as an expression for the political ideas or political visions of the royal author (Sombat 1979).[4] But an important feature of the abovementioned texts is that they place *Traiphum Phra Ruang* within a political space. Departing from this text they try to analyze political developments in modern Thailand. Thus they not only use their analysis to shed new light on *Traiphum Phra Ruang* and the Sukhothai Kingdom from a historical perspective. By regarding the religious ideology found in this text as an manifestation of the origination of an unequal class society and as an guarantee for exploitation and oppression, these studies represent an attempt to understand the political ideology of modern Thailand and the resilience of the premodern symbols that form an important part of this ideology. In this way *Traiphum Phra Ruang* is pulled out of its historical context and becomes part of the modern political discourse.

TRAIPHUM PHRA RUANG: IN SUPPORT OF AN ALTERNATIVE POLITICAL DEVELOPMENT

While Kancana and Lae argued for a re-orientation within the Marxist spectrum, there were many like Charoenkiat who searched for an ideological anchorage within Buddhism. In this connection *Traiphum Phra Ruang* was brought forward and re-interpreted in order to reveal a

---

4 See Thirayuth Boonmi (1983) for another study approaching *Traiphum Phra Ruang* from the perspective of history of ideas.

religious ideology that could support and give legitimacy to an alternative political development of Thailand.[5]

Important in this connection is the analysis of *Traiphum Phra Ruang* presented by the monk Phra Rajavaramuni (Rajavaramuni 1983a). Many Thais view Phra Rajavaramuni as one of the greatest modern Buddhist philosophers, but he is not only well known for his religious and philosophical insight. Phra Rajavaramuni is also well known for his promotion of Buddhism's relevance as a solution for the social problems found in modern Thailand (see for example Rajavaramuni 1987). And it is indeed the social dimension of Buddhism or, rather, the social dimension of the ethics expressed in *Traiphum Phra Ruang*, that Phra Rajavaramuni analyzed at a seminar arranged by the *Group for Study of Buddhism and Traditions* at Thammasat University in 1983.

In his presentation Phra Rajavaramuni argues against academics who hold the view that the religious doctrine found in *Traiphum Phra Ruang* just makes people passive and accepting the world as it is (Rajavaramuni 1983a: 51-52). Instead, Phra Rajavaramuni maintains that the doctrine of non-permanence and *kamma*, the religious teaching with which *Traiphum Phra Ruang* is saturated, exposes the true nature of things (Rajavaramuni 1983a: 55). Through a realization and observance of this doctrine it becomes possible for individuals to change their current situation in a positive way. So even though *Traiphum Phra Ruang* is an old text, Rajavaramuni asserts that the ideology found in it still has a relevance today and can be brought forward to support a just development of Thai society (Rajavaramuni 1983a: 63). In this way Rajavaramuni offers motivation and inspiration for an activation of Buddhism in the quest for an alternative political development of Thailand. Thereby Rajavaramuni plays an important role in stimulating the dialogue between the Buddhist Church and a new generation of progressive Thais.

In his study of the changing attitudes of the Siamese elite towards the Buddhist cosmology, Craig Reynolds has demonstrated how rationalist criticisms initiated by Mongkut lead to re-interpretations of *Traiphum Phra Ruang* in the 19th century (Reynolds 1976). Re-interpretations in which *Traiphum Phra Ruang* is separated from the face value of the cosmology in order to retain the symbolic meanings and ethical teachings of the text. This

---

[5] See Jackson 1993 for a thorough analysis of this theme.

tendency is also found in a later publication by Anuman Rajadhon (Sathiankoset 1954). In this book Anuman liberates *Traiphum Phra Ruang* from the face value of the cosmological notions in order to use the text as a kind of guidebook to the cosmological symbols found in Thai art and literature.

The same kind of distinction is presented by Rajavaramuni, who relates that before the above-mentioned seminar he only knew of *Traiphum Phra Ruang* through a reading of Anuman Rajadhon's rendering of the text. Having read this book he did not read the original text, since he did not believe that this would contribute to an understanding of the "true principles of Buddhism" (Rajavaramuni 1983a: 2). But after having read *Traiphum Phra Ruang* itself Rajavaramuni now brings it forward as a most valuable text, since under its cosmological veneer he encountered a religious and ethical instruction which he finds is identical with the core of Buddhist teaching. In this way Rajavaramuni draws a dividing line between cosmological notions and "true" Buddhism. And by linking *Traiphum Phra Ruang* with a "true" Buddhist teaching this text is separated from the cosmology; thereby the symbolism and ethical teaching of *Traiphum Phra Ruang* is set free to be used in the political discourse.

The same kind of analysis can be found in an article by Phong Sengking published in *Pacarayasara*, which is a journal giving air to this kind of linking between Buddhism and alternative political developments (Phong 1985). Symbols from *Traiphum Phra Ruang* are brought forward in this article to illustrate a criticism of the development (or degeneration) Thailand has experienced, since the country was opened up to the foreign powers in the middle of the 19th century (Phong 1985: 113-114). In contrast, the religious ethics found in *Traiphum Phra Ruang* is brought forward not only to indicate the paradisiacal conditions Thailand experienced before greed, hate and delusion brought an end to this state, but also to show the way out of this nightmare (Phong 1985: 113).

Sulak Sivaraksa appears as one of the best-known representatives of those in Thailand who base their criticism of modern Thai society and their visions for its renewal on ideals drawn from Buddhism. The same distinction between the cosmological notions and the Buddhist doctrine, as mentioned above, can be found in a presentation by Sulak (Sulak 1987). In this article Sulak traces what he regards as the sources of the Thai religious tradition. Since Sulak is associated with a "pure" Theravada Buddhism cleansed of mythological elements, it is of no surprise that "Thai religious tradition" in Sulak's interpretation equals orthodox Theravada Buddhism. Accordingly, in Sulak's view, new religious movements like Santi Asoka and Thammakaya have no place in this tradition (Sulak 1987: 85-86). It is thus notable that Sulak puts *Traiphum Phra Ruang* forward as an important source for this orthodox Theravada Buddhist tradition. As Sulak sees this treatise as expressing a combination of Theravada, Mahayana and Brahmanistic elements, at first glance *Traiphum Phra Ruang* might appear to be beyond redemption (Sulak 1987: 77). But, by stressing that the basic tenet of the text is in accordance with orthodox Theravada Buddhist doctrine and that this has been placed in a cosmological frame in order to make the text more easily understood, Sulak "saves" the text (Sulak 1987: 77). Detaching *Traiphum Phra Ruang* from its cosmological notions sets the text free and it is thus possible for Sulak to place the origins of the Thai religious tradition in the 14th century; a tradition from which Sulak draws ideological ballast for his criticism of modern Thai politics.

TRAIPHUM PHRA RUANG - A CORNERSTONE IN THE NATIONAL IDENTITY

The above-mentioned endeavours to read new meanings into the symbolic sphere of kingship and Buddhism was a challenge to the State's monopoly on the utilization of these symbols. In an attempt to counter these efforts and to re-establish the traditional ideological connotations of these symbols, a marked promotion of Thai national culture took place in the 1970-80s. Accordingly *Traiphum Phra Ruang* and the history of the Sukhothai Kingdom were merged into an important symbol for Thai national identity and cultural heritage, and the religious ideology found in *Traiphum Phra Ruang* was linked with the formation and continued security of the Thai nation.

For example this is the case in an article by Suphani Kancanad published in the *Thai Culture Magazine* which has long served as an important medium for the promotion of Thai culture (Suphani 1971). According to Suphani, *Traiphum Phra Ruang* is the starting point for the cosmological tradition found in later artistic expressions in Thailand. In this way *Traiphum Phra Ruang* becomes a symbol of the utmost importance for the Thai cultural heritage from which lines are established to the artistic traditions and expressions of later periods.

While the *Thai Culture Magazine* had been in circulation since the early 1960s, the magazine *Thai Identity*, first published in 1977, can be seen as a direct outcome of the need to promote and glorify the Thai national identity and the symbols associated with it. This is clearly expressed in an article by Cu'a Satawethin (Cu'a 1977). In this article *Traiphum Phra Ruang* is put forward as the first literary product of the "Thai nation", thus ascribing an illustrious foundation to Thai culture (Cu'a 1977: 5). At the same time it is emphasized that the description of the universe found in the text is of a similar quality as contemporary descriptions composed by philosophers of other nationalities, even if they come from the "developed countries" (*chat caroen*) (Cu'a 1977: 7). Thus:

> We have Pracao Lithai that shows how we Thais too are philosophers capable of expressing profound thoughts. When we talk to philosophers from foreign countries, then we also have something to bring forward, and thereby we will not be discredited. If we did not have Phra Maha Dhammaracha Lithai then we were forced to maintain a profound silence. Therefore the new generation of Thais ought to express great pride about this text (Cu'a 1977: 7).

According to the traditional dating of the Ramkhamhaeng inscription, the year 1983 marked the seventh hundred anniversary of the Thai script. This was celebrated all over Thailand. As part of the celebrations a seminar on *Traiphum Phra Ruang* was arranged by the Department of Fine Arts. In the introductory speeches presented at this seminar, a recurrent theme is how language and literature are important national symbols, reflecting the cultural development of a nation (Prungsri 1984: 6-18). In that context *Traiphum Phra Ruang* inevitably occupies a distinctive position as a powerful symbol of the Thai cultural heritage that, together with the Ramkhamhaeng inscription, signals harmony, unity and national security. In this light even the slightest attempt to question the dating of the text becomes almost an act of blasphemy. Therefore it comes as no surprise that the criticism brought forward by Vickery was not discussed on this occasion.

Finally I would like to direct attention towards the two new editions of *Traiphum Phra Ruang* published lately. Here the introductory remarks by Thawisak Senanarong, leader of the Department of Fine Arts, are noteworthy. Thawisak stresses how *Traiphum Phra Ruang* is linked with the formation and security of the nation:

> In connection with the establishment of the new state it was necessary to unite the population of the nation (*chat*) in order to secure the stability (*mankhong*) of the Thai nation and make it possible to resist the threatening enemies. Therefore there was a need for the population to possess moral (*sinlatham*) and discipline (*yu nai rabiap winai*), they should know good and evil (*ru bap bun khun thot*), and should profess a religion (*mi lak yu't man thang satsana*). [In that connection *Traiphum Phra Ruang* was important] since it is a literary work that aims at disseminating *dhamma* to the population ... (Phitoon 1984: a-b).

Lastly I would like to mention the *Modern Edition* that is included as the first volume in Thailand's contribution to an anthology on the literature of the ASEAN countries (*Traiphumikatha* 1985). It has been left entirely to the individual countries to pick out the literature they would like to bring forward as representative of their literary traditions. The Thai committee's choice of *Traiphum Phra Ruang* forms a sharp contrast to the texts picked by the other countries for the first volume. The texts chosen by the other countries include texts taken from the oral tradition and texts that emphasize the cultural plurality of the various countries. In contrast *Traiphum Phra Ruang* not only represents the written tradition but it is also a text used to signal unity instead of diversity. The choice of *Traiphum Phra Ruang* is motivated in the following manner:

> This cosmological treatise is an impressive text (*mi attharot sung*), that contains a beautiful and complete language (*mi tho'ikham samnuan phasa phairo' ngotngam pranit yangying*) and it reflects the Thais' extrodinary ability and how advanced the literary tradition already was in the Sukhothai period [actually: how advanced the artistic civilization was]. Also with regard to other aspects it is a valuable text. It is a piece of literature from the Sukhothai period, which is the period where the first Thai kingdom saw the light of day. It was a period when it was desired to bring peace to the people and safety to the nation. Therefore an effort was made to create a common ideology that would make the people of the nation

pursue moral (*khunnatham*), a mind that strives for peacefulness (*mi citcai rak sangop*), a harmonious co-existence, and the people should be conscious about good and evil, and only strive for good actions. And as it is generally known legislation and religion are the best tools to make peace in the nation. It is meant that *Traiphum Phra Ruang* or *Traiphumikatha*, as a Buddhist text, in the best manner has served this function. By consolidating (*plukfang*) an ideology based on the belief of good and evil actions, and the belief on goodness and peace, it is counted as a literary work that has had an influence on people's way of living, on the basis for the government, on politics, and on the national culture (*Traiphumikatha* 1985: 8-9).

In this way *Traiphum Phra Ruang* becomes a distant point from which an officially sanctioned interpretation of a national Thai identity can claim legitimacy and the religious ideology associated with the text can be brought forward to support traditional political patterns (see Jackson 1993). Accordingly, the ideological function of *Traiphum Phra Ruang* is also emphasized in this connection. Whereas the Marxist-oriented studies mentioned earlier linked the religious ideology found in *Traiphum Phra Ruang* with the legitimation of an unequal class society and social unjustice, the ideology emphasized here is connected with the formation and security of the nation. But whether *Traiphum Phra Ruang* is seen as an manifestation of the origination of an unequal class society and as a guarantee for exploitation and oppression, or as a manifestation of the birth of the nation and as a guarantee for justice, peace and security, in both instances *Traiphum Phra Ruang* is utilised to locate these developments in time and space. As such the cosmological treatise by King Lithai is a most welcome symbol in both discourses. In this way *Traiphum Phra Ruang* has become an important element not only for the construction of Thailand's history but also as a key to understanding the nature of political ideology in modern Thailand and as a source that lends legitimacy both to factions seeking to reinforce traditional political structures and to those striving for political reform.

LIBERATE THE COSMOLOGY FROM *TRAIPHUM PHRA RUANG*

In my presentation I have outlined the symbolism that surrounds the cosmological text *Traiphum Phra Ruang* and in that connection I have indicated how this text can be viewed as a battlefield for contesting ideologies. But in this battle for the symbolic universe of *Traiphum Phra Ruang* a mythological net have been weaved around the text and the insecure basis for the dating of the text is forgotten. In an uncritical way King Lithai is identified as the author of this text. Likewise is the uncertainty connected with the transmission of the text left unconsidered. Here it is problematic that the ambiguities related to the origin of the text are completely ignored in new official editions of the text. This is something that compares to the re-writing (*chamra*) in earlier periods of historical chronicles.

Besides the problems regarding placement of the text in time and space, we are confronted with a fundamental problem by assigning *Traiphum Phra Ruang* this focal place in the historical and ideological landscape. Thus it is problematic if the cosmological ideas in historical studies narrowly are connected with *Traiphum Phra Ruang*. Not only because of the specific problems related to the dating of the text, but also because this leads to a simplification of the dynamics whereby the Buddhist cosmology has been dispersed in Thai society over time. Therefore, if we want to examine how Buddhist cosmology has influenced people's understanding of society and the world from a historical perspective, it is important to separate *Traiphum Phra Ruang* from these cosmological ideas. This separation implies that the Buddhist cosmology is to be studied using different and much broader source material than merely *Traiphum Phra Ruang*. Studies of this kind could involve using other cosmological texts from the different regions of Thailand and cosmological elements found for example in folktales, classical literature and the ideologies that have justified peasant uprisings at different points in the history of Thailand. Such studies can help etsablish when and where the dissemination of the cosmological ideas in Thailand occured and can present us with a more detailed understanding of the importance of Buddhist cosmology in Thai history, as well as set us free from the problems connected with the specific text *Traiphum Phra Ruang*.[6]

---

[6] In the same book where the article by Piriya is found an article by Somkiat Wanthana appears in which the traditional perception of power in Thai society is analyzed (Somkiat 1990). Although Somkiat discusses the role of cosmological elements in the perception of power, it is noteworthy that his presentation almost solely is based on other texts than *Traiphum Phra Ruang*.

Despite these objections and no matter if it is an authentic text or not, *Traiphum Phra Ruang* should still be regarded as a valuable and colourful presentation of the Buddhist cosmology. Therefore it still has a major value for the study of this subject as long as we do not focus on how these ideas have been acted out in a specific historical context. Several times in this presentation it has been stressed how a demarcation line has been drawn between the "true Buddhist doctrine" and the Buddhist cosmology; whether this has happened to set *Traiphum Phra Ruang* "free" to be used as a "guidebook" to the cosmological symbols found in Thai art and culture, or to save the symbolism and the ethical teaching found in the text. In historical studies it must now be time for the Buddhist cosmology to be liberated from *Traiphum Phra Ruang* in order to open up for a critical study of this treatise and for a more subtle view of Thailand's history.

REFERENCES

Andaya, Barbara W.
   1978   'Statecraft in the Reign of Lü Tai of Sukhodaya (ca1347-1374)'. In *Religion and legitimation of power in Thailand, Laos, and Burma*, Bardwell L. Smith (ed.), South and Southeast Asia Studies, Anima Books, pp. 2-19.

Charoenkiat Thanasukthaworn
   1977   'Religion and the Thai Political System'. In *The review of Thai Social Science. A collection of articles by Thai scholars*, Likhit Dhiravegin (ed.), Bangkok: The Social Science Association of Thailand, pp. 100-143.

Chonthira Kladyu
    1974   'Traiphum phra ruang : rakthan kho'ng udomkan
           kanmu'ang thai'(Traiphum Phra Ruang : Foundation of
           Political Ideology in Thailand), *Warasan Thammasat* 4:1:
           106-121.

Coedès, George
    1917   'Documents Sur la Dynastie de Sukhodaya", *Bulletin de
           l'Ecole Francaise d'Extreme Orient* 17:2: 1-47

Cu'a Satawethin
    1977   'Nangsu' thai ru'ang raek' (The First Thai Story), *Ekkalak
           Thai* 1: 6: 5-8.

Damrong Rajanuphab
    1912   *Traiphum phra ruang kho'ng phaya Lithai* (Traiphum Phra
           Ruang by Phaya Lithai), Bangkok: Sinlapa bannakhan.

    1914   'Athibai hetkan mu'a ko'n sang krung si-ayutthaya"(An
           Exposition of Events Prior to the Establishment of
           Ayutthaya). In *Phraratchaphongsaowadan chabap
           phraratchahatthalekha* (The Royal authograph chronicle),
           Bangkok: Khlang witthaya.

Dhida Saraya
    1984   'Traiphum kap kancat rabiap khwamkhit nai prawattisat
           sangkhom thai' (The Traiphum-Cosmology and the
           Establishment of an Idea in Thailand's Social History),
           Cunlasan Thai khadi 2: 1: 9-19.

Griswold, A.B & Prasert na Nagara
    1973   'The Epigraphy of Mahadharmaraja I of Sukhodaya", *Journal
           of the Siam Society* 60: 1: 91-128.

Hong Lysa
1991 'Warasan setthasat kanmu'ang - Critical Scholarship in Post 1976 Thailand". In *Thai constructions of knowledge,* Manas Chitakasem & Andrew Turton (eds.), London: School of Oriental and African Studies, pp. 99-117.

Jackson, Peter A.
1993 'Re-Interpreting the Traiphum Phra Ruang: Political Functions of Buddhist symbolism in contemporary Thailand 'In *Buddhist trends in Southeast Asia,* Trevor Ling (ed.), Singapore: Institute of Southeast Asian Studies, pp. 64-100.

Jones, J. Taylor
1851 'Some Account of the Trai Phum', *Journal of the Indian Archipelago and Eastern Asia* 5: 538-542.

Kancana Kaewthep
1982 'Bot wikhro' khwamklua nai sangkhom thai duai thritsadi cittawitthaya citwikhro' lae sangkhomwitthaya maksit' (An Analysis of "Fear in Thai Society" based upon Psychological, Psychoanalytical, and Marxist Theories), *Setthasat kanmu'ang* 2: 2: 28-50.

Krom sinlapako'n
1980 *Cakkavaladipani.* Bangkok.

1985a *Traiphumikatha chabap tho't khwam* : (Traiphumikatha - A Modern Version), Anthology of ASEAN Literatures, Bangkok: samnakphim amarin.

1985b *Wannakam samai Sukhothai* (The Literature of the Sukhothai Period), Bangkok.

Lae Dilokvidhyarat
1982 *Transformation and Persistence of Kinship in Thailand* (Research Paper: Institute of Social Studies, The Hague, 1982).

Ling, Trevor (ed.)
1993 *Buddhist Trends in Southeast Asia* Singapore: Institute of
Southeast Asian Studies.

Manas Chitakasem & Turton, Andrew (eds.)
1991 *Thai Constructions of Knowledge* , London: School of
Oriental and African Studies.

Morell, David & Chai-anan Samudavanija
1981 *Political Conflict in Thailand. Reform, Reaction and
Revolution* , Cambridge: Oelgeschlager, Gunn & Hain, 1981.

Nidhi Aeusriwongse
1979 'Lok kho'ng nang Nopphamat' (The World of Nang
Nopphamat),*Warasan Thammasat* 9: 1: 2-31.

Phitoon Maliwan
1984 *Traiphumikatha ru' traiphum phra ruang - phrarachaniphon
phaya lithai* (Traiphumi-Katha or Traiphum Phra Ruang
written by Phaya Lithai), Bangkok: khurusapha.

Phong Sengking
1985 'Sinlapakam an nu'ang kap traiphum' (Art Related to the
Traiphum Cosmology), *pacarayasan* 12: 2: 113-122.

Phraratchaphongsaowadan chabap phraratchahatthalekha
1914 The Royal Autograph Chronicle, Bangkok: Khlang
witthaya.

Piriya Krairiksh
1989 *Caru'k pho'khun ramkhamhaeng: kanwikhro' choeng
prawattisat sinlapa* (The Ramkhamhaeng Inscription. An
Analysis From an Art Historical Point of View), Bangkok:
samnakphim amarin.

1990   'Kho' khit kiao kap traiphum phra ruang: phraratchaniphon
        nai phra maha thamaracha thi nu'ng phaya lithai ru' phrabat
        somdet phracomklao chao yuhua' (Considerations on
        Traiphum Phra Ruang: A Writing by Phra Maha
        Dhammaraja the First or by H.M. King Rama IV?). In
        Thaikhadi su'ksa: ruam botkhwam thang wichakan phu'a
        sadaeng muthitacit acan phan ek ying khun ni-o'n sanitwong
        na ayutthaya   (Thai Studies in Honour of Khun Neon
        Snidvongs Na Ayuthaya), Sunthari Atsawai et.al. (eds.),
        Bangkok: samnakphim amarin.

Prasert na Nagara
    1966   'Kanchamra prawatisat Sukhothai" (A Purification of the
            History of Sukhothai), *Sangkhomsat parithat* 3: 43-51.

Prungsri Wanliphodom et.al. (eds.)
    1984   *Sarup phon kansamana ru'ang traiphum phra ruang - cat*
            phim nu'ang nai okat chalo'ng 700 pi lai su' thai
            (Conclusions from a Seminar on Traiphum Phra Ruang -
            Publised on Occassion of the Celebration of 700 Anniversary
            of the Thai Script), Bangkok: krom sinlapako'n.

Rajavaramuni, Phra
    1983a   *Traiphum phra ruang - itthiphon to' sangkhom thai* (The
            Influence of Traiphum Phra Ruang on Thai Society),
            Bangkok: saeng rung kanphim.

    1983b   *Social Dimension of Buddhism in Contemporary Thailand*
            Bangkok: Thai Khadi Research Institute, Paper No.15, 1983).

    1987   *Looking to America to Solve Thailand's Problems*, Bangkok:
            Sathirakoses-Nagapradipa Foundation.

Reynolds, Craig J.
    1976   'Buddhist Cosmography in Thai History, with Special
            Reference to Nineteenth-Century Change', *Journal of Asian*
            Studies 35: 2: 203-220.

Reynolds, Frank E. & Mani B. (translation and introduction)
1982 *Three Worlds According to King Ruang. A Thai Buddhist Cosmology* , Berkeley: Berkeley Buddhist Studies Series 4.

Santi Mingmongkol
1981 'Thai Communists: Into the 1980s', *Southeast Asia Chronicle* 80: 1: 12-21.

Smith, Bardwell L. (ed.)
1978 *Religion and Legitimation of Power in Thailand, Laos, and Burma*, Chambersburg: Anima Books.

Sombat Chanthornwong
1979 'Phraya cakkraphatthirat nai traiphum phra ruang: kho' sangket bang prakan kiao kap khwammai thang kanmua'ng' (The Universal Monarch in Traiphum Phra Ruang: Some Observations Concerning the Political Meaning), *warasan prawattisat* 4: 1: 1-17.

Somkiat Wanthana
1983 'Traiphum phra ruang: din ko'n diao nai dindaen" (Traiphum Phra Ruang: A Piece of This World). In *Traiphum phra ruang - itthiphon to'sangkhom thai* (The Influence of Traiphum Phra Ruang on Thai Society, Rajavaramuni Bangkok: saeng rung kanphim, pp. 73-100.

1990 'Phuttharat parithat: kro'p kanwikhro' amnat dangdoem nai sangkhom thai sayam" (A Critical Analysis of the Buddhist State: A Frame for the Analysis of the Traditional Perception of Power in Siam). In *Thai khadi su'ksa: ruam botkhwam thang wichakan phu'a sadaeng muthitacit acan phan ek ying khun ni-o'n sanitwong na ayutthaya* (Thai Studies in Honour of Khun Neon Snidvongs Na Ayuthaya), Sunthari Atsawai et.al. (eds.), Bangkok samnakphim amarin, pp. 197-220.

Sthirakoses (Phaya Anuman Rajadhon)
    1954   *Lao ru'ang nai traiphum* (The Traiphum-Cosmology Retold)
            Bangkok: khlang witthaya press.

Sulak Sivaraksa
    1987   'Thai Spirituality', *Journal of the Siam Society* 75: 75-90.

Sunthari Atsawai et.al. (eds)
    1990   *Thai khadi su'ksa: ruam botkhwam thang wichakan phu'a*
            sadaeng muthita cit acan phan ek ying khun ni-'on
            sanitwong na ayutthaya (Thai Studies in Honour of Khun
            Neon Snidvongs na Ayuthaya), Bangkok: samnakphim
            amarin.

Suphanni Kancanat
    1971   nangsu' thai lem raek" (The First Thai Book), *Warasan*
            watthanatham Thai 11: 7: 43-48.

Thirayuth Boonmi
    1983   *Traditional Social and Political Thinkning in Thailand.*
            Polemics on the State (Research Paper: Institute of Social
            Studies, The Hague).

    1985   Samphat Thirayut Bunmi - nakyutthasat mai kho'ng fai
            kaona thai' (An Interview with Thirayuth Boonmi -
            Chiefstrategist for Progressive Thais), *pacarayasan* 12: 2: 47-61.

Vella, Walter F.
    1978   *Chaiyo! King Vajiravudh and the Development of Thai*
            Nationalism , Honolulu: The University Press of Hawaii.

Vickery, Michael
    1974   'A Note on the Date of the Traibhumikatha', *Journal of the*
            Siam Society, 62: 2: 275-284.

    1978   'Review Article. A Guide Through Some Recent Sukhothai
            Historiography', *Journal of the Siam Society* 66: 2: 182-264.

Soren Ivarsson

1990   'On Traibhumikatha', *Journal of the Siam Society* 79: 2: 24-
36.

Wenk, Klaus
1965   *Verzeichnis der Orientalichen Handschriften in Deutschland,*
Supplementband III : Thailändische Miniaturmalereien,
nach einer Handscrift der Indischen Kunstabteilung der
Statlichen Museen Berlin, Wiesbaden: Franz Steiner Verlag
GMBH.

Withayakorn Chiangkul
1975   'Wican nangsu' : wannakhadi kho'ng puangchon' (Review
of "Literature of the Masses"), *Warasan Thammasat* 5: 1: 166-
169.

BIRTH, DEATH AND IDENTITY IN THE WRITING OF
SIDAORU'ANG FROM 1975 - 90

Rachel Harrison

In the fifteen year period under consideration Sidaoru'ang's use of the dual images of birth and death are, though not innumerable, sufficiently diverse to merit comment. That birth and death should appear as subject matter at all in contemporary Thai fiction is not surprising in itself, given that much Thai short story writing of the socially conscious and 'Literature for Life' *(wannakam phu'a chiwit)* genres speaks, inevitably, of the fundamental issues of everyday life. The political and intellectual freedom that was granted in the aftermath of the 14 October, 1973[1] gave rise to a wealth of such stories, focussing their attention upon the plight of the working classes as their principal subject matter. What I intend to examine in this paper is not that Sidaoru'ang alludes to birth and death *per se* but that she continually treats these two antithetical events in unison.

My references are principally to the following works: *Khrang nu'ng nan ma laew* ('Once Upon a Time'), *Phuak nai pa* ('The People in the Jungle'), *Rakha haeng khwamtai* ('The Cost of Death'), *Nam ta lai ngiap* ('Tears that Flow in Silence'), *Tho'i kham lae khwamngiap* ('Words and Silence') and *Banthu'k kho'ng no'ng nu* ('My Diary to Mother');[2] and they must first be set in the. context of Sidaoru'ang's work as a whole.

---

[1] The date marks the culmination of student demonstrations that led to a successful coup deposing the right wing dictatorship of Thano'm Kittikhaco'n and Praphat Carusathian.

[2] *Khrang nu'ng nan ma laew* was first published in the October-November 1975 edition of the journal *Akso'rasat phican*. It was reprinted in the *Kaew yot diaw* collection in 1983. *Phuak nai pa* was also first published in October 1975, this time in the leftist literary magazine *Putuchon*. It too was reprinted in *Kaew yot diaw*. A third story from the *Kaew yot diaw* collection, *Rakha haeng khwamtai* was originally published in the magazine *Chiwit*, in September 1976. It was reprinted in the Thammasat annual *Banthit Thammasat* for 1982 and was also translated into English for publication in the *Bangkok Post* newspaper the following year.

Two much later stories, *Nam ta lai ngiap* and *Thoi kham lae khwamngiap* were included in the 1984 collection of Sidaoru'ang's short stories entitled *Bat prachachon*, the former having first been published in the mainstream women's magazine *Lalana* in 1981, the latter in *Matichon sut sapada* in 1983.

Banthu'k kho'ng no'ng nu was published for the first time in Sidaoru'ang's *Phap luang ta* collection of 1989.

Sidaoru'ang did not begin writing in earnest until she was over thirty years old and her first piece to be published (*Kaew yot diaw* or 'A Drop of Glass') appeared in the January to March 1975 edition of *Sangkhomsat parithat* or the 'Social Science Review'. *Kaew yot diaw* and the eight or so short stories that were published in subsequent months[3] appealed to the journal's progressive, intellectual, urban-based readership, who, at the height of student liaisons with peasant farmers and urban factory workers, were impressed by Sidaoru'ang's authentic rendition of life in a Bangkok glass factory. This response is exemplified by the comments of such literary critics as Duangdu'an Pradapdao[4] when he wrote that:

> One of the good things about Sidaoru'ang is the understanding she shows of the life and thoughts of ordinary country folk and of working class culture (Duangdu'an 1975).[5]

Such credible insights into the lives of the urban and rural poor were the outcome of her own background as the daughter of an up-country railway employee father and market vendor mother. Sidaoru'ang was brought up in the town of Bang Krathum, in Phitsanulok province, where she attended school until the age of eleven. She was then sent away on her mother's initiative to work in Bangkok. Over the twenty years which followed she took a variety of semi-skilled jobs,[6] which included, in the early 1960s, a two year period in a glass factory in Thonburi; and it was this experience which Sidaoru'ang drew upon for the setting and subject matter of her earliest works.

---

[3] The short stories, *Chai pha lu'ang* ('The Hem of the Saffron Robe'), *Pho'* ('Father'), and *Phuak nai pa* ('The People in the Jungle') were first published in *Putuchon* in May, July and October 1975, respectively. *Wao bon fa* ('The Kite'), *Sing thi long thun* ('Investments Worth Making') and *Khrang nu'ng nan ma laew* ('Once Upon a Time') were published in *Akso'rasat phican* in the same year. *Raeng ngan kap ngoen* ('Labour and Money') was published in *Prachachon* in July 1975 and even the well-established women's magazine, *Satri san* ('Women's News') published *Phit wang* ('Disappointed'), in November 1975.

[4] The pseudonymn of Sathian Canthimatho'n

[5] He went on to say that, "Even though her work is not of excellent quality it is still more convincing than that of other petty bourgeois writers."

[6] Her first two years were spent as a live-in nanny, enabling her to send all her wages home to her mother. Having returned temporarily to work in Phitsanulok she again made the journey to Bangkok in 1963, where she took a job as a maidservant in an expatriate American household. Further jobs involved her working as a seamstress and, with her savings, she took lessons in dressmaking. In the years that followed, her work was to alternate between sewing clothes on a piece-work basis at *Pak khlo'ng talat* and working in restaurants, first as a washing up hand, then as a cook and eventually as a cashier.

Although the content of these pieces satisfied intellectual tastes of the times, Sidaoru'ang's own brand of social consciousness soon began to differ from that of her 'Literature for Life' contemporaries[7] and she was to become far less dogmatic in her depictions of 'evil capitalists' on the one hand versus 'virtuous peasants' on the other. Whereas she continued, for many years, to portray the wealthy and powerful as irredemiably disreputable, Sidaoru'ang's lower class protagonists are also less than saintly. The point made by Phinyo Kongthong on her ability to write "in many styles, surrounded by ordinary people, both in the country, the factories and the suburbs of Bangkok", had permitted her, in Phinyo's view, to produce short stories that were "full of realistic and lively images of ordinary folk" (Phinyo 1986: 41). It is this sense of realism, derived from first-hand contact with the people about whom she was writing, that quickly led her into a realm of complex characterization which was often at odds with the doctinaire prescriptions of the 'Literature for Life' movement.

Whilst the heroes and heroines of Sidaoru'ang's first few published pieces are almost beyond reproach, *Su'ng ro' wan ca taek thamlai* ('Which Awaits Destruction'), published only a year later, marks a far less candid attitude. Its chief protagonist, Lung Caew, is an old peasant, irritated to the point of continual and bitter cursing by the failure of the Khu'krit government's 'Tambon Development Scheme'[8] to have effectively improved his lot. Rather than perform an honest day's work he earns his keep by gambling and fish-fighting. In a roughly contemporaneous story, *So'ng mu' rao mi raeng* ('We Have Strength in Our Hands'), a father and his two eldest children devote considerable time to digging a well in order to provide cleaner water for the village in which they live. The other villagers fail to offer their help and instead ridicule this effort to replace the supply of canal water that is also used for washing clothes, for cleaning and gutting fish and by buffalo on their way to the paddy fields. Sidaoru'ang describes the villagers' complacent attitude to the water as follows:

> You can still drink it if it's murky. Just think of it as a kind of medicine. After all, they
> make red ants' piss into medicine. And when people have red eyes they put drops of

---

[7] For example *Wat Wanlyangkun, Prasoet Candam, Wisa Khantap, Seksan Prasoetkun* and *Atsiri Thammachot*, to name but a few.

[8] The Tambon Development Act of 1975 released government funds totalling 2500 million baht to 5023 tambon councils for use in specific local projects such as the construction of roads, irrigation canals, wells etc. For a full account see Chai-anan and Morell, 1981; Girling, 1981: 202-204; and Turton, 1978: 118-119.

kids' pee in them...And this is only buffalo dung and buffalo pee. What's wrong with that? (Sidaoru'ang 1983: 159).

Far from offering a typical 'Literature for Life' eulogy of traditional, bucolic purity *So'ng mu' rao mi raeng* is critical of working class ignorance. While Sidaoru'ang remains largely sympathetic to the plight of the poor she nevertheless condemns their lack of willingness to improve their own situation.[9] Her heartfelt campaign against ignorance and the need for 'education', in the broadest sense of that term, takes precedence as a key theme in her work, explicable, perhaps, in terms of her own lack of formal education and her recognition of its value from an early age. Although Sidaoru'ang was obliged to leave school prematurely she was encouraged by her father to take an avid interest in reading, an interest she pursued throughout her adolescence and which was further stimulated by her acquaintance with the literary critic Suchat Sawatsi, in the early 1970s. It was at this time that she became familiar with the work of the radical literary theorists Intharayut, Bancong Bancoetsin and, more especially, Cit Phumisak and of such fictional writers as Seni Saowaphong and Wat Wanlyangkun. Although inspired to an extent by their socialist-realist views, Sidaoru'ang was never to adopt or immitate them wholeheartedly. Her own work has always retained a preference for social commentary and criticism up until the present day, but even at the height of its political radicalism in 1975 and '76 she was never to advocate the leftist extremism that typified the writing of some of her contemporaries, many of whom joined the ranks of the Communist Party of Thailand following the bloody coup of 6 October, 1976. Sidaoru'ang instead remained in Bangkok at this time, albeit incognito for a six month period.

As a result of these political and domestic upheavals she published only one short story in 1977 but became more prolific in subsequent years, with a total of thirty four of her pieces being published between 1983 and 1986. Recognition that the Communist Party could not fulfill the hopes of the student radicals came by the end of the 1970s and the majority returned to mainstream Thai society in response to the amnesty offered them in

---

[9] The reason for this is largely, I believe, a result of her own upbringing and family background. Interview material and the autobiographical elements of *So'ng mu' rao mi raeng* provide evidence that Sidaoru'ang's own father (who had moved to Bang Krathum from his family home in Bangkok) had considerably more foresight and education than the community in which he came to live.

1978. In parallel to this and to the experience of her own life, Sidaoru'ang's fiction began to occupy itself less and less with the lives of the up-country peasants in preference to those of the suburban middle classes and nouveaux riches. A corresponding rejection of 'Literature for Life' left many of Sidaoru'ang's contemporaries to concentrate upon a more religious veneration of nature and the environment in their writing. By contrast Sidaoru'ang's own life and work became firmly centred on the environment of the home - the house, the garden and her immediate family.

Married in 1976 to the well-known literary critic Suchat Sawatsi, Sidaoru'ang gave birth to a son, Mone, in 1981, having previously had a child who died when only a few days old. The short stories which she produced in the aftermath of these experiences of motherhood focus to a greater or lesser extent on aspects of pregnancy, childbirth, mothering and childrearing. In a significant break with the didactic traditions of Thai literature in general and with her own earlier writing in particular, Sidaoru'ang's later pieces offer a highly personal perspective of the world of mother and child and, in particular, the emotional strains of raising a physically sick child.[10] (Mone, was born with a serious heart condition that has necessitated repeated visits to hospital and major surgery.)

As with most of her earliest works, a strong autobiographical element can be noted in these texts. When Sidaoru'ang first began writing she, on the advice of Suchat Sawatsi,[11] drew largely upon personal experience as the basic material of her fiction. Only when she gained greater confidence in her literary talents and further experience of short story writing was she able to take a more imaginative approach. This becomes evident in her second and third short story collections, *Bat prachachon* and

---

[10] My observations of these trends in Sidaoru'ang's later works are based particularly upon such stories as *Mae kho'ng Pom* ('Pom's Mother'), *Nam ta lai ngiap* ('Tears that Flow in Silence') and *Ta nu* ('Ta Noo') from the *Bat prachachon* collection; *Matsi* ('Matsi'), *Ma hai* ('My Dog has Disappeared'), *Kem phaen thi* ('The Map Game'), *Lok kho'ng Nome* ('Nome's World') and the *Chao yak* series in the collection *Matsi* ; and *So'ng mae* ('The Two Mothers'), *Khon kae, khon liang dek, yai, yai maemot, khun mae, chuay phom duay* ('Mother, Help me Please'), *Phap luang ta kiaw kap kanplian sapphanam* ('Illusions Created by the Change of Pronouns') and *Banthu'k kho'ng no'ng nu* (My Diary to Mother') from the *Phap luang ta* collection.

[11] In an interview Sidaoru'ang revealed that:
After I had met Khun Suchat I once wrote down a dream for him. He was surprised....and that gave me a little more confidence. He advised that if I was interested in writing I ought to start from my experiences. If I started off by using pure imagination without knowing anything about writing then I'd be unsuccessful (Sidaoru'ang, 1988: 246).

Matsi, whilst her fourth, *Phap luang ta* comprises stories that are almost entirely drawn from imagination. Sidaoru'ang attests to this change of technique in the introduction to *Matsi* :

> I think, I write according to how I feel and to my abilities. Initially experience was an absolute essential but as time went on experience became only one aspect of imagination in learning, searching out and experimenting with new ideas. The use of imagination is something new, which I have learnt from books and from people...(Sidaoru'ang 1987: author's preface, n. p.).

Based on this evidence some of Sidaoru'ang's references to childbirth and to motherhood can be interpreted in part as depictions of the author's own life experience. She clearly admits this to have been the case with *Ta nu* and with *Nam ta lai ngiap* [12] and when asked in an interviev with the magazine *No'n nangsu'* or 'Bookworm' to explain her fascination for the characters of mother and child she replied that:

> It's to do with a feeling of attachment (*phuk phan*) which I have had since my first child was born and then died. My second child is not strong and I make use of the feelings which are closest to my heart (Sidaoru'ang 1988a: 11).

Sidaoru'ang's focus on the mother-child relationship provides interesting material for analysis within the framework of recent feminist theories applied to the study of international literature. In terms of 'women's writing' as a distinct category much emphasis has been placed on the expression of the experience in the female text. One of America's best known feminist critics, Elaine Showalter, is responsible for the introduction of the term 'gynocritics'[13], among the primary concerns of which are the 'psychodynamics of female creativity' (Showalter 1979: 25). Showalter's premise that the woman's text is a "transparent medium through which 'experience' can be seized" (Moi 1985: 76), although somewhat reductionist, nevertheless presents an interesting perspective from which to assess Sidaoru'ang's writing. Adopting this 'psychodynamic' approach, the American academic Ellen Moers, in her extensive study of Western women's writing (Moers 1986) locates the inspiration for Mary Shelley's

---

[12] Personal interview with Sidaoru'ang, Bangkok, September, 1990.

[13] From the prefix gyno or gynaeco, meaning 'woman'.

creation of the gothic novel Frankenstein in the writer's experiences of miscarriage and of nurturing weak and ailing offspring. Moers goes on to claim the advent of Naturalism in the late nineteenth century as an indication that the taboo against writing about such topics as pregnancy and labour was beginning to be lifted and she defines Pearl Buck and Sigrid Undset as writers responsible for establishing pregnancy, labour and breast feeding as respectable themes of twentieth century women's fiction (Moers 1986: 92).

The emphasis which both Moers and Showalter place upon authorial experience as a fundamental 'source' of meaning in a text belongs to a liberal traditionalist view of literature, defined below by Toril Moi:

> The humanist believes in literature as an excellent instrument of education: by reading 'great works' the student will become a finer human being. The great author is great because he (occasionally even she) has managed to convey an authentic vision of life; and the role of the reader or critic is to listen respectfully to the voice of the author as it is expressed in the text. (Moi 1985: 78).

Their approach is, however, highly contentious in the light of post-structuralist concepts of the 'death of the author'[14] and the resultant 'birth of the reader'[15] which views the text not as a projection of authorial intention but as an artefact in its own right, to be carefully but disrespectfully interpreted by the reader. Such theoretical perspectives are, however, deeply rooted in the culture of late twentieth century Western criticism and do not transfer smoothly to Thai traditions of discourse, which have evolved in a culture where notions of 'respect' play such an integral role in social cohesion.[16]

Nevertheless, to read Sidaoru'ang's short stories as little more than biographical sketches would be to oversimplify them: although her later stories of childbirth are closely modelled upon experience, the depiction of

---

[14] For the original use of this term see Roland Barthes, 1977: 142-148.

[15] Showalter reconciles this fact by an overall rejection of 'male critical theory', stating on behalf of women, that it "keeps us dependent upon it and retards our progress in solving our own theoretical problems" (Showalter: 1982: 13).

[16] Among the list of 'basic attitudes that are instilled at an early age' in Thai children, the anthropologist Niels Mulder lists *kreng cai* (inhibition, fear of imposing), *kreng klua* (awe, respectful fear), *khaorop* and *napthu'* (respect), politeness and obedience, the acceptance of the wisdom of elders and of tradition and an indebtedness and gratitude to elders, epitomized in the figures of the mother and the teacher (Mulder: 1990: 61).

dual birth and death images in the texts of 1975 and '76 actually predate the author's own experiences of giving birth.[17] In *Khrang nu'ng nan ma laew* a young and carefree prostitute becomes pregnant and is forced, as a result, to take responsibility for her actions. She endeavours to abort her unwanted baby by the various methods available to her, all of which are unsuccessful. Then, through fear of being chastised should she seek medical attention at a hospital, she follows the advice of a friend and visits a local midwife or *mo' tamyae*. After several days of having her stomach massaged by the midwife, the girl still fails to miscarry. She subsequently falls ill and is depicted, at the end of the story, lying in a hospital corridor being told by an angry nurse that the child has died in her womb and that there are no beds available for her.

At its most elementary level *Khrang nu'ng nan ma laew* is a moral tale, woven from the author's own experiences of working with prostitutes as a cashier in a Bangkok restaurant-cum-brothel.[18] The title of the piece and its closing paragraph are indicative of the intention to teach and to warn of the outcomes of recklessness:

> This tale[19] teaches that from that day on sexual oppression as a result of ignorance at every level is a burden which people must join in eradicating once and for all, through education. So please do not hope to derive any pleasure from such a tale as this (Sidaoru'ang 1983 : 124).

Typical of the often artless tendencies of 'Literature for Life' pieces, the above paragraph is intended to be taken precisely at face value. The 'tale' is addressed not, as details of its content might suggest, to a readership of prostitutes and promiscuous teenagers who disregard the needs for contraception at their peril, but to those having benefitted from education. Although, at this early stage in her career, Sidaoru'ang still clung to the hope of being able to address the working classes directly through her

---

[17] It is possible, however, that she may have had both a miscarriage and an abortion as a result of political upheavals during this period.

[18] In the early 1970s Sidaoru'ang worked in a number of restaurants in Bangkok. It was through her work as a cashier at the Nuan Napha restaurant in Saphan Khway that she met Suchat Sawatsi in 1973.
The prostitute in *Khrang nu'ng nan ma laew* receives advice and help from an older, female friend and the relationship between the two characters in many ways mirrors that between the prostitute Oy and her cashier colleague in a later piece, *Mu't laew sawang* ('Light After Dark').

[19] The word used in the text is *nithan*, with the didcatic overtones of a fable or a moral tale.

literature[20] the readership of *Akso'rasat phican* in which the piece was first published, would have comprised students and intellectuals with a vocation to 'inform' the working classes and the socially disadvantaged.[21]

I have already mentioned the importance of education as a theme in Sidaoru'ang's work and of the value placed upon it by a writer who had herself had little formal schooling. Set in this context, *Khrang nu'ng nan ma laew* does not differ in its essential message from such pieces as *Chai pha lu'ang* ('The Hem of the Saffron Robe'), or *Phit wang* ('Disappointed'). What is of interest is Sidaoru'ang's recourse to the image of unwanted pregnancy as a metaphor for ignorance. *Khrang nu'ng nan ma laew* closes without a clear indication of the fate of the ailing prostitute; she herself may or may not die, but her child is clearly dead and rotting in her womb. This somewhat macabre image recurs in a piece published shortly after, entitled *Phuak nai pa* and dealing essentially with the exploitation of mine workers. Open to them is the choice to protest either by joining 'those in the jungle' (the communist insurgents) or by voting against the mine owner when he stands for election as a political candidate. The story traces in part the decision of a young man to join the insurgents following the death of his parents in a mining accident caused by the carelessness of their employer and in which a number of people are killed:

> Workers from other mines ran over. Some simply stood there, stunned, others rushed to help. One man hid his face in horror when he saw a heavily pregnant woman who had

---

[20] This is an idea put forward by the radical Thai literary theoreticians of the 1950s, and which was succinctly reproduced in Cit Phumisak's *Sinlapa phu'a chiwit, sinlapa phu'a prachachon* ('Art for Life, Art for the People'). Although originally published in two parts in 1957, the work received a burst of further attention when it was amalgamated and reprinted by student groups in 1972. It rapidly became a handbook on the meaning of literature and art among student radicals in the aftermath of the 1973 uprising.

Although never a fully fledged member of this student radical movement Sidaoru'ang was vicariously involved in it through her connections with Suchat Sawatsi. She had a clear desire to write for people of the same background as herself and she alludes to this not only in interview material but in her short story *Tam pai kha Suriya nai pa oei* ('Go Slay Suriya in the Jungle'), first published in 1978.

[21] This is a theme particularly dear to Sidaoru'ang's heart, given her own lack of formal education and her subsequent efforts to compensate for this, be it by taking evening classes, by reading or by writing fiction. Much of her earliest stories return to the persistent theme of the need for education and the methods in which knowledge is disseminated, or they serve to highlight the benefits of 'education' in the broadest sense of that term. See, for example, *Chai pha lu'ang* ('The Hem of the Saffron Robe'), *Sing thi long thun* ('Investments Worth Making'), and *Phit wang* ('Disappointed'), all of which were first published in 1975; and *So'ng mu' rao mi raeng* ('We Have Strength in Our Hands'), *Bang thi wan nu'ng khang na* ('Perhaps, One Day in the Future') and *Su'ng ro' wan ca taek thamlai* ('Which Awaits Destruction') published in 1976.

been crushed on her stomach by a rock. Both the child in the mother's womb and her intestines flowed out and lay in a pile beside her body. Some workers had broken their arms or legs. Some people could not be identified but were covered in blood and amongst these fifteen unfortunate workers lay the remains of the young man's parents. Both had died beneath a large boulder, their bodies flattened to the ground. When the mine workers took the bodies to the temple the next day the corpses of the two old people were already swollen and distended (Sidaoru'ang 1983: 130).

A predilection for macabre imagery that, to a Western reader, has reminiscences of the Gothic, seems often to be present in radical Thai short story writing, and may be symptomatic of the background of political unrest against which it was written. In addition to regular reports of industrial accidents (which still persist even today) numerous political killings also took place in the 1974-6 period, among the most shocking of which was the burning by Border Patrol Police of the north eastern village of Ban Na Sai in January 1974. One thousand three hundred inhabitants were ordered out of their homes and several villagers were burned to death, including a six year old child.[22] The two year campaign of 'public intimidation, assault and assassination' referred to by Ben Anderson (1977: 13) as the precursor of the bloodshed of 6 October, 1976 ensured the persistence of high levels of violence. Anderson provides detailed references to the polarization of left and right wing groups in Thai society in the mid 1970s, and of the aggression that was articulated against the latter by the former. He draws particular attention to the assassination by professional gunmen of Dr Boonsanong Punyodana in February 1976, to the launch of the slogan by Pramarn Adireksan in the Spring of 1976 of "Right Kill Left", and to the views of the Buddhist monk Kitti Wuttho that no demerit would be gained by the murder of communist sympathizers (Anderson 1977: 13 and 24; Chai-anan and Morell 1981: passim and, in particular, Chapter 9).

Although Sidaoru'ang was not actively involved in leftist demonstations, her writing during this period clearly testifies to her radical sympathies, as does her association with Suchat Sawatsi and the circles in which he moved. Nowhere is this better expressed than in *Phu'an chan yang mai klap ma cak nai mu'ang* or 'My Friend Has Not Yet Returned From The City', written in the immediate aftermath of 6 October and which catalogues the fear felt by the author/narrator as she awaits the return of

---

[22] For further details see Chai-anan and Morell, 1981: 169.

her partner from the October demonstrations at Thammasat University. In her attempt to protect her friend from danger she buries his books at night in the garden, in constant fear of detection by a neighbouring Village Scout. Both Sidaoru'ang and her readers would doubtless have felt intimidated by the campaigns of rightist groups such as the Village Scouts and the Red Gaurs. *Phuak nai pa* for example, is one of her most politically prescriptive pieces, one in which Sidaoru'ang comes closest to extolling the virtues of the Communist Party. Moreover, the flavour of the literary magazine *Putuchon*, in which the story was first published, (in the very month of October 1976), appealed to the extremes of youthful, radical fervour. Its pages were filled not only with politically committed articles, short stories and poems but also with pictures of such 'revolutionary heroes' as Che Guevara and cartoons which portrayed capitalists as bringers of death to an innocent and oppressed working class.

It is against this political background that the representation of the dead workers in the mining accident of *Phuak nai pa* was created by the author and understood by its readers, so that it is, at one level, symptomatic of the very violent times in which it came to be written.

It remains, however, to be noted that among the vicitims of this accident the prime symbol of its brutality is (in the above extract) not so much the corpses of the two old people, who are integral to the plot, but the crushed body of the pregnant woman, the horror of which is so profound that it causes a witness to avert his eyes.

There is an implication here about the sacred place awarded to the mother in Thai society (the woman is referred to in the text by the pronoun 'mother' or *mae*) that may also account in part for the potency of the image of the dying 'mother' in *Khrang nu'ng nan ma laew*. In his analysis of everyday Thai life the anthropologist Niels Mulder defines the mother as the symbol of moral goodness (*khunngam khwamdi*), ever-giving, caring and self-sacrificing towards "her dependents who rely on her for stability and continuity in life. She is a refuge, a haven of safety.....At mother's side one is safe (Mulder 1990: 25).[23] Mulder goes on to describe the mother-child

---

[23] Mulder also points out that the sustaining earth, rice and water are all represented in the feminine in Thai, as in *mae thorani, mae phosop* and *mae nam*. To this list I would also add the figure of *mae phra khongkha*, to whom Sidaoru'ang refers in two or three of her stories. In *Phrapheni thi yok loek* for example, a young woman, Cinta, is unhappily married to a man who beats her. During the *loi krathong* festival she stands alone in the river water and prays to *mae phra khongkha* to witness her bruised body and to give her the strength to persevere in her duties as a wife.

union as "a pivotal relationship and an ideological pattern that gives stability to the Thai experience and way of life (Mulder 1990: 64).

If the image of 'mother' does have its place in the Thai psyche as one of stability and safety as Mulder suggests, then the reference to a dead or dying mother with a dead child in *Phuak nai pa* and *Khrang nu'ng nan ma laew* is a fundamentally destabilising one, characteristic of the political and social environment in which both these stories were written.

Traditional perceptions of the mother as a stable, all-loving figure are not, however, the ones that match Sidaoru'ang's references to her own mother. Sidaoru'ang instead presents her, in interview material, as essentially uncommunicative and punitive, in contrast to a much gentler father figure. She comments on her childhood, for example, that:

> We always had to do exactly what mother told us and if there was anything we didn't understand, like where she was going, then we couldn't ask since that was adults' business and children were not supposed to ask about it. If mother had visitors we had to go and play under the house and not interfere with the adults. So I loved my father more than my mother. Even though I wasn't all that close to him and we didn't see much of each other my father never hit us or told us off.
>
> ......When my mother used to tell me off she used to beat me. She was always beating me and it was a terrible thrashing she gave every single time. Sometimes she used to use a great big long stick that she'd take hold of in both hands. We would all get a beating.....but I knew that she loved us all the same (Sidaoru'ang 1988b: 242)[24]

Evidence of Sidaoru'ang's autobiographical writing would suggest that the role of a tender, caring mother was largely usurped by her grandmother. The latter is portrayed with obvious affection in such stories as *Yai kap thahan num* ('Grandmother and the Young Soldier', first published in 1978), *Krasae samnu'k kho'ng yai* ('Grandmother's Stream of Consciousness', first published in 1982), *Lan yai* ('Grandmother's Grandchildren', first published in 1983) and *Rakha kho'ng yai* ('Grandmother's Worth', first published in 1985). By contrast, Sidaoru'ang's mother only makes insignificant appearances in her fiction and portrayals tend to be either indifferent or even rather negative. One of the few examples of writing with reference to her mother is *Rakha haeng*

---

[24] Other references to Sidaoru'ang's relationship with her mother are given in interviews with the magazines *Thanon nangsu'*, year 2, number 9, 1985 and *No'n nangsu'*, year 1, number 3, 1988.

khwamtai, published a year after *Phuak nai pa* and which again returns to the linked imagery of birth and death. Sidaoru'ang's fear of her mother which Sidaoru'ang has noted in interview material is similarly articulated in the text:

> When I walked through the darkness, past the railway station, Father was still working in the control room, but Mother hadn't given me instructions to stop by and tell him she had gone into labour so there was no way I dare call in and let him know. I always did as my mother told me, even though there were many occasions when I wanted to speak out. But the minute my eyes met with hers my mouth would be firmly closed (Sidaoru'ang 1983: 217).

There is sufficient evidence in *Rakha haeng khwamtai* to indicate that the story is a recollection of the author's own family; it takes place in a small market town that so often provides the rural setting of Sidaoru'ang's texts; the father of the family is a worker on the local railway; and it is related through the eyes of a young girl called Yong, the nickname used for Sidaoru'ang by her own relatives. *Rakha heang khwamtai* narrates the birth of a child and his subsequent drowning in an accident at the age of nine. Taking up a common theme of socially conscious literature, Sidaoru'ang presents the child's death as a consequence of a local doctor's refusal to provide treatment before prior payment.[25] But beneath this standard social message of rural poverty and the inhumanity of a money-orientated medical profession lies a much more emotionally committed work, one that bears similarities to such tender character portrayals as *Pho'* ('Father') and *Lan kho'ng yai* ('Grandmother's Grandchildren'). A large part of the narrative comprises a detailed description of childbirth in rural Thailand, one which Phinyo notes for its informative value, on a subject matter of which few members of the younger generation would have had knowledge (Phinyo 1986: 42-43).

Although the new-born baby is in fact Yong's brother, Yong assumes responsibility for him in the role of a surrogate mother. It is she who runs to fetch the midwife when her mother goes into labour, she who helps with and watches the birth intently, she who feeds the child with water on the tip of her finger while her mother sleeps. In the text she refers to him as the

---

[25] This theme is also present in the work of such writers as Siburapha and Wat Wanlyangkun.

baby "for whom I had done everything save give birth to" (Sidaoru'ang 1983: 223).

Rakha haeng khwamtai speaks, in part, then, of the author's own sense of frustrated maternity. Given the closeness of her bond with her little brother, his subsequent death is especially traumatic for the narrator. For Sidaoru'ang the two images of her brother's birth and of his death appear inseparable (even the descriptions of the pain of the mother's labour and the copious amounts of blood that are spilt convey a sense of horror and violence more fittingly associated with death), and nowhere is this better illustrated than by the identical opening and closing paragraphs of the piece:

> He was once a child in my arms. Yes. He was one of my little brothers, a little brother whom I had looked after ever since he was born. But now I was stroking his distended stomach until the water flowed out. His body was beginning to rot and would soon be leaving me. Now he had died. But I was thinking of the night that he was born (Sidaoru'ang 1983: 215 and 226).[26]

Rather than conforming to Buddhist notions of the inevitability of impermanence, the tragedy with which the deaths and failed births in this story and in *Khrang nu'ng nan ma laew* and *Phuak nai pa* are portrayed by Sidaoru'ang reveal a poignant sense of loss. What I am edging towards in highlighting this is a recognition of the input of Western ideas in Sidaoru'ang's work and in Thai prose fiction as a whole. Whilst Sidaoru'ang operates from within a wholly Thai environment and has always rejected any opportunity to travel abroad, Western literature and cultural values have nevertheless made felt their effects in the development of her writing career. Her husband, Suchat Sawatsi, is moreover reknowned as an intellectual in the Western mould, venerated among the Thai *literati* for his promotion of the philosophical values of Jean-Paul Sartre and Albert Camus.

It is for these reasons that the application of some aspects of Western literary theory cannot be excluded as a tool in the analysis of Sidaoru'ang's writing. For an insight into the themes of birth and death in writing I want here to concentrate upon the work of the French theorists Helene Cixous

---

[26] The paragraphs differ only by the inclusion of the final sentence, which appears at the close of the story.

and Julia Kristeva.[27] Drawing heavily upon the principals of Freudian and Lacanian psychoanalysis the former has postulated that writing can operate as a way of coming to terms with death, of reviving the dead and of mourning for them. The death of Helene Cixous' own father gave her the following conviction:

> From the outset, writing serves as a necessary means of repairing the separation from a place or a person caused either by exile or death. Writing does the work of bereavement, of reconstituting the loss, and of keeping the memory of the precarious (Cornell 1990: 32).

This view applies not only to the person who creates the text but also to the audience that reads it. Cixous goes on to say that:

> Writing is very violent. Death is implied in writing: the redeeming from death but also the giving of death......Note the ambivalence: writing both buries and evokes; it's in the text that dead people or forgotten people can come back, be recalled, and find a kind of resurrection......Actually you write thanks to death, against death, beginning with death, and at the price of death (Cixous 1990: 18-19, my editing).

Sidaoru'ang's own *Rakha haeng khwamtai* or 'The Price of Death' serves to recall the memory of her drowned brother, while at the same time permitting his final 'burial', via the text. Nowhere greater is this sense of mourning through writing experienced, however, than in one of Sidaoru'ang's earliest short stories, *Pho'* or 'Father' (her fifth piece to be published in 1975). While Cixous places considerable emphasis on the death of her own father in reference to her own 'birth' into writing there is also a temporal link between the suicide of Sidaoru'ang's father and her desire to write her first short story for a local newspaper competition when she was fifteen years old. This story, entitled *La ko'n khon bap* ('Farewell to the Sinner') concerns a naughty child whose disobedience drives her mother to become ordained as a nun as her only means of escape. In an interview conducted with Sidaoru'ang in 1990 she claimed to have written this piece

---

[27] Although Cixous and Kristeva are the key proponents of 'French feminist criticism' neither of them is technically French. Cixous is the daughter of a German Jewish mother and Spanish Jewish father and was herself born in Algeria. Kristeva is half Burmese, half Bulgarian. Both women migrated to Paris, where they now live and work.

in order to 'punish herself' for what she considered to be disrespectful behaviour towards her mother.[28]

Sidaoru'ang's somewhat fraught relationship with her mother is in contrast to a less troubled one with her father. This is implied in *Rakha haeng khwamtai* but is much more clearly stated in *Pho'*. The latter provides a detailed character portrayal of Sidaoru'ang's own father and documents her separation from him as a result of her mother's instructions that she leave home to work. As the little girl in the story boards the train for the city she sees her father coming after her; ill health, however, prevents him from catching up with her before the train departs. This is the last time that she is to see him, for shortly after he commits suicide. The impact of his death is noted in interviews with the author:

> Usually I'm a fighter, so there's nothing really terrible in my life. The time I was most upset was when my father hanged himself. I wasn't living at home then and by the time I got back he had already been cremated. I was so disappointed, for I had not seen how ill he was. I knew nothing about it. This is just the way that country folk think - that however the person dies you just want to be able to see them and to touch them for the very last time. But I wasn't able to. By the time I arrived all I saw were his ashes and we sprinkled them in the canal (Sidaoru'ang 1988b: 250).

The sudden death by suicide of Sidaoru'ang's father was evidently not fully resolved in her mind and she had been unable to properly mourn him. In light of this event, and of its relationship to her writing, it is noteworthy that Sidaoru'ang traces the origins of her pseudonym back to her father. She does this not only in interview but in the text of *Pho'* itself:

> The children noticed that Father had stopped going to work at the station. Nowadays he just stayed at home and whiled away his time growing chillies and aubergines, and rearing chickens. He gave Mother a hand making sweetmeats, and he also liked growing flowers.
>
> "Hey, look what I've got" his daughter called to him one day, waving a plant at him that had come out in little yellow flowers with serrated edges.
>
> "What sort of plant's that ? he asked.

---

[28] The importance of the respect owed to the mother in Thai society is highlighted by Niels Mulder and is the subject of Sidaoru'ang's second short story to be published, *Chai pha lu'ang* ('The Hem of the Saffron Robe'). Natsini Witthuthirasan claims this text to be based upon Sidaoru'ang's own mother (Natsini, 1976: 258).

"I've no idea. I got it over by the jetty . There's loads of them over there."

Father came out of the house, looking intrigued.

"Don't you know what kind of flower it is? he asked her. "Well, we'd better give it a name, hadn't we?...... How about *Daoru'ang*?"

The girl laughed happily.

"Hey! That's *my* name." she said.

Both father and daughter laughed and he patted her gently on the head.

(Sidaoru'ang 1983: 96-97).

This is literary licence. Whilst *'daoru'ang'* flowers or marigolds are reminiscent of Sidaoru'ang's childhood, their name was in fact identified to her by Suchat Sawatsi and not by her father:

> Both Khun Suchat and I thought of my pen name. I thought of this, that and the other. I thought of flowers. I thought of my father...I think I thought of[29] my father a lot. I used to collect flowers for him and they were yellow. Khun Suchat worked out that they must have been *daoru'ang* flowers. That was my father. And then the *Si* was a bit from him as well. All the famous, old writers had *si* in their names. So Khun Suchat called me *Sidaoru'ang* (Sidaoru'ang 1988b: 241).

The evidence of *Pho'* and of the above extract would suggest that Sidaoru'ang owed much, in her writing, to the memory of her father. Whilst this can, in part, be attributed to the sense of gratitude to parents and their elders instilled in all Thai children (Mulder 1990: 64) (Sidaoru'ang's second book is dedicated to both her father and her mother), it was her father who first encouraged her to read as a child by returning from Bangkok with books for his children; and it was from this that she derived her love of literature.

The psychoanalytical approach to the analysis of writers and writing that enjoys considerable popularity in contemporary studies of Western literature places much emphasis on the concept that *all* writing is an attempt to come to terms with the loss of a love object, to in some sense retrieve it and to maintain control over it.[30] At the heart of this theory lies Freud's observation of his grandson playing what he came to call the *fort-da*

---

[29] The words 'thought of' in Thai (*khit thu'ng*) can also be translated as 'to miss' or 'to long for'. This sentence could therefore alternatively be translated as, "I think I missed my father a lot."

[30] For further details of these concepts see Eagleton, 1989: 185-186.

game. Freud saw the preverbal infant playing with a cotton reel, throwing it down and shouting *fort* or 'gone away' and then pulling it back towards him with the cries of *da* or 'here'. Freud interpreted this as a ritual method of expelling and recalling the mother, whose absence was, in reality, a source of great distress to the child (Freud 1922: 11-14). The significance of this very need for ritual in light of the mother's absence is adequately described by Juliet Mitchell:

> The child is dependent on its mother (or her substitute) for the satisfaction of his needs - her absence means growing internal tension because the needs cannot be satisfied, and the baby is helpless. It is this situation which recreates or rather creates *a posteriori* the so-called anxiety of birth. The child learns that the presence of the mother can save it from this birth-like danger, hence the loss of her means danger to which the child gives the signal of anxiety, an act of self-preservation as it is intended to prevent her loss. The biological separation of the act of birth is replaced and reinterpreted by the psychical relationship with the mother. But then the baby has to learn to master the absence of the loved and needed object (Mitchell 1974: 82).

Within the dynamics of this *fort-da* principle are the linked notions of the fear of metaphorical 'death' through the absence of the 'mother' figure, coupled with the anxiety of birth. Although what Freud and Mitchell are referring to here is based on essentially Eurocentric perceptions of social organisation, Niels Mulder, in his work on Thai society, also testifies to the strong bonds between the child and its mother (or surrogate mother). In drawing attention to mother's milk and mother's indulgence, late weaning and undemanding toilet training in patterns of Thai childrearing Mulder notes that:

> There are no good reasons why the experience of indulgent nurture and tolerance should not engender high dependence, personal insecurity, doubt, vulnerability....(Mulder 1990: 61).

Not only may death be implied in writing then, but also notions of anxiety with regard to the loss of a mother figure and with the 'rebirthing' of a distinct and separate 'self' that this necessitates and implies. For both Cixous and Kristeva it has therefore become important, as part of this rebirthing process, to recognize in turn the maternal relationship which the writer has with a text. While observing that writing is both being born and dying (Cixous 1990: 20) Cixous goes on to equate the desire to write with "a desire to live the self from within, a desire for the swollen belly, for language, for blood" (Cixous 1975 quoted in Jones 1985: 90). For Kristeva also, an understanding of the association between maternity and female creation is essential (Kristeva 1990: 298).

In light of these ideas there is some validity, I believe, in interpreting Sidaoru'ang's desire to write as part of a struggle for a separate identity and a voice that had previously been denied her, to which the sense of frustrated maternity that is expressed in *Khrang nu'ng nan ma laew, Phuak nai pa* and, most implicitly in *Rakha haeng khwamtai* is thematically related.

One of the fundamental difficulties in applying to Thai literature notions of identity in writing that are particularly crucial to feminist and psychoanalytical literary theory lies in their essentially Eurocentric emphasis on the centrality of the individual.[31] The emphasis placed by Western philosophical tradition upon the need for a strong sense of Self stands in sharp contrast to Buddhist concepts of destruction of the Self as the path to happiness and well-being (Netnapha 1993: 7). This point of difference can be counterbalanced, however, by the fact that contemporary Thai writers, artists and intellectuals frequently define themselves as social marginals, operating only to a limited degree within the traditional structures of Thai society and heavily influenced by Western philosophy and Western literature. Novels and short stories have themselves been introduced into Thai culture from the West, though this is not to say that they have not evolved in their own idiosyncratic fashion. Much of Sidaoru'ang's own work can, in fact, be seen as an attempt to balance the old ways of her country upbringing with the quasi-Western intellectualism of Bangkok's literary avant-garde. Stories such as *Prapheni thi yok loek* or 'Passing Traditions', for example, deal, as the title suggests, with changes in social attitude. This text, first published in 1978, tells of a young woman who moves from an unhappy, traditional marriage into a new-style cohabitation, though the conclusion testifies to her ambivalence about whether this will really prove a success. Again with autobiographical resonances, the latter relationship corresponds with that suggested to

---

[31] To set the work of the French feminist theorists in their own cultural context see Spivak, 1987: 134-153.

Sidaoru'ang by Suchat Sawatsi shortly after they met. Having spoken, in a magazine interview, of the efforts she made to follow Suchat's political thinking when she first met him, Sidaoru'ang continues:

> He suggested that we should try living together for a while and he gave me a book to read about new approaches to marriage (by Witthayako'n Chiangkun). When I had read it I went along with his idea that if we loved each other it didn't matter if we lived together first. Providing I attached no financial value to virginity then as long as we got on well we could carry on living together. And if we didn't get on then we wouldn't need to start working out costs and damages. The choice was ours. (....) And he also said that he was worried about my background. We hadn't known each other long and he must have felt afraid I was the kind of woman who would tie him down. And he had his eyes on other women too. We tried living together first but we weren't sure whether or not he'd have to leave. He warned me about this. When we talked about it I understood his reasoning. (....) If I tried to keep up with him it might work out but if not we would grow apart and we should not stay together. But when I was alone I used to think that one day he would leave for I was nothing and he'd be bound to go off and live with someone more suitable (Sidaoru'ang 1988b: 244).

Sidaoru'ang's sense of inferiority is evident in this extract, as is her keen desire to understand and to follow Suchat's ideas as crucial to the survival of their relationship and to greater self esteem. Her wish to assume an identity in writing must be examined in this context. Sidaoru'ang became a successful writer against all odds, having had a minimal formal education and having worked in semi-skilled and poorly paid jobs ever since. Moreover, until the death of her mother she had had little opportunity to choose the direction which her life should take. As I have demonstrated earlier in this paper, Sidaoru'ang has interpreted her own 'silence' as the consequence of her mother's severity but even after she began her relationship with her husband she was obliged, to a certain extent, to maintain a subordinate role.[32] In reference to the the time when they first began living together she says:

> When Khun Suchat met his friends he didn't introduce me to them. He said nothing. Sometimes we'd be standing side by side and they'd be chatting away. He didn't

---

[32] Whilst there is no denying that Sidaoru'ang's husband is progressive in his attitudes to women's place in society, several of Sidaoru'ang's short stories can be interpreted as, albeit humorous, expressions of his traditionalism.

introduce me and I'd slip away. Sometimes I'd stand behind him. Because he didn't introduce me no one dare ask who I was (Sidaoru'ang 1988b: 245).

The significance to Sidaoru'ang of writing can be argued to have furnished her not only a with a chance to 'speak' for herself that was otherwise denied her, but also to belong to an intellectual community with which she had established peripheral and vicarious contact through her well-respected husband but which had failed to acknowledge her. publicly. The need for acceptance into social groups in Thailand has been recognized by anthropologists such as Herbert Phillips and Niels Mulder; the former dedicates a section of his ethnographic interpretation of modern Thai literature to a discussion of the Thai community of writers (Phillips 1987: 39-60)[33]; the latter comments more generally:

> To suffer rejection means that one has to operate in a dreaded, unreliable, amoral world and consequently to live in the equally dreaded area of personal loneliness. The desire for positive acceptance and identity within a trusted small world is therefore enhanced by the spectre of loneliness... (Mulder 1990: 69).[34]

The 'spectre of loneliness' and of isolation are features which characterize much of Sidaoru'ang's life as a suburban housewife and which have earned her the nickname among literary circles as *ai mong* or 'the ghost'. Both her desire for a metaphorical 'child' in writing and her wish for a real child appear to offer an antidote to this sense of isolation. This is documented in *Nam ta lai ngiap* (or 'Tears that Flow in Silence'), the autobiographical tale of a woman giving birth to a child who dies shortly after. A flashback in the second chapter of the piece refers to her wish to conceive, long before her husband feels ready to begin a family:

> It took several years for the couple to agree to have a child - a child who was the greatest desire a family could have. Warmth, gladness and joy. The family would be united. In fact, the wife had really wanted to have a child ever since they had first begun living together, but her husband did not agree (Sidaoru'ang 1974: 99).

---

[33] An analysis of Thai attitudes towards the community is also offered in Phillips, 1974: Chapter 5 and passim.

[34] Mulder points out the threat to young children of 'being given away', either to the monkhood or to foster parents of even being sold. His notes serve to highlight the sense of rejection and confusion that Sidaoru'ang must have felt as a child when she was sent away from her family to work in Bangkok.

In this extract the woman is referred to as 'the wife' or *phu pen phanraya,* though her title changes at different points in the text: once she has given birth she becomes 'mother' or *mae,* only to revert to her title as 'wife' when she is told that her child has died. By contrast the story opens with a description of the woman in premature labour in a private hospital and in which she is alternately 'the thing lying on the bed' (*sing thi no'n bon tiang)* and 'she who is tied by the arms and legs' (*thoe phu thuk mat khaen kha*) (Sidaoru'ang 1974: 95-96):

A heavily pregnant woman who was lying on the bed was turned over on her side with her back arched. A man holding a needle came up close and said to her,

"Brace your back to take the needle. Don't shrink away from it."

The sharp needle was jabbed and pressed into her backbone two or three times until the person administering the treatment was satisfied. She gritted her teeth and braced her back to take the needle as she had been ordered, although it did did not hurt for long. Her legs and her stomach began to go numb and heavy.

"How is it?" one of the men in green robes asked.

"I feel a bit sick", she replied. She stared up at the two enormous clusters of lights which were hanging above her as if in observation of her empty, naked body which was presently tied tightly by hands and feet to the bed.

"If you feel sick then breathe deeply. The doctor's bringing you a urine tube."

She who was tied by the arms and legs nodded and at the same time someone placed a plastic mask over her nose. Following orders, she began to breathe in and out deeply.

Shortly afterwards her senses told her that only her mouth, her ears and her thoughts remained in operation. She could hear the voices of the people in green robes who surrounded her. They were chattering on about the day to day events that were happening in the outside world, that lay beyond this place. Although she could only faintly hear their voices the green cloth which separated her head from her body meant that she could not actually see them (Sidaoru'ang 1974: 95-96).

Alienation and isolation are implicit throughout this extract, not merely in terms of content but also of form. The use of the passive (which I have endeavoured to retain in the translation) is uncommon in Thai and reserved only for instances where the action is considered by the recipient to be unpleasant. The hospital staff address the patient in brusque and unemotional tones, as though she were less than human. Her low status is implied not only by the earliest reference to her as 'a thing' lying on the bed but also by the way in which she is told to roll over on her side and in which she is literally tied down. Through this restraint of her physical freedom she is effectively subordinated to authority and denied free will. Her body belongs not to herself but to the medical staff who attend to her. This is epitomized by the green cloth which separates her head (and her remaining senses of speech, hearing and thought) from her numbed, desensitized body that lies within the boundaries the medical staff, of authority and 'split off' from the remainder of her 'self'.

The sense of fragmentation that this implies is pertinent to analysis under current literary theories which view the literary text as a projection of the soma.[35] For feminist critics the question of a woman's access to her own body is a crucial aspect of the struggle to establish her own identity since, in patriarchal societies, she is always defined as 'other' to the dominant male. Consequently marginalized, she is able only to speak from a space outside the prevalent discourse. According to Luce Irigaray[36] women can therefore only experience themselves fragmentarily, as waste or excess in the margins of the dominant ideology (Foster 1990: 66). As a result a sense of her own body is denied her and she is silenced. "Censor the body and you censor breath and speech at the same time" writes Cixous (quoted in Shiach 1991: 18).

Writing is seen by these theorists, then, as an act of translating ones true self into the body of the text: it is an attempt to create new identities, to break free of fixed categories, to rediscover what has been actively repressed and to challenge the culturally produced category of 'woman' (Shiach 1991: 26).

All these ideas are underpinned by European notions of a child's psychological development and on theories of sexual identity which have been constructed with reference to Western society. The key concept here is that of the 'Mirror Stage', first outlined by the French psychoanalyst Jacques Lacan, and of its relationship to the construction of individual identity. Lacan proposes that an infant between the age of 6 to 18 months sees its image in a mirror or has the equivalent experience of identifying itself in

---

[35] These theories based on the connections between the body and the text have grown out of the post structuralist movement of the past twenty years and are heavily based upon Freudian and Lacanian psychoanalysis. For a general introduction to these concepts see Wilcox eds, 1990; Moi, 1985; Brooks, 1993; and Eagleton, 1993: 7-8.

[36] French feminist philosopher and author of 'Women's Exile' in Cameron ed, 1990: 80-96.

the body of another child. As a result fragmented body images begin to merge and produce an identity based on the infant's perception of other identities. It perceives itself as a separate entity from the body of its mother (with which, until now, it has been involved in an all-consuming psychological relationship) and begins to gain control over its own motor functions. In actual fact what it recognizes as the embodiment of its 'self' or ego in the mirror is never tantamount to its real self, which, can never fully be attained.[37]

The description of the pregnant woman in *Nam ta lai ngiap* as detached from her body is, in Lacanian terms, reminiscent of her own struggle to attain selfhood. Rather like the child in quest of its own identity in the bodies of others, the woman's search for confirmation of her 'self' in the form of the medical staff who surround her is frustrated by the fact that she cannot actually see them but only hear their faint voices and even then to know they are talking not of her but of subjects that are totally unrelated. Moreover, the administration of a local anaesthetic, so that the baby can be removed by Caesarian section, causes "she who is tied by her arms and legs" to lose all sense of that part of her body beyond the green cloth and which she cannot see. As a result she is denied not only a visual perception of her body but a physical awareness of its existence. Finally the cries of the new-born child are heard and "she who is tied by her arms and legs" is referred to for the first time in the text as a "mother", although she is unable to exhibit physical joy at the realization of her motherhood. Even her mouth is too numb for her to be able to smile. Someone comments that the child is underweight and the fading sound of its crying cause the mother to realize that it is being taken away without her even having seen or touched it. Not only is access to her own body denied her, but also access to her that of her child. As the anaesthetic wears off her numbness begins to disappear, but she still has no real awareness of the birth. In keeping with the persistent association of birth and death in Sidaoru'ang's work, the mother's thoughts are occupied by a sense of her own impending death as she slips in and out of consciousness. Having given birth it no longer matters to her whether she lives or dies. In the event it is the mother who survives and the baby who dies, several days later and without her ever having seen it.

As I have defined in my arguments above, *Nam ta lai ngiap* deals with the concepts of identity, creation, silence and isolation - albeit not

---

[37] For further details see Sarup, 1992: 62-66; and Bowie, 1991: 21-27.

necessarily at the level of authorial intention. The story closes with the nurse's enquiries about how the parents would like the child's body to be disposed of. Whilst the father's response to this insensitive request is an angry and vocal one, the mother's is one of silence and of 'tears that flow in silence'. As she comes to terms with the reality of her loss the woman, now referred to as 'the person who is a wife', contemplates her once swollen stomach.

> Yes, there was no question of it. It was empty and had gone. She felt as if it had
> disappeared, as if there had never been anything there except for emptiness...and scars
> (Sidaoru'ang 1984: 120).

Following the death of her child the mother's only sense of her own body is in terms of the damage done to it and of its emptiness. The silent tears which she sheds speak not only of her bereavement but of her own relationship to her 'self' and to her body.

This equation between the post-partum body and the notion of silence is nowhere more clearly evidenced than in *Thoi kham lae khwamngiap* (or 'Words and Silence'), the story of a young woman who takes the difficult decision to have an illegal abortion in the light of difficult political circumstances. The text deals entirely with the abortion procedure and with the young mother's related apprehension and confusion. As the abortion is being performed she reminds herself of her deeply felt desire to have a child at some time in the future:

> She was coming to a clear understanding about all the confusion she felt inside her.
> Even though it was too late this time, on this particular occasion, this was something
> every daughter could understand, and now she too understood. She felt as though she
> wanted to cry out to her heart's content when suddenly the doctor stiffened, spoke and
> drove out all these beautiful feelings with the distant words - "That's it. All over
> now."
> The words and the silence seemed so distant from each other, like dreams and
> reality, separated by long and distant memory (Sidaoru'ang 1984: 339-340).

From amongst the set of antonyms presented in this extract Sidaoru'ang equates pregnancy with words, abortion with silence. When viewed in relation to Sidaoru'ang's own career as a writer and the struggle to locate her own literary voice, success is measured in terms of the ability to give birth, failure in terms of death. To follow this analogy through to its conclusion brings me to the observation that it was not until 1989, some fourteen years after the publication of her first short story, that Sidaoru'ang produced a text in which the combination of birth/death imagery was to result in the survival of the child (though not of the mother). I refer here to *Banthu'k kho'ng no'ng nu*, written in the form of a confessional diary by a young woman addressed to her mother. It reveals that, in the knowledge she is dying of an incurable disease, the young woman has had sexual intercourse with several men in order to become pregnant and to gain the best of all their qualities for her child. (Also implicit here is the notion of fluid or multiple identities which I have not attempted to address in this paper.) As she dies she assures her unborn child that soon he will make his appearance in the world in her place. Following her words is a drawing of a child in a womb and beneath it the cries of, "Mother. Wait. Please don't die yet. Let me out first." The author then intervenes in her own text with words that are printed in parenthesis and in a smaller type-face:

> This final sentence was not in the diary but was added by the author herself because when the doctors operated to remove the child the mother died. May she rest in peace and if the spirits and the stars in the sky really do exist then now the child's mother will know that her heir is strong, lovely, clever, ambitious and a little cunning, just as she had wished (Sidaoru'ang 1989: 113).

These words - strong (*khaeng raeng*), lovely (*na rak*), clever (*chalat*), ambitious (*mi fai raeng*) and a little cunning (*mi le liam lek noi*) - provide the most apt description of all the stories in the *Phap luang ta* collection, appropriately subtitled as 'short stories to defy the ideas of the reader!' (*ru'ang san tha thai khwamkhit phu an*).

I have attempted to demonstrate in this paper the various reasons why Sidaoru'ang has frequently linked depictions of birth and death in her texts. This task has been executed both at face value and via the application of essentially Western perceptions that are rooted in psychoanalytical and feminist literary theory. The extent to which such theories are appropriate to an analysis of Thai literature has also been investigated here. Since my attempt has been to imply a strong parallel between the body and the text and of the maternal relationship of the writer to her work it is in this regard that I should have liked to close with the ultimate example of a truly successful birth in Sidaoru'ang's oeuvre, one that went completely unchallenged by the presence of death. As yet, however, she has not produced such a text, though her increasingly firm foothold in the Thai literary world may act as an incentive for her to do so in the future.

REFERENCES

Anderson, Benedict
1977 'Withdrawal Symptoms: Social and Cultural Aspects of the October 6 Coup' *Bulletin of Concerned Asian Scholars*, 9: 3: 13-30.

Barthes, Roland
1977 *Image, Music, Text.* London: Fontana.

Bowie, Malcolm
1991 *Lacan.* London: Fontana.

Brooks, Peter
1993 *Body Work.* Cambridge, Massachusetts and London: Harvard University Press.

Cameron, Deborah
1990 *The Feminist Critique of Language: A Reader.* London: Routledge.

Chai-anan Samudavanija and Morell, David
1981 *Political Conflict in Thailand: Reform, Reaction, Revolution.* Cambridge, Massachusetts: Oelgeschlager, Gunn and Hain.

Cixous, Helene
> 1990 'Difficult Joys' in Helen Wilcox *et al* (eds.), *The Body and the Text. Helene Cixous, Reading and Teaching*. London: Harvester Wheatsheaf, pp. 5-30.

Cornell, Sarah
> 1990 'Helene Cixous and *les Etudes Feminines*' in Helen Wilcox *et al* (eds.), *The Body and the Text. Helene Cixous, Reading and Teaching*. London: Harvester Wheatsheaf, pp. 31-40.

Duangdu'an Pradapdao
> 1975 'Ru'ang san 18. Thu'ng yuk kho'ng Sidaoru'ang laew ru'?', *Prachachat Daily Newspaper*, 14 September.

Eagleton, Terry
> 1989 *Literary Theory*. Oxford: Basil Blackwell.

> 1993 'It is not quite true that I have a body, and not quite true that I am one either,' *London Review of Books*, 27 May, pp. 7-8.

Foster, Shirley
> 1990 'Speaking Beyong Patriarchy: The female voice in Emily Dickinson and Christina Rossetti,' in Helen Wilcox *et al* (eds.), *The Body and the Text. Helene Cixous, Reading and Teaching*. London: Harvester Wheatsheaf, pp. 66-77.

Freud, Sigmund
> 1922 *Beyond the Pleasure Principle*. London and Vienna: The International Psychoanalytical Press.

Girling, John S
> 1981 *Thailand, Society and Politics*. Ithaca and London: Cornell University Press.

Jones, Ann Rosalind
    1985   'Writing the body: toward an understanding of l'ecriture
           feminine' in Judith Newton and Deborah Rosenfelt (eds),
           Feminist Criticism and Social Change. New York: Methuen,
           pp. 86-101.

Kristeva, Julia
    1990   'A New Type of Intellectual: The Dissident', in Toril Moi
           (ed.), *The Kristeva Reader*. Oxford: Basil Blackwell, pp. 292-
           300.

Mitchell, Juliet
    1974   *Psychoanalysis and Feminism*. London: Penguin
           Books.

Moers, Ellen
    1986   *Literary Women*. London: The Women's Press.

Moi, Toril
    1985   *Sexual, Textual Politics*. London and New York: Routledge.

Mulder, Niels
    1990   *Inside Thai Society: An Interpretation of Everyday Life*.
           Bangkok: Editions Duang Kamol.

Natsini Witthuthirasan
    1976   *Wikhro wannakam naew prachachon*. Bangkok: Sayam
           wannakam.

Netnapha Kumthong
    1993   'The State of Being 'Happy and Well' in a Central Thai
           Village', unpublished seminar paper given at the Centre of
           South East Asian Studies, School of Oriental and African
           Studies, University of London, 5 May.

Phillips, Herbert
  1974 *Thai Peasant Personality. The Patterning of Interpersonal Behavior in the Village of Bang Chan.* London: University of California Press.

  1987 *Modern Thai Literature. An Ethnographic Interpretation.* Honolulu: University of Hawaii Press.

Phinyo Kongthong
  1986 'Watthanatham chao ban naew prachachon', in *Phasa lae nangsu'*, April-September, pp. 41-52.

Sarup, Madan
  1992 *Jacques Lacan.* London: Harvester Wheatsheaf.

Shiach, Morag
  1991 *Helene Cixous, A Politics of Writing.* London and New York: Routledge.

Showalter, Elaine
  1979 'Towards a feminist poetics', in Mary Jacobus (ed.),*Women Writing and Writing About Women.* London: Croom Helm.

  1982 'Feminist Criticism in the Wilderness', in Elizabeth Abel (ed.), *Writing and Sexual Difference.* The University of Chicago: The Harvester Press, pp. 9-35.

Sidaoru'ang
  1983 *Kaew yot diaw.* Bangkok: Met sai.
  1984 *Bat prachachon.* Bangkok: Met sai.
  1987 *Matsi.* Bangkok: Than tawan.
  1988a Sidaoru'ang, phua ko khian, mia ko teng, kheng kan phim', interview in *No'n nangsu'*, 1: 3: 3-11.
  1988b 'Bai wan sao kap Sidaoru'ang', interview in *Dichan*, 12: 276: 241-251.
  1989 *Phap luang ta.* Bangkok: Kamphaeng.

Spivak, Gayatri Chakravorty

 1987   *In Other Worlds. Essays in Cultural Politics.* New York and
        London: Methuen.

Turton, Andrew

 1978   'The Current Situation in the Thai Countryside,' in Caldwell,
        Fast and Turton, *Thailand, Roots of Conflict.* Nottingham:
        Spokesman Press, pp. 104-142.

FEMALE CHARACTERS IN THAI NARRATIVE POETRY

Ruenruthai Sujjapun

The purpose of this article is to study the features, roles and characteristics of the women who appear in the literature of the Ayutthaya to the early Rattanakosin period (1350-1851). Emphasis is placed upon narrative poetry, with specific reference to *Lilit Phra Lo'*, *Sepha Khun Chang Khun Phaen*, *Sangtho'ng* and *Phra Aphaimani*.

A study of these works reveals that the female characters in narrative poetry are not merely introduced as accomplices to men but are often key protagonists in the plot and theme in their own right. Their characterization is based upon the ideal concept of woman as expressed in didactic poetry. Nevertheless, elements of realistic human nature are also reflected and the actions of some characters may be in contrast to ideal behaviour. Significant is their flexibility, indicating the complexity of their character and of human nature in general. Since narrative poetry entertains its audience by relating the adventures of its protagonists the characters are often atypical and do not hold the same standards of morality that are found in didactic literature and in *nirat* poetry. The audience accepts the behaviour of the characters and participates enthusiastically in their adventures. Because Thai society endows men with greater importance than women it might follow that female characters should play less important roles than men. Some female characters continue to conform to the traditional image of women, as the obedient, loyal and dutiful property of men; following on rather than taking the lead. Some literary works, however, reflect another aspect of women's image, that is, as the equal of men. Above and beyond this, they are complex characters with conflicts in terms of their personalities, emotions and actions. They impress their audiences in their representation of real human beings.

CONCEPTS OF THE IDEAL WOMEN IN THAI LITERATURE

Both didactic literature and *nirat* poetry reflect the concepts of the ideal woman in Thai society. In the former female characters conform to social expectations, i.e. they are virgins until they marry, after which time they are duty bound to love and remain faithful to their husbands. They must keep their houses clean and tend to their husbands' needs, waking before them in the morning and going to bed after them at night.Thus didactic literature reflects the social code of a woman's way of life that is expressed by Sukanya Sukhachai:

> Thai society is patriarchal. From the Sukhothai to the Rattanakosin period men were higher in status than women. Mostly, women have only functions and not rights. In this kind of society men establish many traditions and social values in order to keep women in the position that they wish. This culture is taught particularly through law and through didactic literature such as the *Suphasit Phra Ruang, Owat Kasattri, Tamrap Thao Srichulalak, Krisna So'n Nong* and *Suphasit So'n Ying*. Such didactic literature controls women, rendering them obedient to tradition from one generation to the next (Sukanya 1982: 102).

Because the status of women is lower than that of men marriage offers itself as a way for women to improve this. For this reason poets tend to use precious objects as a metaphor for husbands; in *Kritsana so'n no'ng*, for example, references are made to royal flags, a crown and a diamond ring; and in *Klong Lokkanit* it is a hair pin.

In *nirat* poetry love-longing is always the key theme of the work, in which the poet laments his separation from his beloved. The role of the woman is therefore central to the plot and it is the ideal beauty and behaviour of women that evoke such depths of love-longing. The poet expresses the passion of his feelings, his suffering at being parted and his deep-felt desire to be reunited with his lover. Unlike in tales and dramas, the female characters in *nirat* poetry have no 'self' and no clear actions; they are merely projections of the poet's imagination, based, perhaps on some elements of real women. Prince Bidhyalangarana had stated that the female characters in *nirat* poetry are not essentially real women but only figments of the imagination, created for the purpose of producing a sweeter tone to the lamentation (Bidhyalangarana 1970: 88). The most important aspect of *nirat* therefore, is its potential to touch the emotions of its audience. However, the description of the close relationship between the poet and his lovers in *nirat* poetry persuades the audience to feel that the female characters are in fact, alive, passionate and real. The concept of the ideal woman is therefore clearly reflected in tangible characters in *nirat* poetry: beyond applying the standard concepts of ideal beauty and behaviour to their female characters poets also reveal the complexity of their minds. Some actions result from frustrated emotions, self-conflicts or the pressure of circumstances. The thoughts and deeds of the characters may sometimes be in conflict with the ideal but do manage to reflect real human nature.

AN ANALYSIS OF SOME FEMALE CHARACTERS IN NARRATIVE LITERATURE

The female characters under survey here are Phra Phu'an and Phra Phaeng from *Lilit Phra Lo'*, Wantho'ng from *Khun Chang Khun Phaen*, Rotcana from *Sangtho'ng* and Laweng from *Phra Aphaimani*.

Lilit Phra Lo'

The epic poem*Lilit Phra Lo'* has long been considered one of the great masterpieces of Thai literature. Written during the early Ayutthaya period the plot is believed to have been drawn from a romantic Northern Thai legend. It concerns the fate of the three lovers whose uncontrolled passion leads them to a tragic end.

Phra Phu'an and Phra Phaeng are the main female characters in this work. Both are princesses from the Kingdom of So'ng who, on hearing of the valour and beauty of Phra Lo', King of the neighbouring enemy Kingdom of Suang, fall madly in love with him. Unable either to eat or to sleep, they wait to hear news of him and pray to all the gods that he will come and seek them out. They are willing to give their money and their treasures in reward for a visit from Phra Lo' and they vow to marry no one else but him:

> Ah! Great King,
> From the first moment we heard of you,
> We could not eat for thinking of you,
> We could not sleep. We are sick from waiting to hear from you.
> We pray to every God in every mountain and every tree,
> Asking them to destine the King to come to us.
> If we are successful, we will pay our respects to them all.

> We will donate much money,
>
> Elephants with golden ivory and white oxen to fullfil our vow.
>
> If we cannot be your beloved, then we will not marry.

The strength of their intentions can be taken as an illustration of the two princesses' self confidence in making an independent choice of husband. This breaks with the social and cultural mores of the day, in which parents chose a husband for their daughters.

Having expressed their intention to become Phra Lo''s brides Phra Phu'an and Phra Phaeng procure the help of their two faithful attendants in luring Phra Lo' to the Kingdom of So'ng. When they send their men to sing a song in praise of the princesses' beauty Phra Lo' desires them as his wives. Having no shame, Phra Phu'an and Phra Phaeng use their magical powers to succeed in forcing Phra Lo' to leave his kingdom, his devoted mother and his loyal wife and journey to the Kingdom of So'ng.

The two princesses' actions demonstrate a conflict between love and social acceptability. They have clearly broken with convention in the expression of their desire, their use of taboo magical powers and in falling in love with an enemy of their kingdom. Knowing that tradition and culture operate as methods of social control Phra Phu'an and Phra Phaeng act in defiance of this and understand the liklihood of being punished. Nevertheless, the power of their love overrules reason and it is the depth of this passion that inevitably leads them to such a tragic end.

Phra Phu'an and Phra Phaeng's step-grandmother, whose husband, the former King of So'ng, was killed by Phra Lo''s father, sends guards to capture the prince. Dressed as men, Phra Phu'an and Phra Phaeng choose to stand by their husband and defend him when he is attacked. Smiling as they fight, they are happy to die as they are willing to risk their lives in defence of their dignity. As a result the death of the three lovers evokes a very beautiful picture and encourages the audience to be brave and face up to fate.

In former Thai society women's lives were controlled by tradition and social values. The conflict faced by women that is reflected in the heroines of *Lilit Phra Lo'* depict a conflict between human nature and social tradition.

Sepha Khun Chang Khun Phaen

Sepha Khun Chang Khun Phaen is believed to have been based upon real events which took place during the reign of King Bo'rom Trailokanat in the early Ayutthaya period (Damrong 1967: 12-15). It was originally told as a tale and later narrated in the form of sung oral poetry known as *sepha* (in which the rhythms are provided by a pair of bamboo pieces held in one hand and called *krap*). *Sepha Khun Chang Khun Phaen* was very popular until the early Rattanakosin period. Although few texts of the *sepha* survived, the plot and some of the verses were memorized and, during the reign of King Rama II, the text was revised and recomposed in the form that we currently know it. King Rama II composed some parts of this *sepha* and other parts were written by court poets and professional *sepha* narrators of the day, over a lengthy period of time. Despite the input of several authors the main theme and characterization remains consistent. The plot is long and complex, involving three generations of characters. However, the love of two men - Khun Chang and Khun Phaen - for one woman - Phim or Wanthon'ng - is the best-known part of the story. The characterization of women in this *sepha* is influenced by the ideals of the literary conventions of the Ayutthaya period.

At the centre of the action in this *sepha* is Wantho'ng for she is loved by both Khun Chang and Khun Phaen and is wife to them both. Firstly she becomes the wife of Khun Phaen but after he has gone away to war Khun Chang tries to trick Wantho'ng into marrying him. Khun Phaen returns from battle in time to help Wantho'ng but they quarrel because he brings with him a new wife, Laotho'ng. Much hurt by the fact that her husband has a new wife Wantho'ng is forced to become Khun Chang's wife against her will. As time passes, however, she comes to appreciate Khun Chang's love and loyalty. When Khun Phaen takes revenge on Khun Chang by abducting Wantho'ng she again becomes the wife of Khun Phaen and is happy with him, despite the difficulties of their life. When Wantho'ng becomes pregnant, Khun Phaen surrenders himself to the King. The wily Khun Chang takes advantage of this opportunity to force Wantho'ng to live with him and lovingly care for her. Fifteen years pass and Camn'un Wai, Wantho'ng's son by Khun Phaen, forces Wantho'ng to leave Khun Chang, whom he hates. Khun Chang appeals for justice and Wantho'ng is executed by order of the King.

While it is possible to consider Wantho'ng as the source of conflict in this *sepha* she can also be seen as a character who is affected by conflicts caused by others. The various roles she plays as the wife of Khun Phaen and of Khun Chang, as the mother of Camu'n Wai, as the daughter of Sipracan and as an ordinary citizen all reflect the multiple dimensions of her character.

Wantho'ng is condemned to be the prototype of the fickle woman in Thai literature because she has two husbands. Yet Wantho'ng is known not to be a woman of sexual greed, but rather one who is pushed into circumstances beyond her wishes. Her suffering is caused by those characters who have power over her, namely her mother, her husbands, her son and the King. These people have no regard for her feelings and responses and they do not accept reason. Wantho'ng can therefore be seen as an unlucky woman. She is a typical Thai woman who is powerless to determine her own fate and whose life is commanded by men and controlled by tradition and social values. Nevertheless, Wantho'ng's charm has long captured the sympathy of audiences and it is significant that she is a deeply 'human' character; Wantho'ng is always impressed by other people's goodness and always forgives the wickedness of others. Instead of being angry with Khun Phaen, who abducts her from Khun Chang and causes her much trouble, she is instead impressed by the strength of his love. Feeling no love for Khun Chang Wantho'ng is still able to respect his love for and loyalty towards her and is a good wife to him. When Khun Phaen forces her to leave Khun Chang she is concerned about how he will feel and how he will survive so she writes him a letter to tell him that she must go, otherwise Khun Phaen will kill her. She explains that she is not leaving because she is an unfaithful wife and that she will miss him. As she is leaving Wantho'ng asks Kaew Kiriya to soothe Khun Chang and take care of his meals in the way that she would. Wantho'ng's lamentation when Khun Chang is beaten unconscious in a quarrel with her son reveals her great tenderness and delicacy:

> Oh! My dear husband. If you die I will die too.
>
> It's only you who are so kind.
>
> Living together for fifteen or sixteen years, you never hurt me, even with one word.
>
> While I was giving birth you helped me to sit leaning on your knee.

When I cried, you cried too.

When I was sick and unable to eat, you sat beside me and fed me.

When you saw that I was unable to sleep, you too were unable to sleep.

In summer you fanned me from the heat.

In winter you embraced me and covered me with a blanket.

In the rainy season you closed the windows to let me stay inside.

Among all the men on earth who love their wives, no one can

compare with you.

Even though you are ugly, your mind is as bright as the moon.

Thus, it is Karma that gives you death.

It is the impression that Wantho'ng gives of Khun Chang's great merit that is partly responsible for causing her own death. When the King orders her to choose one man to live with, being afraid of the King's anger, Wantho'ng is unable to tell the truth. At the same time, the audience is aware that while Wantho'ng loves Khun Phaen she feels a sense of obligation towards Khun Chang for all his devotion. It is Wantho'ng's indecisiveness that leads to her death. Wantho'ng calmly accepts all the circumstances of her life, including her death, without blaming anyone. The King accuses her of lust. Public opinion condemns her as an unfaithful wife but the truth is far from this; and it is this contradiction which immortalizes Wantho'ng in the Thai literary tradition.

Sang Tho'ng

Sang Tho'ng is a well known dance-drama composed by King Rama II. As a royal lako'n no'k or folk play reconstructed as court drama it differs from others of its genre in its emphasis on humour. Even during the reign of King Rama II, at a time when society was still not modernized, the female characters created in this literary work portray a combination of the ideal woman of traditional Thai literature and a woman who is an individual with an independent mind, self confidence and intelligence.

Princess Rotcana's father, King Samon is liberal in the sense that he does not wish to force any of his seven daughters to marry men they do not love. He therefore allows them to choose their own consorts. Unlike her sisters, Rotcana does not choose a husband on grounds of appearance but instead selects a negrito who is in fact a prince in disguise. Rotcana's choice disappoints her father and he, her mother and her six sisters are infuriated by the dishonour she has brought to the royal household. Rotcana is a dutiful daughter and a loyal and faithful wife. At the same time she is strong, intelligent, independent and self-confident in dealing with conflict with others. When she chooses the negrito for her husband she goes against the opinion of others and yet is steadfast and courageous enough to wait until the truth reveals itself. She is the only one who sees that beneath the ugly disguise is the golden figure of Prince Sangtho'ng.

Because of her choice Rotcana and the negrito are banished from the city and forced to live outside. Rotcana acts as a perfect wife, taking care of her husband according to the ideals portrayed in didactic literature, believing in him and obeying him. Rotcana tries to destroy his negrito disguise since this is the only way she can let others know that her husband has a golden figure, but when her husband orders her not to do this she obeys him.

In order to get rid of his negrito son-in-law King Samon orders his seven sons-in-law to bring him a hundred fish and then a hundred deer. Being thought of as foolish, the negrito is able prove his intelligence and later, he saves the kingdom by winning a polo match against Indra. Rotcana is finally able to prove that she has made the right choice.

Rotcana's mother, Queen Montha is also an interesting character in that she reflects the other side of the woman's role in the Thai family. As a queen she always gives advice and sometimes makes decisions and she is more sensible and understanding than King Samon. Thus the poet can be seen to create characters from his understanding of woman's nature.

Phra Aphaimani

This extremely popular epic-romance was composed by the poet Suntho'n Phu during the Rattanakosin period and is a highly imaginative and exotic piece of poetry. The distinguishing point of this work lies in its ability to integrate the traditional conventions of classical literature with modern creativity. The work is heavily influenced by classical literary tradition and draws also upon stories which were popular or events which took place at the time. The hero of the piece, Phra Aphaimani, is said to be "like a thread which binds the other characters and the action together because every character and every situation relates to and concerns this character (Suwanna 1975: 13)." In actual fact, however, many of the situations in which Phra Aphaimani finds himself are caused by the female characters in the poem. Firstly, the sea ogress seizes Phra Aphaimani and forces him to become her husband. Then he is later rescued from the sea ogress by a young mermaid. The next woman who steps into his life is Suwannamali, who refuses to marry him and who runs away to become a nun. Wali, an ugly but highly intelligent woman helps Phra Aphaimani to marry Suwannamali and to fight in the war. Wali also causes the death of the King of Langka and Usaren, his son. Laweng, the King of Langka's daughter, begins a war of revenge. She and Phra Aphaimani fall in love during battle. Unlike the female characters in many traditional Thai literary works, those who appear in *Phra Aphaimani* are strong, intelligent and courageous. Not only are they equal to men in ruling the country and in fighting but they are also, in many ways, superior to men and able to have influence over them.

The female characters in *Phra Aphaimani* play interesting roles and they are often the equals of men, many of them being brave warriors, capable of commanding their armies. When Laweng initiates a war in order to avenge her father and brother, she trains three thousand women as her soldiers. Suwannamali, Wali, Saowakon and others are also great leaders, although they are, to some extent, influenced by the concepts of the ideal woman in traditional literature; despite their strength and bravery they also follow their husbands.

Laweng's role in this story is an important one. She is the sister of Utsaren, who is the fiance of Suwannamali. When her father and brother die at the hands of Phaluk's women, she declares war to avenge their deaths, never expecting that she herself will fall to the power of love. Laweng is a kingly leader, but she is also beautiful and during the battle Phra Aphaimani falls in love with her. When Laweng realizes that she too loves Phra Aphaimani she becomes confused and is faced with the conflict between passion and duty. She attempts to reject her love because Phra Aphaimani is both an enemy and a foreigner, but the depth of her affections brings her to realize that she will not marry another man until the day she dies. As the text says:

> Thinking of Phra Aphaimani causes shame.
> What misfortune.
> He is a foreigner, and an enemy, of a different religion.
> It is impossible to marry him.

Yet I will not love another man until I pass into the next world.

Because of her love Laweng loses the courage to kill Phra Aphaimani, despite the fact that she has an opportunity to do so. She is angered by her own failure to fulfill her duty but this is lessened when she reads a book written by a priest named Pipo. Part of the book tells her not to kill Phra Aphaimani since he is her consort from a previous life. On learning this Laweng brings Phra Aphaimani to her palace without anyone's knowledge and stays with him, although she is not his wife. Laweng faces the conflict of love and shame that this situation provokes and thus illustrates her strength of mind.

Considering female characters in *Phra Aphaimani* we can conclude that they are a combination of the traditional concepts of the ideal woman and the realities of human nature.

CONCLUSION

Female characters in Thai narrative poetry differ from those in didactic literature and in *nirat*. In didactic literature women follow the traditions of the ideal woman; in *nirat* they are created from the poet's imagination of lust and desire rather than existing in their own right; in tales and dramas the characters are more complex. They continue to be influenced by the traditional concepts of the ideal woman that are to be found in didactic literature and *nirat*, particularly in terms of standards of beauty and behaviour: but at the same time these female characters reflect human nature, especially the complexity of personality, behaviour, action and emotion. Female characters may often be the victim of circumstances and sentiments that are another's making and their actions are therefore sometimes in conflict with the ideal. For instance, despite the value attached by society to virginity, Phra Phu'an, Phra Phaeng and Wantho'ng all lose their virginity before marriage. Despite the tradition that daughters should obey their parents, Rotcana chooses her husband, against her parents wishes. Despite the taboo of using magical powers to win love, Phra Phu'an, Phra Phaeng and Laweng are brave enough to disobey. Their conflict with traditional moral values proves the strength of their reaction and shows how human and how universal they are as characters. Phra Phu'an and Phra Phaeng experience a conflict between passion and the honour of the royal family. Laweng's conflict is between desire and duty.

The fate of Wantho'ng reveals that she faces a conflict between human freedom and social institutions, including the power of the King, tradition and morality. In finding the best answer for the King she must hide her true wishes. This portrays the limitations of freedom, even in choosing the best solution for the problems one faces in life. Thus the deaths of Phra Phu'an, Phra Phaeng and Wantho'ng are engraved in the memories of Thai readers.

Female characters in Thai narrative poetry accepts life's suffering and frustrations with great courage and patience. Yet even in the face of death these women are both enduring and dignified. It appears that the poet questions how much freedom one has to determine the course of one's own life. We may say that Thai poets appreciate the value of human beings. Furthermore, as the poets are men, they appear to be broad-minded in their treatment of women as human beings and exhibit a sound understanding of every facet of human life. People are normally used to judging others by their own standards and ethics, but poets urge us to realize that we cannot evaluate them from a narrow viewpoint. This humane and understanding approach to the characterization of women only serves to enhance the charm and immortality of the Thai poetic tradition.

REFERENCES

Bidhyalankarana, Prince
1970 "Pathakatha Ru'ang Nirat Narin" (A Lecture on Nirat Narin). In Pho' Na Pramuanmak (ed.)*Nirat Narin Kham Khlong Lae Nirat Plik Yo'i.* Bangkok: Phrae Phitthaya, pp. 3-72.

Damrong Rajanubhap, Somdet Kromphraya
1967 "Introduction". In *Sepha Khun Chang KhunPhaen,* Bangkok : Sinlapa Bannakhan, pp. 12-15.

Sukanya Sutchaya

    1982   *Pleng Patipak : Bot Phleng Patiphan Kho'ng Chao Ban Thai.*
            (So'ngs of Intellectuality of Thai native people). Bangkok :
            Office of the committee of national culture.

Suvanna Kriengkraipetch

    1975   *Phra Aphaimani: Kan Su'ksa Nai Choeng Wannakhadi Wican*
            (Phra Aphaimani: A Critical Study). Bangkok : Samakhom
            Ho'ng Samut Haeng Prathet Thai.

Phuttha Loetla Naphalai, King.

    1970   *Bot Lakho'n No'k Ruam Hok Ru'ang.* Bangkok : Sinlapa
            Bannakhan.

Ruenruthai Sujjapun.

    1991   "Female Characters in Thai Literature of the Ayutthaya
            and early Ratanakosin Period (1350- 1851)". Ph.D Thesis,
            Chulalongkorn University.

Sinlapako'n, Khrom.

    1967   *Khun Chang Khun Phaen.* Bangkok: Sinlapa Bannakhan.

Suntho'n Phu.

    1966   *Phra Aphaimani Kham Klo'n.* Bangkok : Sinlapa Bannakan.

CHARACTERS IN THAI LITERARY WORKS
'US' AND 'THE OTHERS'

Suvanna Kriengkraipetch

This paper aims to study the concept of 'otherness' expressed intentionally or unintentionally by poets of the Early Rattanakosin period, through the characters they created, described or criticized in their work.[1]

This study originated in the provocative question often asked by colleagues who are involved in various Thai studies programs at my university.[2] That question is: "What is being Thai?" My usual and honest answer is "I don't know". However, the question still bothers me and, as the teacher of Thai literature, I would like to find a clearer and more convincing answer from the area of my training and experience-- literature.

My idea is that, an analysis of the implicit and explicit categories used to describe and discuss characters may help us understand how poets thought about differences between the group with whom they identified (us) and those with whom they contrasted themselves (the others), in this case, the 'Thai' and the 'non-Thai'. I will use these categories to classify attitudes taken towards particular groups of characters. This should help provide both a broader and firmer background for understanding possible answers to the question, "What is 'being Thai?"

This essay suggests that people of the Early Rattanakosin period experienced the interactions between 'Thai' and 'non-Thai' group differently than did people in late Ayutthaya period (Nidhi 1986: 2-4). Their attitudes towards 'the other' and 'otherness' during their time may provide us with a deeper background to better understand our concept of 'otherness' today. As will become apparent in this study, the characteristics contrasting with those used to identify 'others' and 'otherness' also help to

---

[1] I would like to express my deep gratitude to Associate Professor Pornrat Damrung and Mr. Lowell Scarr. Without their help this paper could not have been finished.

[2] Chulalongkorn University offers many special programmes on Thai language and Culture, for example, Perspectives on Thailand, Knowing Thailand, and Intensive Thai Language, offered by the Faculty of Arts.

identify the defining characteristics of the 'us' group. These classification systems are always integrated into the social practices of different social groups, which change over time and are expressed in different ways.

In many literary works, for example, *Khun Chang Khun Phaen*, and *Phra Aphai Mani*, poets note many characters who were obviously non-Thai, while the chief protagonist and his group of characters were mostly Thai. In *Inao*, the main characters were supposed to be Javaneses and some characters were described as people of the other group, with different religions and languages. In Suntho'n Phu's *Nirat*, the poet often mentions people who belonged to other ethnic groups such as the Chinese, Lawa, Mo'n, Karen and so on. However, the poet's tone here sounds different from that of *Khun Chang Khun Phaen*. An analysis of these smaller differences should enable us to see a set of criteria through which poets created or described their characters both for the 'us' group they identifed with, as well as 'the others' group. This set of criteria can be seen as a system of classification through which poets understood other groups of people and, in this process, understood themselves.

Another dimension concerns the issue of the level of society indicated by the separate groups of characters. In Early Rattanakosin literature, the concept of separating the ruler from the ruled is very obvious and common. This notion of characterizing separate groups might not seem to be directly linked with the main question of 'being Thai', yet it is crucial, since it is only in relation to other groups that another can be defined. Defining 'the others' helps to define 'us'.

This paper will limit itself to preliminary considerations of two genres: firstly, literature with a 'story' of the tale, narrative, and dance-play types, which originated as a tale; and secondly, lyrical literature based on the more 'genuine experience' of its author (Nidhi 1986: 31). For the latter I will focus on Suntho'n Phu's *Nirat* lyrical poems, whose emotion and experience bring both the poet and his readers closer to the outside world of foreign peoples, different languages and cultures. Both 'story' and 'experience' literature usually allow the authors to exercise their imagination freely and expressively (Sombat 1986: 45-46).

The literary works explored in this study are as follows:

1. *Inao*
2. Six Dance-Plays by King Rama II
3. *Khun Chang Khun Phaen*

4. Four Literary tales by Suntho'n Phu: *Kho But, Laksanawong Singha Kraiphop,* and *Phra Aphai Mani*

5. *Nirat* poems by Suntho'n Phu: *Nirat Mu'ang Klaeng, Nirat Phrabat, Nirat Phukhaothong, Nirat Mu'angphet, Nirat Wat Caofa, Nirat Suphan,Nirat Phra Prathom* and *Ramphan Philap*

INAO : THE COMPOSITION OF 'OTHERNESS'

In the introduction explaning the stories, written by their editor Prince Damrong Rajanubhap, there appears the following explanation:

> ".....Besides being good literature as already mentioned, this book is also suitable as information for the study of the ancient Thai tradition. ...[the authors] wrote exactly to the test of court tradition, and changed only what really disagreed with the story. For example, Buddhist monks were changed to rishi. All concerned with the country tradition and even the habits and behaviour of the people was noted according to whatever was observed during the time of the writing, except those that disagreed with the story, which had to be changed. ..."
>
> (Damrong 1965: (5))

From this we can assume that the group of protagonists or the 'us' group were representatives of the Thai nobility of their period; and the narrator's actual descriptions of these characters include only two characteristics for the identity of the Javanese (or the Melayu): namely, the name and title of the character and the *Kris* which was assumed to be the special, personal identity mark for each particular male character, and for the ruling class only. This was undoubtedly the condition the editor mentioned before as what agreed (or disagreed) with the story which had its origin in the Javanese tale.

Another interesting characteristic of the male, ruling class characters in this story is that all members were classified into two main groups: the *Raden* and the *Ratu* The first group were believed to be descendants of the Ancestor-god and thus they were collectively called *Asanyadaewa*. These ruling class members were described as a special group whose distinctive sub-culture became the basis of the theme and plot of the story, since they could not marry outside their own group. However, this condition was observed strictly on the one hand and loosely on the other. Some members of this higher class who appear in this story married into the *Ratu* group, and so were actually related to each other by marriage. More confusing than this, sometimes a *Ratu* father had a daughter who was given a *Raden* title as with *Ratu Manya* and his daughter *Raden Chintara*, *Ratu Lasam* and his daughter *Raden Kusuma*, and also *Ratu Kamangkuning* and his son *Raden Wiyasakam*.

On the other hand, this condition was rigorously applied in the case of the hero and the heroine, who had been matched to marry each other from birth, according to group rule. And when the hero broke this agreement by getting involved with the *Ratu's* daughter (who actually related to him through his mother's line), the father of his fiancee then gave his daughter to the ugly, inferior ruler of the *Ratu* group, and then the Ancestor-god was very angry. This conflict lies at the root of the whole story.

Undoubtedly, the concept of the two groups of ruling class based on the idea of the ancestor-god was not part of the Thai way of thinking, and thus, the narrator could not observe this particular notion critically.[3] More convincing for the narrator was the notion that the powerful ruler or the hero was marked with special superior qualities. This is why the narrator continues to mention his magical weapon, his special appearance, his braveness and so on. Reminding ourselves of the editor's explanation that only 'whatever disagreed with the story would be kept', it is clear that we are reading only what the prince considered to be 'Thai'.

Although the notion of the two distinct groups within the ruling class was not held consistently, the divide between the ruling class and the common people was more strictly observed. In this story, the ruling class as well as their officials and servants kept a clear separation between themselves and the common people, whether they were from the city or the countryside. The narrator always clearly marks the distance between these two social levels. The inferior and least respectable characters tended to be from the countryside and were referred to elsewhere by the ruling class as *forest people* or *remote outsiders*. Surprisingly, whenever the

---

[3] In *Inao* the narrator used the word *thao* (ท้าว) for kings or rulers of various cities, either big or small. Otherwise, the word *Sipatala* (ศรีปัตหรา) which means 'king' in Javanese would be used.

heroes and heroines disguised themselves in order to travel around for particular purposes, they would become *panjuret* or bandits. Thus, according to the story, those who wandered in the forest or outside the city and its suburbs were reasonably thought to be thieves, bandits, or outlaws. Even though these forest thieves were very powerful and did not need to comply with any rules, they were still regarded as the lower class, or the outcasts by the royal story-writers.[4]

One criterion that the narrator generally applied to this confusing situation was the concept of appearance. When *Inao*, the hero, and *Busba*, the heroine, had to disguise themselves as *panyi* and *unakan*, other characters were suspicious of their graceful, powerful, and refined appearance, which made them think they belong to the nobility. This open suspicion confirms the concept of being born superior, which is often mentioned in Thai literature. Common people or the less respected forest and outlaw group, would never have the refined appearance believed to be the result of the wisdom and good upbringing of the upper classes. Therefore, those who did not know the truth usually pitied them since they could not accept the graceful, powerful and apparently good bandit as a member of their 'us' group.

It is worth noting that, while disguising themselves as bandits, these characters changed their names. The narrator was so conscious of this issue that sometimes more than ten lines were used to give the "forest people's name" to the main characters and all their entourage. That indicates the difference between the names for the ruling class and that of the common or forest people. Thus, names were thought of as attributes which could match the status and the appearance of their bearers.[5]

Another dimension of the 'us' and the 'other' group differentiation in *Inao* was the concept of non-Javanese groups mentioned in the story when *Inao*, the hero, travelled across the sea from Java to Malaca Island. It was noted that the people of the Malaca Island spoke Melayu, while the

---

4 ปันหยีนี้*ชาวอรัญวา* สุริยวงศ์พงหาไม่แจ้งใจ
   จะให้น้องนี้ขึ้นไปเฝ้า พี่เจ้าเอ๋ยจะไปกระไรได้
   จะต้องไหว้*โจรป่าพนาลัย* อายใจเป็นพ้นพันทวี
                                    (Phuttha Loetla Naphalai 1965: 169)

5 จงกำชับโยธาทุกหมวดกอง ให้เรียกน้องว่ามิสารปันหยี
   แล้วเปลี่ยนนามพหลมนตรี เป็นชื่อชาวพนาลีจงทุกคน
                                    (Phuttha Loetla Naphalai 1965: 123)

others spoke Javanese, thus preventing mutual understanding. This notion is different from that discussed earlier, since it shows that 'other' group could be identified in terms of race and language and also religion. However, it is obvious that the narrator was not much concerned with this criterion. Only once did he mention both language and religion as identifying characteristics, in the royal wedding scene at the end of the story that, the *Khaek differed from the Thai since they did not eat pork/ Even looking at pork made them feel disgusted* (Phuttha Loetla Naphalai 1965: 1024). Actually both hosts and guests in this scene were from the Great Four Cities which were always counted as part of the same 'us' group.

Besides this particular group outside the Javanese were other groups mentioned in the city market scene. There were *Chinese* , *Cham* , *Acae*, *Hollanders*, and *Indians*. Other groups mentioned were the volunteer soldiers made up of English, Japanese, *Melayu*, *Hollanders* , and *Tani* , supposed to be the southern people. The description here was very similar to those in other literary pieces in which various racial groups were mentioned to show the glory and wealth of the city. Thus, readers could not really tell whether the city market being described was in Java or elsewhere.[6]

The last criteria to be discussed here is that custom which, referring back to the editor's explanation, intentionally became Thai as opposed to the original Javanese. Two special non-Thai customs were highlighted in this story: the *Tunangan* or the arranged marriage of the ruling class, and the *baela* ceremony or the wife's suicide after the death of her husband. The first one was used to enrich the plot and was more understandable and acceptable to Thai readers, but the second was quite opposed to Thai conceptions. This ceremony was mentioned only once in full detail in the whole story, in which many hamths were the results of this ceremony. Thus, this might be counted only as exotic decoration to add Javanese flavour to the story.

In conclusion, the concepts of the 'us' and the 'other' group in *Inao* are based mainly on the grounds of people separated into groups in the same society or the same race. Morever, while the story originated from a

---

6   ลูกค้าวาณิชทุกนิเวศน์   มาแต่ต่างประเทศเขตขัณฑ์
     สำเภาจอดทอดท่าเรียงรัน   สลุปแขกกำปั่นวิลันดา
     จีนจามอะแจแซ่ซ้อง   ดับคั่งทั้งสิบสองภาษา
                                   (Phutha Loetla Naphalai 1965: 5)

Suvanna Kriengkraipetch

Javanese tale (through a Melayu narrator in the Ayutthaya period), it mainly used the Thai way of thinking to distinguish between the royal 'us' and the non-royal 'others' and thereby identify the protagonist with the 'us' group of the nobility. The citreria used by the narrator to classify the various groups were concrete and clear enough for both sides to identify themselves as either 'us' or the 'others'; but it is important to remember that this story appeared among the royalty and nobility and was used to identify their ways of life as the essence of being Thai, only through contrasting themselves with the foreigners and common people. In this case being Thai was a royal prerogative. Even though relationships between groups seemed uncertain, members of each group certainly knew their expected roles and patterns of behaviour. The attitude of the narrator observed through the words used to call or classify the various groups (especially those of the forest people) obviously shows that the narrator identified himself and the ruling, upper class as 'us', while the common folk and forest people were on the side of the 'others'.

SIX DANCE PLAYS: THE FOLK KING AND 'US'

In these six poetic plays, composed in the reign of King Rama II, but originating from earlier folktales, one can clearly see the influence of folk elements on the main characters. That is, the king and the reyalty are portrayed as less removed from the common people and foreigners than *Inao*.

Distinct standards for classification are not so significant in these plays. However, concerning marriage with the ruling class, it is clear that there were at least two distinguised groups; the ruling class and the common people.

The most complete story among these six plays was *Sangtho'ng*, in which the protagonist disguises himself as a stupid, ugly forest person or *ngo'*. The protagonist's appearance became the narrator's tool to satirize the usual hero's qualities as a ruler or leader. In fact the hero's genuine skin was covered with gold.[7] The narrator reconfirms the importance of

---

7 เหลือแต่เงาะป่าทรพล   หน้าตาผิดคนทั้งหลาย
ห้วพริกหยิกยุ่งหยาบคาย   ตัวลายคล้ายกันกับเสือปลา
ใครจะบอกจะเล่าไม่เข้าใจ   พูดจาไม่ได้เหมือนใบ้บ้า
(Phuttha Loetla Naphalai 1962: 110)

136

appearance, but it shows up more subtley than in many of the earlier stories.

In another scene, the city people looked at the disguised king (ท้าวศวิมล) and his wife (นางจันทรา) and criticized the two strangers who were different from them because they looked like those well-to-do aristocrats who never worked hard, and more specifically, their hair-style really differed from that of the poor people.[8] Here, the narrator gave a more specific criteria for distinguishing the appearance of the rich, elite class and the poor common people.

Another interesting comment on the hero's qualities was made by his rivals, who said he was so mighty that he must be a vampire or a ghost, and not a human being. The hero was further distanced from them by being classed as non-human.[9]

The most interesting and significant criteria distinguishing the ruling group from the common people is found in the heroine's description of her changed life after marrying the hero, when she was chased to live in a hut outside the city. She complained that she had been pampered all her life in the palace and had never learned how to cook for herself.[10] This sudden change thus seemed deadly to her. However, after a while, she was able to live like other common people and appeared as happy as the others. In this way the heroine was able to adjust and identify herself to the group of 'others', and not the 'us' with whom she identified

---

8 บ้างว่าข้าเห็นยายก็ชอบกล   ชะรอยคนจะมั่งมีผู้คือเก่า
   ถึงทั้งแก่แลดูยังพริ้มเพรา   ไรจุกโตแทบเท่าสองนิ้ว
                                          (Phuttha Loetla Naphalai 1962: 246)

   กูไรจุกไรก้านพานชอบกล   จะว่าคนยากจนเห็นผิดนัก
   ผิวพรรณรูปทรงส่งศรี   น่าจะเป็นผู้คือมียศศักดิ์ก็
                                          (Phuttha Loetla Naphalai 1962: 253)

9 ชะรอยเป็น *ปีศาจ*ประหลาดใจ   กูตามันมีใครจะกระพริบ
   วิปริตผิดมนุษย์นักหนา   ข้าเห็นว่าไอ้นี่เป็นผีดิบ
   มีพลังถึงกินทิพย์   เนื้ออยู่สิบหาบมาถึงธานี
                                          (Phuttha Loetala Naphalai 1962: 168)

10 น้องนี้แต่ก่ำเนิดเกิดมา   จะหุงข้าวหุงปลาก็มิเคย
   แต่ก่อนร่อนชะไรอยู่ในวัง   วิเสทหามาตั้งให้เสวย
   ไม่เข้าเนื้อเข้าใจอย่างไรเลย   อกเอ๋ยผักรรมก็จำเป็น
   ว่าพลางนางทรงโศกี   ครั้งนี้ยากแค้นแสนเข็ญ
   ถึงหนึ่งเลือกตาจะกระเด็น   จำเป็นจำใจจออกไปพลัน

137

before marriage. This new role was not longlasting though. The hero and heroine were restored to their previous genuine status and role. And the feeling of having been one of the 'others' vanished.

The other plays apply similar criteria to those in *Sangtho'ng*. However, one word appears in the *Sangsinchai* story in which the female vendors call the king, the hero's father, the village official (พระยาบ้านนอก)[11] because of his nervous look, which seemed like one of the remote countryside people who came into the city.[12] This word, as well as the other comments mentioned above, were combined to show the classification system and the attitude of the narrator.

Critical remarks on people of different races is mostly limited to the Chinese people who were merchants or rich officials. This was surely taken from the real experience of the Early Rattanakosin period in which the Chinese, as rich merchants or entrepreneurs, became a powerful new group in Thai society (Nidhi 1986: 11-12). On the other hand, there were also comments on the inferiority of the Chinese, for example,

ถูกเจ็บเข้าไม่ได้ทั้งใจเจ๊ก	You are just like the Chinese who cannot bear the slightest pain
แต่เด็กเด็กมันก็คึกกว่ามึง	Children are braver and can tolerate more compared to you.

And also,

ชาติเจ๊กกินหมูจะสู้ไทย	The Chinese, eating pork, wanted to fight with the Thai.

(Damrong 1962: 155)

The dual image of the Chinese is found not only in these plays but also in many other literary works. And this clearly shows the unsettled attitudes of the narrators toward the 'us' (Thai) and the 'others' (Chinese).

It is obviously seen that in these poetic plays, the narrators were teasing the king and the royalty for acting in a manner improper to their status. The narrators did not firmly identify themselves with the ruling

(Phuttha Loetla Naphalai 1962: 129)

---

11 ฝูงนางแม่ค้าก็ร้องหยอก   นี่ *พระยาบ้านนอก*จะไปไหน
                                       (Phuttha Loetla Naphalai 1962: 688)

12 In Inao this notion appeared very clearly, for example:
    คอยแต่จะตี นอยู่ อัตรา   ทั้งชาวป่าไม่เคยเข้าเวียงชัย
                                         (Phuttha Loetla Naphalai 1965: 1107)

class in these stories as the us group. Meanwhile, the distinction between the ruling class and the common people was not firmly established and their relationship seemed unclear. It was possible that perhaps the narrators, who were mostly from the court poets and even the king himself, sided with the commoners and foreigners as much as with the ruling class. Equally, the dual portrayal of the Chinese as 'others' who were respectable show a more duplicitous attitude the narrators took to this group of foreigners.

KHUN CHANG KHUN PHAEN : POLITICO-CULTURAL ASPECTS OF OTHERNESS

This well-known literary work of the early Rattanakosin period is perhaps the most famous. It was composed by a group of poets from various backgrounds, ranging from the king himself to court poets to folk singers, many of them living at different times. Given this fact, the diversity of the poets' attitudes toward their characters seems impossible to explore in this essay. However, I was interested to discover a remarkably consistent set of attitudes toward 'us' and the 'others' in this collection.

Since most characters in this story are common people, the classification of such criteria as the ruler and the ruled is less significant. The more interesting point is the criteria used to identify the rich and the poor, the city people and the country people, and last but not least, the Thai and non-Thai groups.

Khun Chang, the antagonist, was a rich man who was always aware of his wealth and usually defined himself as a ผู้ดี (the aristocrat). Others, on the contrary, often made fun of him and had criticized his ugly, vigorous appearance since he was very young.[13] Interestingly, Phim, the heroine, once classified herself as a ผู้ดี because of her mother's wealth.[14] In a later part of the work, Phlai Ngam, Khun Phaen's son, made a comment to

---

13   ส้มสูกลูกไม้ใส่ของสวน   ให้ดีด้วนถูกแพงก็ไม่ว่า
     อย่าทำใจทมิฬเขานินทา   เขานับหน้าว่ากูเป็นผู้ดี
     เกินยองไปส่องกระจกใหญ่   ทุกหัวจังไรเหมือนร่องขี้
     ถึงหัวชั่วแต่ตัวเป็นผู้ดี

                                (Damrong 1960: 58)

14   อนิจเราเขาก็ว่าเป็นผู้ดี   มั่งมีแม่มีให้ลูกอายเพื่อน
                                 (Damrong 1960: 74)

himself that Srimala, who later became his wife, was beautiful, prim and had the genuine appearance of a ผู้ดี.[15] Kaewkiriya, whose father was in debt, sent her to Khun Chang for money, telling Khun Phaen that she was a slave, and not part of the ผู้ดี class like Khun Phaen and Wantho'ng. It seems that the meaning of ผู้ดี was loosely related with the concept of the rich in the mind of the narrator, not with the concept of having proper, good manners and not even of being born into a high ranking family as most of us tend to think today.

Secondly, there was a separation between groups in the city and in the village. Interestingly enough, the village people and the forest people here were groups of ethnic minorities who were moved from their home country after the war. Those groups mentioned regularly in the story are the Karen, the Lawa, the Mo'n, the Laotian, and sometimes the Kha and the Lue. According to this political background, these minority groups were scattered around the border. Here, the distinction was obviously between Thai and non-Thais, or in other words, between 'us' and the 'others'.

The ethnic group frequently referred to in this story was the Laotian of Chiang Mai who were enemies in the two wars between the Ayutthaya and the Chiang Mai kings. Other Laotian groups such as the Chiang Tho'ng and the Vientien people were not counted as enemies, but still were part of the 'other', non-Thai group.

Details of the characteristics of the Laotians as 'the others' are consistently given. The most regular one was the hairstyle of the Laotian women. The narrator never failed to note that these women, whether of high or low class, had their hair tied up in a bun and fastened with ornaments. While Thai women had their hair either long or short with the mark of hair part left from the topknot they had in their youth and not yet reached maturity. Other details were also described, such as food, household utilities, as well as language and custom. However, the hairstyle seemed to be the most impressive detail.[16] Even when Khun

---

15   ทั้งพระจันทร์วันเพ็ญเมื่อผ่องผูก   บริสุทธิ์โอภาสสะอาดเอี่ยม
         สองแก้มแย้มเหมือนจะยิ้มเรียม   งามเสงี่ยมราศีผู้ดีจริง
                                 (Damrong 1960: 636)

16   This notion was repeated regularly in Suntho'n Phu's Nirat.

Phaen was imprisoned for a long time, his friend teased him that his hair was long and made him looked like the Chinese or the Lawa.[17]

Hence, the criteria used to define 'the other' group was always concerned with the ethnic characteristic. The attitude towards these groups was shown through words used to insult or tease all the time. Examples are the words always added to the calling of the Laotian in-law, So'i Fa, whose husband's grandmother always used to insult her with words such as, อีลาวชาวกอน, อีลาวกอน, อีลาวชาวป่า and so on. Actually she was the daughter of the king of Chiang Mai, but because of her status as a war slave, she was treated as inferior to Srimala, the major wife. Only one strange situation was mentioned when Phlai Ngam's grandmother wanted to arrange a *Tham khwan* ceremony (ทำขวัญ) for him; she called upon her Laotian servants to perform music and song for the ceremony.[18] However, given the fact that the *Tham Khwan* ceremony was popular among Laotians of the northeast more than the central Thai, this might be understandable.

From details described in the story, the narrator as the resentative of the Thai group, must have known the non-Thai, or, to be more specific, the Lao, quite well. However, such familiarity was still used to produce a sense of political and cultural superiority with regard to the Lao. Hence, the concept of 'otherness' in this famous piece of literature was obviously constructed by the political and cultural criteria towards the ethnic minorities who were taken to be the inferiors in spite of their refined appearance and culture.

---

[17] เกลออเอ่ยน่าอกสูกูเผ่าผม   ทำรุงรังช่างสมอ้ายใจแข็ง
จะเป็นเจ๊กก็ใช่ไทยก็แคลง   มันระแวงคล้ายละว้าน่าขันคร้าน
(Damrong 1960: 611)

[18] ให้สาวสาวลาววัยที่เสียงดี   มาขอปี่ออชั้นทำขวัญนาย

....

แล้วพวกมอญซ้อนซอเสียงอ้ออ้อแอ้   ร้องทะแยย องกะเหน่าะย่ายเตาะเทย
ออระหน่ายพลายงามพ่อขามเขย   ขวัญเอ่ยนกกะเนี่ยงเกรียงเกลิง
ให้อยู่กินคิมีเมียสาว   เนียงกะราวกนคละเลิงเคลิ่ง
มวยบามาขวัญจงบันเทิง   จะเปิ้ยยี่อิกะปีปอน
(Damrong 1960: 528)

141

PHRA APHAI MANI AND NIRAT : NEW RELATIONS WITH 'OTHERS'

Suntho'n Phu, the author of the four poetic tales discussed in this paper may be considered as a leader of the new generation who had to cope with a new experience of 'otherness'.

His various literary works also brought new experiences to his readers, not only the elite, who were well educated or close to the traditional court, but also to the common people outside the court, especially the rising merchant class (Nidhi 1986: 13). These latter people comprised a new reading public, and Suntho'n Phu, especially in the second half of his life as wandering poet, began to realize this new socio-economic situaltion. Thus, his works brought new experiences which audiences could not have read or known before. Despite his outstanding poetic ability, he was unfortunately driven from the court and thus achieved a new understanding of the non-noble 'others' and how they interacted with the noble 'us' group.

In his poetic narratives, *Kho But, Singha Kraiphop, Laksanawong*, and the most famous of all in its genre, *Phra Aphai Mani*, Suntho'n Phu developed an idea of 'otherness' which was expressed through various kinds of characters. In *Singha Kraiphop*, the interaction between the ruling class and the villagers, especially those who spent their whole lives in remote areas, was seen from the point of view opposite to that on which he was raised and expressed in his earlier literary pieces. When the king and his wife were thrown out by the rebels, they went into the forest and took refuge with the forest villagers. Here, the ruling class was criticized for being unable to live on its own like the others. Briefly speaking, the 'us' group here were the forest villagers who were proud of their self-maintained lives. While 'the others' were the king and queen who represented the helpless, hopeless persons and did not know even how to find food for themselves.[19] They became 'the others' in their own land.

Throughout the story, Suntho'n Phu set an inverted scene and situation and thus revealed new aspects from a new standpoint, in which the new set of interactions was also concerned. Even the criteria of separation which was used to praise the beautiful, refined appearance of the ruling class and their entourages as the court people or ชาววัง was mocked in

---

19   เกิดมาเปล่าต่ายข้าวไม่แตกกาก   ค่ารมมมากพูกล้วนแต่สรงเสวย
        ออผัวไปก็ไม่ได้อะไรเลย   มิงเสวยเกลือเถิกทั้งผัวเมีย
                            (Suntho'n Phu 1962: 25)

this story.[20] Intentionally or not, the narrator revealed his sympathy for the poor, but proud and happy, villagers who used to be called ชาวป่า ชาวดง in literature prior to his works.

Searching through his *Nirat* which introduced new experience to both the author and his comtemporary readers, one can clearly see the origin of his attitude. This court poet might have been the only one who travelled around his country and thus, gained the experience of getting to know the 'others' who existed beyond his former 'us' group. In his first few *Nirat*, the author still shows his insulting attitude towards villagers in the countryside and certainly the forest people, including the minority group such as the *Chong* (in *Nirat Mu'ang Klaeng*) who was mentioned to his own relatives. He insulted and made fun of their food, pronunciation and habits whenever he noticed differences[21] but in the later *Nirat* such insulting tones and the concept of the superior/inferior vanished.[22] The author expressed a new attitude towards villagers and ethnic minorities. These people, in the eyes of the author, were sincere, straight forward, co-operative and helpful. Even the women of the other, non-Thai group whom he used to make fun of by means of unintentionally courting them, became those he would be happy to let his son marry.[23]

---

20   พ่อเจ้าขามาไยพ่อทุนหัว   ล้วนแต่งตัวหรือเขาหาไปเล่นโขน
                                   (Suntho'n Phu 1962: 38)

       กูขาวผ่องเป็นละอองระโอคองค์   ทั้งทรวดทรงสลับก้านกัยวายาว
       ที่เด็กหมันคะนองก็ร้องแช่   อีผ่อแม่เอ่ยมากูอ้ายคนขาว
       มันนุ่งผ้าตาลายคล้ายแมงคราว   บ้างถามท้าววว่ามึงไปข้างไหนมา
                                     (Suntho'n Phu 1962: 22)

21   เห็นสาวสาวชาวไร่เขาไถที่   บ้างพาทีอือเออเสียงเหนอหนอ
       แลขี้ไคลใส่ตาบเป็นคราบคอ   ผ้าห่มหอหมากแห้งตะแบงมาน
                                     (Damrong 1973: 52)
       ทั้งแย้บึ้งอิ่งอ่างเนื้อค่างคั่ว   เขาทำครัวรั้นไปปะชยแขยง
                                       (Damrong 1973: 56)

22   มาตั้งขายผ่ายเจ้าของไม่ต้องถือ   ผลเรือล่องร้องว่าซื้อทับทิมเหนอ
       จะพูกจาการวะทั้งคะเออ   เสียงเหน่อเหน่อหน้าตาน่าเอ็นดู
       นึกเสียดกายหมายมั่นใครผันผูก   ไว้เป็นลูกสะใภ้ให้เจ้าหนู
                                    (Damrong 1973: 177)

23   ที่แพรายหลายนางสำอางโฉม   งามประโลมเปล่งปลั่งอลั่งเหลือง
       ผมั่นเอ่ยเคยใช้แต่ในเมือง   มาฟุ้งเฟื่องฝ่ายเหนือทั้งเรือแพ
                                     (Damrong 1973: 214)

In short, the distance between the author and the others outside his former group decreased. Getting to know his fellows in the remote, poor area, had widened his eyes to the fact that there were certainly differences between 'us' and 'the others', but these differences did not prevent their mutual understanding.

Then, in *Phra Aphai Mani*, the best-known of his works, he introduced a new set of criteria to define 'the others'. In this marvellous story, the narrator brought his readers to the world of various races and languages, without notions of superiority/inferiority. All the differences were both simple and interesting. Thus, the characters show the readers a new way to interact with 'the others'. With details of the concept of territories, boundaries, races, and cultures, the narrator brought his readers an outside world which, as the matter of fact, he himself learned from the others' experiences, by means of listening, and also perhaps reading (Suntho'n Phu 1967: 379). Thus the world of his imagination did not have to be real, but was nonetheless genuine.

As the story was told, the main character groups, with *Phra Aphai Mani* at the centre, were always aware of the distance between these groups. Differences of language, religion and culture were noted and then, the narrator revealed his attitude once again by letting his supposedly Thai characters learn, and thus, enjoy different cultures.

It is worth noting here that the criteria the narrator set for defining 'the other' group were mostly related to clothing style, some details in everyday life such as eating habits, and more significantly, religion and language. Since Buddhism is quite flexible in tolerating other religious groups, the difference in the case of religion was not a problem. As well as language, the main characters learned a new language in order to communicate with 'the others' without a feeling of disregard or insult. This aspect revealed the concept of the narrator that the interaction among different groups could be developed through cultural learning without any notion of superiority or inferiority on either side.

เอ็นกูหนูพี่น้อง	สองสาว
คิดใครได้เลี้ยงลาว	ลูกสะใภ้
แต่ลูกผูกรักขาว	วันลา เจ้าเอย
จะเจ็บเล็บเขาไว้	ช่วนร้ายคลายเสือ

(Suntho'n Phu 1973: 277)

In conclusion, one scene should be mentioned (Suntho'n Phu 1967: 214-219), where all the enemies in the battle listened to the teachings of the great rishi in order to call a halt to protracted fighting. After the teaching, which concerned Buddhist ideas, those who listened to this teaching explained their understanding in their own way, based on the religious beliefs and the cultural practices of each group. Suntho'n Phu, as a Buddhist himself, did not clarify the meaning of this teaching, as if he wishing to suggest that differences between 'us' and 'the others', when considered from all aspects of interaction, had no need for set criteria to distinguish each group, permitting one to enjoy the differences and become acquainted with each other.

Certainly, there was a distinction between 'us' and 'the others' or 'Thai' and 'non-Thai', but that concept was used to support the idea of getting to know each other, and not preventing a more flexible and adaptable form of identity in this world of difference.

OTHERNESS : CONCERN FOR 'US' AND 'THE OTHERS'

The literary work discussed in this paper leads me to conclude that identifying oneself with a particular group 'us' can sometimes be reduced to a clear set of criteria to classify each group's characteristic features. In the literature of the Early Rattanakosin period, from *Inao* to *Phra Aphai Mani*, it seems the narrator used clear (and traditional) criteria, therefore, there was no hestitation to define oneself with the 'us' group and set the others into a contrasting group. This usually followed an attitude towards the group of 'us' and 'others' which could not avoid a notion of the interaction of a superior with an inferior. However, sometimes these implicit criteria are insufficient for the complex interactions of everyday life, as is seen in the case of Suntho'n Phu, who once belonged to the court poet group, but then became a 'free poet' who lived by readers' patronage. This latter difference between sets of criteria and the complexities of everyday life help bring us back to the opening of this paper.

Recalling the question 'what is being Thai?' the criteria used to classify the 'Thai' and 'non-Thai,' while important initial markers seem unable to delineate the rich interactions we have with people of either the group of our 'others' or our 'us' group about the 'others'. The concept of 'the otherness' helps us to understand and then to define ourselves as belonging to a particular group. A colleague of mine once said, 'Being Thai is not a set of criteria, but for me it is a life-long process.' And I would like to confirm her suggestion that however helpful criteria may be, they are only relevant in the concrete circumstances of living and imagining human beings.

REFERENCES

Damrong Rajanubhap, Somdet Krom Phraya (ed.)

1960 *Khun Chang Khun Phaen.* Bangkok: Sinlapa Bannakhan.

1973 *Prachum Klo'n Nirat Tang Tang Kho'ng Suntho'n Phu* (Collection of Suntho'n Phu's Nirat in Klo'n Verse). Bangkok: Soemwit Bannakhan.

1965 "Introduction". In Phuttha Loetla Naphalai, Phrabat Somdet Phra, *Inao.* Bangkok.

Nidhi Aewsriwongse

1986 'Suntho'n Phu : Mahakawi Kradumphi' (Suntho'n Phu : The Great Bourgoisie Poet). In *Sinlapa Watthanatham : Suntho'n Phu Du Lok Lae Sangkhom,* Special Issue on Suntho'n Phu, 1-35.

Phuttha Loetla Naphalai, Phrabat Somdet Phra.

1962 *Bot Lakho'n No'k Phraratchaniphon Ruam Hok Ru'ang* (Six Dance Plays by King Rama II). Bangkok: National Library.

1965 *Inao.* 2 Volumes. Bangkok: National Library.

Sombat Chanthornwong

1986 'Lokathat Kho'ng Suntho'n Phu' (The Worldview of Suntho'n Phu). In *Sinlapa Watthanatham : Suntho'n Phu Du Lok Lae Sangkhom,* Special Issue on Suntho'n Phu, 40-166.

Suntho'n Phu

    1962 *Nithan Kham Klo'n Suntho'n Phu* (Suntho'n Phu's Poetic Tales). Bangkok: Soemwit Bannakhan.

    1967 *Phra Aphaimani.* 2 Volumes. Bangkok: Khlang Witthaya.

    1973 *Nirat Suphan Chabap Sombun* (Nirat Suphan, the Complete Version). Bangkok: Krom Sinlapako'n.

THE GREEN WORLD OF ANGKHAN KALAYANAPHONG:
A VISION ON NATURE AND ENVIRONMENT

Suchitra Chongstitvatana

NATURE AND THAI POETRY

Thai poets have always been very much attached to nature. To describe nature in elaborate details is probably one of the outstanding characteristics of Thai classical poetry. Nature plays an important role in *Nirat* poetry composed as a lamentation of love when the poet is separated from his loved one. As *Nirat* is one of the most popular type of poetry in Thai literature from the past to the present, we can rightly state that nature is one of the most essential elements of Thai poetry. Even in modern Thai poetry various modern poets still express their attachment to nature or use nature as one of their main themes. Angkhan Kalayanaphong, one of the most unique contemporary Thai poets, employs nature as his main theme both in the traditional convention and in his own unique style.[1]

ANGKHAN'S VISION ON THE BEAUTY OF NATURE

Like most of Thai poets from the past to the present, Angkhan is very much inspired by the beauty and the marvel of nature. As a painter-poet he is capable of "painting" nature with the beauty of the language as well as with the beauty of colours. Angkhan's description of nature is vivid and unique. He uses a lot of personification to render more liveliness and gentleness to nature. The poet declares in his masterpiece-- *Lam Nam Phu Kradu'ng* that love for nature is the most important inspiration for him in composing poetry.

> Thus ends my *Nirat* Phu Kradu'ung,
> Composed from the deepest love for nature.

---

[1] For more detail see Suchitra : 1984.

No matter how many existences to come,
The same love may I feel forever!
Humbly would I always recognize
The real value of the Earth and the Sky!

(Angkhan 1969: 163)

His deep love for nature makes him admire the apparent beauty of nature he
describes very vividly by creating beautiful images with details and colours.

Far beyond the wide horizons are the mountains lines,
With the cliffs and valleys intertwined.
Forlorn and lonely are the clouds uphigh,
And on each mountain shines the blue, pale gray divine!

(Angkhan 1969: 96)

Flowering indeed are these wild green screens,
Full of buds and blossoms, yellow, red, white, and cream,
With young and tender leaves ravishingly adorning,
Thus render divine and beautiful the whole surrounding!

(Angkhan 1969: 121)

This soft golden moss, gleaming in orange beams,
Is like a magic carpet on the rocks' recesses.
Precious ornaments of the mountains are they all
With wonderful wild flowers of every kind!

(Angkhan 1969: 98)

Besides, the poet also sees beyond the surface of nature to the spiritual beauty
of nature that is normally overlooked by others. The poet looks at nature
closely and gives equal value to all elements in nature for he sees that all
elements are interrelated and interdependent.

Thousands of grains of dust and sand
Creating the Earth for us to live
Are, no doubt, more virtuous and precious
Than any gems or diamonds!
Why look down on small wild flowers?

Are they not the precious gifts from Heaven
To beautify and adorn this Earth?
Why praise only gold, neglecting lead and iron?
A tiny drop of water, though, like a dewdrop,
Surely helps to create the great ocean!
Without sand, stone and earth,
What is the value of gems and diamonds?
Even the lowest creatures, insects or worms,
Are worthy of our appreciation,
With the heart free from contempt,
We can learn the values of all things!

(Angkhan 1969: 14)

The poet clearly express his respect for nature especially when he declares that nature is in fact his great teacher or Guru.

My divine teachers are all over the Sky,
The Moon and bright Stars in heaven
Kindly tell me the wondrous mystery of Night
And various universes, glittering like diamonds!
The Mountains teach me the taste of loneliness,
And the Clouds train my forlorn heart to wander.
The falling Dew teaches me how the heart can freeze
When love and hope fade away like Night.
The flowing stream, weeping to the pebbles.
Invites me to cry silently for my broken dreams!
For Cupid wakes me up to Love
Only to show me all its sweet sufferings!
Even the smallest wild flowers are like friends
Who help to enlighten and sharpen my mind.
Thus will I devote my life to all Nature Teachers
Trying to realize the divinity of poetry!

(Angkhan 1969: 101)

For the poet, nature is more than just beauty but a source of spiritual wisdom. The beautiful big trees in the forest never protest the cruelty of men who slaughter them. They only give fragrant flowers, fruits, and even their lives to all men without discrimination. In fact they are like a Bodhisattva who sacrifices all for the benefit of others.

Thus the poet believes that to learn from nature the way to live without greed would be the ideal solution to the crisis of modern men. If we appreciate and respect nature enough we could save all natural environment and know how to exploit nature within limits for the common good of all. If we follow the noble example of nature we will not only save our environment and our world but we will also save humanity from dehumanizing themselves. The poet views modern men and modern advanced technology with suspect and horror. For he clearly sees how these things change humane hearts into calculating hearts. Genuine kindness becomes a luxury that modern society cannot afford. Everybody has to fight and compete with each other just to accumulate more and more, not realizing how their greed will affect others and the world. The modern comfort and convenience blind men from the possible danger of technology to the world. The poet sees the problem of modern men as the problem of spiritual illness. He claims that the lack of sympathy and compassion is the cause of all problems in modern society. Be sides, he warns us that sciences can also be destructive even to the point of destroying all humanity. In fact to be more precise, the poet even mentions the danger of nuclear war in his poetry.

> Alas inhuman and dry is now our world!
> The infernal fire will sweep over Earth and Sky
> All our tears can hardly help to cool
> Nor calm nor subdue the burning fire! Marvellous though
> sciences seems to be
> Equally dangerous it can also be
> Even to destroy all human race
> Thus all creature can disappear with no trace!
> (p. 41) Then the world would be without happiness.
> Night and day the Heart would suffer,
> Just because of wicked cleverness,
> Indulging in sins and impure labour!
> Behind the arrogance of the brains,
> Lies the wicked nature of wild animals,
> Full of mysteriously evil influences,
> Burning like the infernal flames!

151

> Unable to know one's self,
> The meanings of life are empty and gone.
> Thus ruined is the whole world,
> Where virtues and morals see no dawn.
>
> (Angkhan 1969: 41)

MEN AND NATURE : A BOND OF LOVE AND WISDOM

It is essential to point out that the poet's attitude towards his human fellows is far from being positive. He abhors the greed and ignorance of men especially men of modern civilization. He criticizes modern way of life as inhumane and wicked. The most important proof of his judgment on modern civilization is the lack of respect for nature that men in the old days used to have. Modern technology makes men believe in their false power to control nature and thus they are not capable of feeling any real respect for nature except viewing nature as a source of their material comfort and wealth. The poet tries to endear nature to men by "painting" the exquisite beauty of nature through to his mastery in literary arts. He emphasizes that to be able to see and perceive the real beauty of nature is a basic quality of any human being. He persuades his readers to emulate the noble example of nature. He tries to "wake" men up from their blindness and ignorance towards the invaluable beauty of nature by advocating the teaching of the Lord Buddha as the ideal way of life.

> Now awake, let us find the divine path
> Of our noble and great Buddha.
> With our whole heart let us sacrifice
> And truly give for joy, day and night.
> Come, let us change beliefs and ways of life
> To create a heavenly world well-purified.
> Pray, never kill, have mercy on others.
> Instead use the blood to grow flowers!
> Raise our heart as high as the bright stars
> Let it be shining with brilliant noblesse
> With bravery and sound wisdom,
> And immortal heart, forever timeless!
>
> (Angkhan 1969: 15)

The poet's attempt to link the spiritual aspect of nature to the ideal of Buddhism can be considered as an effective means to convince his readers. The poet often praises the beauty of nature as an element to make this earth as exquisite as a paradise. He declares his love for this world in the " Poet's Pledge" that he will not even enter nivarna as he will stay on to compose poetry for this marvellous world.

> Let others soar beyond the infinite skies
> Or thread cosmic paths of moons and stars;
> But to this living world my heart is pledged
> To Earth bonded in all my lives and deaths.
> I shall even refuse Nirvana
> And suffer the cycling wheel of rebirths
> To translate the multitudes of wonders
> Into poems dedicated to this Universe.
>
> (Angkhan 1986: 23)[2]

In this poem the poet literally tries to idealize the importance of poetry and the bond of love between men and nature. In the Buddhistic context nivarna is the ideal goal of life and Thai poets of the past used to declare the purpose of their work as to help them attain the ideal goal of nivarna. Here, Angkhan makes it clear to his readers that he is willing to sacrifice even the most valuable thing in life just for his love for this world. Yet, the poet's greatest love lies in his love for nature and not for mankind. In his famous poetic prose "Grandma", the poet conveys a strong message of nature's benevolence towards men through the story of a lonely old grandma who is loved and cared for by nature without anyone else to look after her. The poet subtly criticizes the selfishness of men towards nature and towards each other.

However, the tragic ending of the story where grandma is killed by a poisonous snake reflects the poet's deep insight of nature. The description of grandma getting decayed and de- stroyed by worms and insects illustrates the ultimate truth of life and the bond between men and nature. Human beings belong to nature and in the end must return to nature. Thus in the poet's eye the bond between men and nature is the bond of love and wisdom.

The red ants are feasting on the black eyes of

---

[2] This English translation is by Chamnongsri L Rutnin (Chamnongsri 1988: 193).

Grandma. They are gathering in big groups.
In a few days, the corpse will get rotten and
swollen. The crows and vultures will come to
devour the bones that are scattering around.
What a pityful and fearful sight!

(Angkhan 1964: 177)

ENVIRONMENT OF VICES AND VIRTUES

Angkhan is probably one of the first poets who show a concern on the problem of environment such as the problem of pollution and deforestation. As an artist and a poet he is very sensitive to beauty and ugliness. He perceives the exquisite beauty of nature as well as the inhumane abuse of nature by men. For the poet, nature represents both beauty and virtues. Nature only gives without asking anything in return.

Moreover, nature is the source of inspiration and wisdom for men who care enough to learn. Unfortunately, men of modern civilization have lost their respect for nature. They blindly abuse nature with greed and ignorance. As the result, they are now suffering from their own misdeed. Therefore whereas nature is the environment of virtues for men, men are the environment of vices for each other.

The poet's solution to the problem of environment mainly depends on human awakening to the real value of nature. Angkhan urges us to see the danger of our own greed that affects the environment. He tries to advocate the ideal attitude towards life- to work for one's own ideal and to sacrifice for the common good of all just like nature. We can say that the poet is trying to create an ideal world of utopia- a green world of perfect nature in harmony with virtuous men. It is quite clear that the poet sees the problem of environment as the problem of men's selfishness. The solution he emphasizes always is the kindness and wisdom of human's heart gained through the right understanding of nature.

Compared with nature, even a stone or a grain of sand, human life is so short and so insignificant. The poet warns us to be modest to nature and realize our own limitations.

This sand is from great mountain long ago,
Falling down, transforming into small grains.
This is the law of the three characteristics of existence.

154

> To be modest like earth is to attain real prominence.
>
> (Angkhan 1972: 27)

The poet further warns us against the danger of the nuclear war which will destroy the whole world. He portrays the catastrophe after the nuclear war in "Tears from the stars" one of his poetic prose in a most passionate manner.

> The atom is singing a lullaby to the ashes of
> humanity. "Don't feel sorry. Those past sorrows
> are but bad dreams. Don't feel ashamed. I- the
> great atom is going to lead you in the future.
> Just trust me.
> Is it not for my marvellous power that caused
> the end of humanity? Now all humanity has
> become like lost dust ... just like the state
> of void."
>
> (Angkhan 1964: 182)

Here we can see the poet's concern for humanity in general and also his deep love for this earth as he often emphasizes in his poetry.

THE POET'S GREEN WORLD : A SOLUTION OR AN IDEALISM ?

Considering from the context of Thai literature, Angkhan's poetry on nature is more than just a lyrical type of poetry but a serious "didactic" poetry. The poet conveys his serious engagement to "salvage" the soul of humanity through strong criticism of their selfishness and passionate persuasion to change their way of life. It is not uncommon for Thai poets to try to convey a message of the Buddha's teaching in their work. Yet Angkhan's poetry is far from conventional didactic poetry. The poet is passionately sincere in his love for nature and his contempt for modern civilization. His poetry reflects his confidence in the solution he offers. He vigorously suggests a solution to the problem of modern world- to change the attitude towards life and nature.

According to the poet, an ideal man in his ideal world is a man of enlightenment- a man without greed and malice but with refinement. The poet's ideal man is one who is content with doing good for all and is willing to sacrifice all for the sake of others. In fact, the poet is almost demanding an ordinary human being to become a Bodhisattva in order to preserve this beautiful world. Maybe, this sounds like an impossible demand on the poet's part. However, while all men are not enlightened yet, what can we do to solve the problem? The poet suggests that we should adopt the ideal and attitude of a Bodhisattva. Hence a passionately "didactic" tone in his work. To convey the teaching of the Lord Buddha may be common enough in Thai poetry. Yet to advocate the idea that everyone should try to become a Bodhisattva or at least to be a man without greed is something quite different. The poet's strong contempt for modern civilization and modern technology is somewhat quite disturbing for his readers. For even when the reader agrees with the idea that modern technology can be harmful to humanity, it is not quite valid to see almost no use of technology at all. However, it seems natural that the poet appears one sided as he is trying to convince his readers with an ardour quite unusual for a Thai poet. Despite his strong commitment and the mastery of his language use, his "message" seems to reach the heart of his readers only as a moving poetry and not a feasi- ble solution to the crisis of humanity. Perhaps, this is a common fate of all great poets. Yet the greatness of the great poets lies in their determination and not the fulfilment of their dreams.

REFERENCES

Angkhan Kalayanaphong,

    1964   *Kawiniphon kho'ng Angkhan Kalayanaphong.* Bangkok: Su'ksit Sayam.

    1969   *Lam Nam Phu Krad'ung.* Bangkok: Su'ksit Sayam.

    1986   *Panithan Kawi,* Bangkok: Carat Books House.

Chamnongsri L. Rutnin (trans.)
1988   'A Poet's Pledge', In Prasert Na Nagara et al (eds.)
       Treasury of Thai Literature : The Modern Period. The
       National Identity Board Office of the Prime Minister,
       Bangkok: Amarin Printing Group.

Suchitra Chongstitvatana,
1984   "The Nature of Modern Thai Poetry". Unpublished Ph.D.
       Thesis, School of Oriental and African Studies, University
       of London.

THE *KĀMADAŚA* IN CLASSICAL THAI POETRY

Thomas John Hudak

Western scholars and critics often describe Thai poetry written between the mid-thirteenth century and 1932 as classical, suggesting perhaps a time when poetry was of superior caliber and works created during this 700 year span as masterpieces of literature. A general assumption about these classical works is that they were all in one way or another influenced by the classical literatures of India. Influences range from the borrowing of plots to the adaptation of the meters known as *chan,* one of the primary meters used during the Ayutthaya period (1351-1767). Not as readily recognizable in Thai poetry are the many individual Indic poetic techniques and tropes. However, a quick survey of any dictionary of Sanskrit or Pali poetics reveals techniques familiar to and chracteristic of classical Thai poetry.

Catalogues, in many cases simply lists, form one of the hallmarks of classical Thai poetry, and in Thai poetry they are known collectively as *bot chom* 'stanzas of admiration'. Linguistically, there appear to be five general types of catalogues (Hudak in press). The first has no internal organization other than the grouping of items with a similar semantic content such as all birds or fish. A second more sophisticated type has the item arranged by consonantal or vocalic rhyme, sequences of alliterating, for example. A slight variation, the mixing of consonantal and vocalic rhyme, comprises the third. In the fourth type, punning is used as the organizing principle. One of the most famous examples of this type occurs in *Samutthakhot kham chan,* a poem written in the *chan* meter begun in the seventeenth century and completed in the nineteenth. In this composition, the prince, having lost his beloved, wanders through a forest where every tree and flower reminds him of his lost love. Each plant name has a secondary meaning that describes his emotion. Thus, seeing the *sawāt* tree he is reminded of the love and pleasure (*sawāt*) that he found with his beloved. The last type of catalogue is in effect a descriptive passage (Hudak 1988). With these catalogues someone, generally a woman, or something is described in minute detail. Frequently these descriptive catalogues appear when a love is lost or when love is unrequited. In these cases, the catalogues take on the form and the characteristics of the Indic sequence known as *kāmadaśa* or the lovelorn condition.

In the compact *A Dictionary of Sanskrit Poetics* by Nagendra, the *kāmadaśa* consisting of ten phases, is described as the pining of a lovelorn person for union with the loved one. A variety of different ways of using the *kāmadaśa* can be found in the poem *Samutthakhot kham chan*.[1] In brief, the poem, a Buddhist birthstory, describes Prince Samutthakhot's courting and marriage to Princess Phinthumadi and the adventures the couple encounter visiting the heavens with a magic sword. The plot of the story allows for the meeting of a new love as well as the lose of a love, all of which are described through the ten phases of the *kāmadaśa*. While various phases of the *kāmadaśa* are employed to describe the meetings and separations of Samutthakhot and Phinthumadi, the most elaborate and complete use of the *kāmadaśa* is found in the lament of the phitthayathorn for his abducted wife, a poetic sequence that clearly demonstrates each of the ten phases.

Sequentially, the lovelorn condition begins with *abhilāṣa*: longing or pining (Nagendra 1987: 3). The explanation of the phase maintains that the condition arises after the first sight of the beloved, and the viewer desires a quick union. This is certainly the case when Samutthakhot first meets Phinthumadi and is then separated from her. However, it seems appropriate to expand this phase to include the lose of a beloved which also arouses deep pain and longing. In the pitthayathorn sequence, the first two lines of stanza 1401 (see Appendix A for the complete sequence) succinctly describe the pain and longing of the devastated diety:

1401   Great sorrow and mourning
        Shook the ruined heart.

The second two lines of the same stanza and the following stanza complete the second phase *cintā*: pondering, worry, or anxiety (Nagendra: 1987: 46).

1401   Anxiety arose from the thoughts of his beauty
        But the thinking never stopped.

---

[1] Translated as "The Tale of Prince Samuttakote" (see Hudak: 1993).

1402   "O god, now I must endure great sorrow
        Separated from my bride
        My heart's always lost
        In suffering, sorrow, and longing.

In the third phase *smṛti* meditation or recollection of past experiences is usually called forth by the association of a similar experience (Nagendra 1987: 164), although in this sequence there is simply the recollection of past events.

1405   When I embraced you, my beauty,
        Hugged you, we went off
        To frolic in the forest
        To find joy in every corner.
1406   I embraced you tightly, noble one,
        And took you to the garden
        At majestic Meru
        And Himaphan, the mountain of pleasure.
1407   And then we entered the forest
        To admire the precious blooming blossoms,
        The golden lotuses, the red lotuses,
        And there we picked them.
1408   And then I caressed you,
        Embraced you, my precious,
        Arrayed your perfect body,
        O my lovely one.
1409   And then we went to play in the forest.
        We saw a pool and went to bathe
        At that jeweled bathing place,
        O precious jewel.
1410   We two were content and filled with joy.
        We didn't dare leave.
        What evil could come
        And separate you, my glory?

In the fourth phase *guṇakathana* praise and talking about the virtues of the loved one appear because the recollection in the third phase is not enough (Nagendra 1987: 62) It is this phase that frequently forms the descriptive passages so characteristic of classical Thai poetry.

1412   "O my young love, my youthful loved one, you
        with the face of the young moon,
1413   No heavenly nymph can match your alluring, your
        captivating form.

This same phase is repeated later in the lament when an even more detailed recollection is given:

1438   I remember her face, an unsullied spotless moon.
        I remember her night-dark hair.
1439   I remember her dark sapphire eyes, blooming lotuses,
        purple dark. Her ears golden lotus petals.
1440   I remember that flower's skin, delicate as the
        blossoms of the blue climber. Each side with grace-fully
        arched eyebrows--she with the eight desires.
1441   I remember the fragrance of her cheeks, the perfumed
        essence of blossoms in full bloom. None to compare
        with that beauty.
1442   I remember her nose, an incomparable curve.
        I remember its splendid tapering.
1443   I remember her luscious lips. My appreciation never stops.
        Her sweeping smile's now gone, no longer here to admire.
1444   Like the God of Love with a joyful woman, all through
        night and day glorious scents arise.
1445   O my heart, my jewel shining through the night, must
        you bear this burden?
1446   I remember her angelic voice, the melodious cooing
        bird--now distant from my ears.
1447   Her throat, the throat of a deer. Her chin, the chin of a lion.
        Her breasts, round like the moon.
1448   Her swaying arms, elegantly curved elephant trunks.
        I remember her shape, a beautiful woman, delicate and
        smooth.
1449   I remember her waist and stomach. Her beauty excites love.

Pure and innocent she is.
1450   I remember her legs, her lotus-like feet, like those
        of the apsaras, spotless and pure.

In the fifth stage, *udvega* agitation arises, caused by the separation and the lack of solace reached through the recollection in phase three and praise in phase four (Nagendra 11987: 176).

1426   Anguish mounted upon anguish because of our
        separation, our calamity. My heart's scorched,
        parched, withered, shriveled from the heat.
1427   Ruin mounted upon ruin because of defeat by this enemy.
        Boldly he came firing anger, generating shame.
1428   Shame before all of the deities, shame before all of the
        demons. If my life ends, I am happy.

Phases six through eight are all closely related and are not always recognizable as separate stages. In the sixth phase, *sampralāpa* , lamentation, wailing, and incoherent talk result from the inability to bear the agitation in phase five (Nagendra 1987: 153). Phase seven, *unmāda*, is hysteria from the weeping and inchorent talking of phase six. And, finally, in phase eight, *vyādhi*, bodily ailments such as fever and bodily aches begin. Nagendra notes that frequently an unberarable burning pain is described (1987: 202). In the Thai example the pain appears in stanza 1435. In the passage under discussion all three of these stages quickly follow one another.

1434   I moan, I groan, I search for you, my lost bride, my
        auspicious beauty. My heart will break,
        my mind's overwhelmed.
1435   I long to meet you, but I do not. I only meet sorrow
        like fire. Better death than separation from my beloved.

A similar set of stanzas can be found in 1451-1453.

1451   O god, I've reached my end, helpless and forlorn.
        My aching heart almost shatters.

1452   Sleeping, I used to cling to my beloved's body.
    Now I sleep alone in the forest.

1453   O god, my heart's in torment. O don't think of my life.
    I think only of my beloved. I can't forget her beauty.
    O god, I lament.

In the ninth phase, *jaḍatā,* swooning and unconsciousness occur, both a result of the agitation and the disappointment.

1436   I die, but I do not. Sorrow and memories are the same.
    My strength gone, what'll I think of next,
    reflections nearly gone.

The final phase is death *mṛti,* a death caused by the unbearable physical and mental agony. This death, however, is only temporary and is generally removed by some miracle. In the phitthayathorn passage there is an initial call for death.

1437   Cease heart, heart without joy, heart with its
    everlasting memories of her beauty--memories that
    remain with me.

This cry is echoed at the end of the lament:

1456   I'll die, die alone. Who'll see me? My jewel and I
    we do not see each other.

The death is averted by the appearance of Prince Samutthakhot and his retinue.

In this rather lengthy breakdown of the *kāmadaśa* passage, all ten phases are readily apparent. What makes the entire passage so exquisite is that the phases do not simply follow one another in quick succession. Rather they are interwoven with other aspects of the entire poem. For example, once phase five has been completed, part of the plot is reviewed or expanded (stanzas 1429-1433).

Another characteristic feature is the repetition of phrases. This passage appears to be unique in that the entire *kāmadaśa* sequence is completed and then partially repeated. One complete sequence occurs in stanzas 1401-1437 while a second one beginning with phase four starts with stanza 1438 and continues through the remaining phases through stanza 1456.

While complete sequences are generally long and involved, other phases are often used to help delineate the characters and to further the plot. In the poem, Prince Samutthakhot and Phinthumadi are first magically brought together by a spirit and then separated. When Prince Samutthakhot awakens remembering his love affair with Phinthumadi only the first four phases occur: he remembers his love, grows agitated, remembers his past experience, and then praises her beauty. Once these phases have been described the lovelorn condition is completed and the plot continues with the Prince's search for Phintmumadi.

In another sequence the *kāmadaśa* begins but then moves into a different type of poetic technique. Early in the poem the prince has left his first wife, Surasuda, to hunt in the forest, and as evening approaches he begins to long for her (phases one and two). Phase three, recollection, is introduced when the prince sees all of the birds with their mates flying home for the eveneing. While this generates a longing to be with his wife, it is also a means by which the poet demonstrates his skill with the language, for the poem quickly moves into a series of stanzas with alliterating bird names, the second type of catalogue described earlier.

The *kāmadaśa* sequence appears to have three main functions in classical Thai poetry. First, it is used to delineate the emotions of a lover whose love has been lost or left behind, as when the phitthayathorn's wife is abducted. Secondly, the sequence is used to describe the longing that occurs when lovers first meet and then are seperated as when the spirit removes Prince Samutthakhot from the arms of Phinthumadi. Finally, some phases are used to describe a single emotion as well as to further the plot, as when Prince Samutthakhot begins his search for Phinthumadi. In addition, certain phases provide the opportunity to include other formal poetic techniques, as when the recollection generates the alliterating catalogue.

It is hoped that this rather brief examination of a common Indic poetic sequence used in classical Thai poetry will demonstrate that Indic poetics is a rich source for Thai poetics. Ideally this study will also suggest further avenues of exploration and study.

REFERENCES

Hudak, Thomas John.

    1988. "Organizational Principles in Classical Thai Poetry." *Bulletin of the School of Oriental and African Studies* 51: 1: 95-117.

    1993. *The Tale of Prince Samuttakote: A Buddhist Epic from Thailand.* Monographs in International Studies, Southeast Asia Series, No. 90. Athens, OH: Ohio University.

    (in press). "Repetition and Text-Building in Classical Thai Poetry."

Nagendra.

    1987. *A Dictionary of Sanskrit Poetics* . New Delhi: B.R. Publishing Corporation.

APPENDIX

The following passages have been taken from *The Tale of Prince Samuttakote*, pp. 143-47. They describe the anguish of the phitthayathorn after he has been defeated in battle and his wife abducted by another phitthayathorn. Numbers at the end of the stanzas indicate the corresponding sections of the *kāmadaśa*.

1401   Great sorrow and mourning   (1)
    Shook the ruined heart.
    Anxiety arose from the thoughts of his beauty   (2)
    But the thinking never stopped.

1402 "O god, now I must endure great sorrow
   Separated from my bride
   My heart's always lost
   In suffering, sorrow, and longing.

1403 "O god, now I must endure great sorrow
   Separated from my bride.
   My heart's always lost
   In suffering, sorrow, and longing.

1404 Oh, I went out and met
   That enemy attacking with evil intent,
   Ripping away my beloved beauty,
   My bride, and flying away.

1405 When I embraced you, my beauty,
   Hugged you, we went off
   To frolic in the forest
   To find joy in every corner.

1406 I embraced you tightly, noble one,
   And took you to the garden
   At majestic Meru
   And Himaphan, the mountain of pleasure.

1407 And then we entered the forest
   To admire the precious blooming blossoms,
   The golden lotuses, the red lotuses.
   And there we picked them.

1408 And then I caressed you,
   Embraced you, my precious,
   Arrayed your perfect body,
   O my lovely one.

1409 And then we went to play in the forest.
   We saw a pool and went to bathe
   At that jeweled bathing place,
   O precious jewel.

1410 We two were content and filled with joy.
   We didn't dare leave.
   What evil could come
   And separate you, my glory?

1411   Then Ronapimuk's face
        Filled with great despair,
        Pain and sorrow,
        Great despair from the separation.

1412   "O my young love, my youthful loved one, you   (4)
        with the face of the young moon,

1413   No heavenly nymph can match your alluring, your
        captivating form.

1414   We two found happiness and pleasure journeying through
        the flower-filled forest.

1415   Filling us with desire, fragrant flower garlands spread
        their perfumes about you, O enraptured beauty.

1416   We marveled at the trees, the waters, the forested
        mountains; we delighted in the lotus blossom pools.

1417   Flowers and bright-petaled lotuses diffused their pollen
        and their luscious perfumes.

1418   Bees swarmed like flawless black sapphires; ruby red
        blossoms resembling lotuses grew scattered about.

1419   Tiered green leaves sparkled like emeralds; limpid water
        shone with rays of the cat's eye.

1420   Turtles teeming in the water swam with fantastic fish,
        crabs, tortoises--complete contentment in the pool.

1421   Enraptured prattling parrots flew overhead; peacocks
        danced and strutted by the brimming pools.

1422   Cicadas sang out like melodious instruments; waters
        mingled their powerful sounds, lulling us to sleep with song.

1423   Elephants, tigers, lions, and other animals in pairs
        wandered side by side filled with joy.

1424   Embracing you, O noble one, we flew through the air in
        fun, in happiness, in everlasting delight. What evil
        could come and force us to separate?

1425   Then--the phitthayathorn, wicked and wanton, savage and
        fierce, ripped you away from me, my beauty.

1426   Anguish mounted upon anguish because of our   (5)
        separation, our calamity. My heart's scorched,
        parched, withered, shriveled from the heat.

167

1427	Ruin mounted upon ruin because of defeat by this enemy. Boldly he came firing anger, generating shame.
1428	Shame before all of the deities, shame before all of the demons. If my life ends, I am happy.
1429	So the battle would be unfair, without form, without propriety, that evil enemy boldly attacked.
1430	Because I was carrying you, my beloved, he had power and strength. So out he came fighting and attacking.
1431	Superior he was, but who flatters a felon? No one! In ignominy and disgrace I shrink.
1432	I think of only you, my beloved--the purest on the earth, O fragrant one.
1433	My heart, my bride with everlasting beauty, how will you endure the torment?
1434	I moan, I groan, I search for you, my lost (6,7,8) bride, my auspicious beauty. My heart will break, my mind's overwhelmed.
1435	I long to meet you, but I do not. I only meet sorrow like fire. Better death than separation from my beloved.
1436	I die, but I do not. Sorrow and memories are (9) the same. My strength gone, what'll I think of next, reflections nearly gone.
1437	Cease heart, heart without joy, heart with its (10) everlasting memories of her beauty--memories that remain with me
1438	I remember her face, an unsullied spotless moon. (4) I remember her night-dark hair.
1439	I remember her dark sapphire eyes, blooming lotuses, purple dark. Her ears golden lotus petals.
1440	I remember that flower's skin, delicate as the blossoms of the blue climber. Each side with grace-fully arched eyebrows--she with the eight desires.
1441	I remember the fragrance of her cheeks, the perfumed essence of blossoms in full bloom. None to compare with that beauty.
1442	I remember her nose, an incomparable curve. I remember its splendid tapering.

1443   I remember her luscious lips. My appreciation never stops. Her sweeping smile's now gone, no longer here to admire.

1444   Like the God of Love with a joyful woman, all through night and day glorious scents arise.

1445   O my heart, my jewel shining through the night, must you bear this burden?

1446   I remember her angelic voice, the melodious cooing bird--now distant from my ears.

1447   Her throat, the throat of a deer. Her chin, the chin of a lion. Her breasts, round like the moon.

1448   Her swaying arms, elegantly curved elephant trunks. I remember her shape, a beautiful woman, delicate and smooth.

1449   I remember her waist and stomach. Her beauty excites love. Pure and innocent she is.

1450   I remember her legs, her lotus-like feet, like those of the apsaras, spotless and pure.

1451   O god, I've reached my end, helpless and forlorn. (5,6, My aching heart almost shatters. 7,8)

1452   Sleeping, I used to cling to my beloved's body. Now I sleep alone in the forest.

1453   O god, my heart's in torment. O don't think of my life. I think only of my beloved. I can't forget her beauty. O god, I lament.

1454   Bathed in blood, bathed in tears, my heart's bathed in utter sorrow that seeps through my whole body.

1455   Now, my beloved, I'm maimed and wounded. It's difficult to see you, my bride.

1456   I'll die, die alone. Who'll see me? My jewel (9,10) and I, we do not see each other.

THE THAI TALE OF *ANIRUDDHA*: POPULARITY AND VARIATIONS

Cholada Ruengruglikit

The story of *Aniruddha* has been widely known among Thai people since ancient times. At least, there is clear evidence that it was already popular in Thailand around the 20th century B.E., and was referred to in the old law and many old literary works of that period. The Thai tale of *Aniruddha* is found in every part of the country and in various styles and versions, with emphasis on different details. This is due to the purposes of the composition which have resulted in variations of the contents and types of tales such as myths, Jatakas, fairy tales and local tales.

THE GENESIS OF THE STORY OF *ANIRUDDHA*

The story of *Aniruddha* is of Indian origin and appears in the *Purana*, in the *Mahabharata* and in the *Bharatamanjari* written by Ksemendra. It also exists in poetic and dramatic forms of later periods, namely *Usaragodaya*, *Usakalayana*, *Usa-bhilasa*, *Usaharana*, *Okhaharana*, *Usaparinaya*, *Usaniruddha*, *Usa-Aniruddha and Banasura* (Sahai: 1978: 10-11). India's oldest version of the story is in the *Vishnu Purana* presumably composed during the first or the second century A.D. - the fifth century A.D. (Mani 1975: 617).[1]

The story of *Aniruddha* appears in chapters 32-33 of the *Vishnu Purana* (Wilson 1961: 465-469). Its purpose is to praise the god Vishnu (reincarnated as Krishna) as supreme among the three gods - Siva, Brahma and Vishnu. It described the battle between Krishna and Siva with the subjects of each side in which Siva's side is defeated. Siva himself is unable to overcome Krishna, either. Besides, Krishna is victorious in his fight against the demon king Bana or Banasura who is not only Usa's or the heroine's father but also Siva's devoted disciple. His faithfulness towards

---

[1] R.C. Hazra places this work in the last quarter of the third or the first quarter of the fourth century A.D. See R.S. Hazra "The Date of Visnu Purana" Annals of Bhandarkar Oriental Research Institute Vol. 18, 1937, p 617 (quoted by Sahai: 1978: 4). J.N. Farquar places the work in the fourth century A.D. See J.N. Farquar, Outline of the Religious History of the Indian Literature p. 143 (quoted by Sahai: 1978: 4). M. Winternitz places it in the fifth century A.D. (Winternitz: 1927: 545).

Siva is so great that Siva and his subjects help Banasura in warfare in order to protect him from harm, although this is to no avail. The war between Krishna and Banasura is sparked by the romance between Aniruddha and Usa, the hero and the heroine, the love that goes against tradition since he has enjoyed her without her father's knowledge. When Banasura learns about this, he flies into a rage and makes Aniruddha his captive. Krishna, who is Aniruddha's grandfather learns of this some time later and leads his people to Aniruddha's rescue. After winning the war, he takes the couple back to his city.

The *Harivamsa*, an appendix to the *Mahabharata*, contains a similar story. The date of its composition is between 300 and prior to 1046 A.D. (Jiraphat 1990: 60),[2] presumably later than the composition of the 18 chapters, which form main story of the *Mahabharata*. In 1046 A.D. Ksemendra had already added the story of *Harivamsa* to the last part of his work, *Bharatamanjari*, which was written as a summary of the *Mahabharata*.

As mentioned above, the original Indian story of *Aniruddha* portrays the love between Aniruddha and Usa as well as describing in detail the battle between the gods Vishnu (in the form of Krishna and Siva), and the fight between Krishna and Banasura.

However, if one studies Indian poems and plays of later periods, one will find that the love affair between Aniruddha and Usa is a distinct subject matter, and the two names of the main characters are used in the titles such as *"Usaniruddha"* and *"Usa-Aniruddha"*.

The Indian story of *Aniruddha* has spread to Southeast Asian nations, namely Laos, Cambodia and Thailand.

In the ancient Laotian kingdom of Lanchang, a literary work on *Aniruddha* was produced at the time of written literature of the earliest period when the *akso'n tham* (dharma alphabets) were used, around the 19th-20th century B.E. The story is called *Usabarot* (Phouvong 1958: 343).

As for the ancient Cambodian kingdom, there is evidence that the *Aniruddha* story was known there since the 17th century B.E.. This is shown by a bas-relief in the first-floor gallery of Ankor Wat which was built in 1690 B.E. in honour of King Suryavarman II. It portrays a duel between Krishna and Banasura. At the end of the picture is an additional detail of the story of *Aniruddha*, of Siva begging Krishna to spare Banasura (Narisa

---

2 See Vaidya, Harivamsa as quoted in Sahai (1978: 5)

1979: 61-63). This corresponds to the end of the story of *Aniruddha* which shows Krishna's great victory over Banasura and the god Siva at the same time.

THE POPULARITY OF THE *ANIRUDDHA* STORY IN THAILAND

There is no clear evidence as to when the Indian story of *Aniruddha* was introduced into Thailand. All that is known is that it has existed extensively in the North, the Northeast and the Central Region since the ancient times.

The Northern Thais have known the story since the 20th century B.E. as shown by the evidence of an old Northern law during the reign of King Kuena, the ruler of Chiengmai from 1910-1931 B.E.. It refers to a man informing an official that his wife was neglecting the household work, indulging in reading *Khlong Ussabarot* (Singa 1976: 1). This indicates an existence of a Thai literary work entitled *Ussabarot*, which is the *Aniruddha* story written in the *Khlong* style.

One of the North's oldest literary works - *Khlong Nirat Hariphunchai* which was written by a Northern poet in 2060 B.E. during the reign of King Ramathibodi I of the Ayutthaya kingdom (Prasert 1960: ch) - mentions the parting of Barot or Barasa and Usa in the *Usabarot* story or actually Aniruddha and Usa in the story of *Aniruddha*. This represents another piece of good evidence that the story was widespread in the Northern region since ancient times.

The *Aniruddha* story in the north of Thailand is found in various versions. The important versions are *Khlong Dan Usabarot* of the National Library version, *Khlong Usabarot* of Pa Hin Temple version, and *Ussabarasa Jataka* version.

In the Northeast, the popularity of *Aniruddha* story is evidenced by an ancient Northeastern literary work titled "*Thao Hung Thao Cueng*" or by another name "*Thao Ba Cueng Epic*", which is presumed to belong to the late 20th-21st century B.E. (Prakong 1992: 361). It contains an episode in which Bamarat parted from Usa Soikongphan; both of whom are actually Aniruddha and Usa in *Aniruddha* story.

At present, several versions of the manuscripts of *Aniruddha* story have been discovered in the Northeast. In most cases, names like "*Phra Kut Phra Phan*" or "*Usabarot*" appear in the titles, i.e. "*Lam Phra Kut Phra Phan*" of Ban Nong Paen version, "*Phra Kut Phra Phan*" of Khok Klang

Temple version, *"Phra Kut Phra Phan"* of Phra Ariyanuwat Khemmajari version, *"Phra Kut Phra Phan"* in the *Urangathat* legend version, *"Usabarot"* in the book titled *The History of Phra phutthabat Buabok Temple* and *"Usabarot"* which is written specifically for children.

The main content of the *Aniruddha* story in the above-mentioned versions concerns a highly-intelligent deformed man named *"Ai Salunkun"* who can answer the question posed by the god Indra. As a result, Indra castes his body with the mould that had been used in casting his own. This gives the man an appearance identical to that of Indra and leads to his seduction of Suchada, Indra's wife.[3] Indra then punnishes him by having him abandonned on the bank of the Mekong River in the kingdom of Sri Sattanaga. Later on, he becomes its king, Phra Phan. As for Suchada, she bids farewell to Indra and is reincarnated as Usa in the human world. She is born in a lotus flower and later becomes an adopted daughter of Phra Phan. Indra himself is reincarnated as Barot and enjoys Usa without Phra Phan's permission as a result of which Barot and Phra Phan fight. Eventually, Phra Phan is defeated and killed and Suchada succeeds in taking her revenge against Phra Phan or Ai Salunkun. Subsequently, Usa goes to live with Barot and is bullied by his other jealous wives. In the end, she returns to her hometown and dies of a broken-heart. The story closes when Barot comes after her and also dies.

It is the author's assumption that the story mentioned above could have originated from an ancient story in the Laotian Kingdom. The *Aniruddha* story exists in the old Laotian literary works. The content of the *Aniruddha* story in the Northeastern versions and in the Laotian version are exactly the same. Laos is Thailand's neighbour. There is also historical evidence of remnants of the influence of ancient Laos or the kingdom of Lanchang in Thailand's Northeastern region, along the Mekong River in the areas of the provinces of Loei, No'ng Khai, Udo'n Thani, Sakon Nakho'n and Nakho'n Phanom (Phaithun 1991: 111-114).

However, it is notable that the Northeastern versions of the *Aniruddha* story are quite different from the Indian original.

In the Central Region, the *Aniruddha* story is found in many styles and many versions and in larger number than those existing in the other parts of the country. It is remarkable that the story is extensively rewritten

---

[3] The name *Suchada* in the North and the Northeastern version is called *Sujitra* in the Central version.

for various kinds of performances - *Bot Lakho'n Nai, Bot Lakho'n No'k,* classical Thai dances (บทจับระบำ) *Bot Lakho'n Du'k Dam Ban* and tableau vivant. Besides, there are some works which are not intended for performance, i.e. the *Aniruddha* story for reading, the *Aniruddha* story representing the legend of Vishnu's reincarnation and the *Aniruddha* story in the form of a lullaby.

The story of *Aniruddha* was already widespread in the Central Region around the reign of King Bo'rom Trailokanat. Some of the Ayutthaya poets referred to the episode when a deity takes Aniruddha away from Usa in *"Thawa Thotsamat Khlong Dan"* and in *"Samutthakhot kham chan"*, important literary works of the period.[4] The story in these versions is the forerunner of *"Aniruddha Khamchan"*.It is possible that the story of *Aniruddha* of that time was simply a piece of oral literature, had not yet been written down, or possibly already written down, but then later disappearing. Quite notably, the story shows the influence of Sanskrit literature in that the two main characters are called by their names, preceded by the word *"Sri"* - *"Sri Aniruddha"* and *"Sri Usa"* - like the names of important characters in Sanskrit literature, such as *"Sri Rama"*, and *"Sri Krishna"* etc..

Another thing to be noted is that in the description in *Samutthakhot Khamchan* of Aniruddha entering Usa's bedroom, the old version refers to Phra Sri Phromrak[5] as the one who carries Aniruddha to her room. This is different from *Aniruddha Khamchan,* in which the guardian spirit in a banyan tree (พระไทรเทพารักษ์) is the carrier.

The worship of Phra Sri Phromrak was prevalent during the late Sukhothai Period and the early Ayutthaya Period (Maneepin 1980: 192-194).

---

[4] In *Thawathosamat Klong Dan,* there is clear evidence of the prevalence of the *Aniruddha* story as shown in the following *khlong:*

ศรีอนิรุทธราศร้าง	แรมสมร
ศรีอุษาเจียรไคล	คลาศแก้ว
เทวานราจร	จำจาก
ยังพร่ำน้ำวน้องแก้ว	คอบคืน

Apart from this, in *Samutthakhot kham chan,* the important episode of the carrying of Aniruddha to Usa by Phra Sri Phromraksa, is mentioned as follows:

กุศรีพรหมรักษตระกอง	อนุรุทเปรียบปอง
ไปสมอุษาเทพี	

[5] Sri Phromraksa is a character in Sanskrit literature called Sri Brahmaraksasa, a subject of the god Siva.

People called him "Phromrak Yakkuman" or "Phra Phanasabodi Sri Phromrak Yakkuman", guardian spirit of the forest.[6] There is evidence of this in Inscription No.45 of Sukhothai made in 1935 B.E. in"*Prakat Chaeng Nam Khlong Ha*" and in *"Lilit Phra Lo'"* which were important literary works of the early Ayutthaya Period.

There are presumptions that the tradition of worshipping Phra Sri Phromrak among Thais was passed down from ancient Cambodia where Phra Sri Phromrak was revered as a lesser god, ranking under principal gods like Vishnu and Siva. This is indicated by the *Yasovarman* Inscription, made between 1432 and 1433 B.E. (Maneepin 1980: 193).

For the above reason, it is possible that the Indian story of *Aniruddha* spread to ancient Cambodia which, in turn, passed it on to Thailand and this would explain why Phra Sri Phromrak is depicted as the matchmaker. This presumption is extremely likely because there is clear evidence that Brahmanism was adopted in ancient Cambodia and one or both of the religion's sects, *Vaisanavaite* and *Saivaite* were followed at one time or another. So it is possible that the Indian story was introduced into ancient Cambodia through its adoption of Hinduism.

The Central Region's written story of *Aniruddha* is found in many literary styles, as follows :

1. *Aniruddha kham chan* of the early Ayutthaya Period (Cholada 1992: 25).
2. *Bot Lakho'n Nai Unarut* in an abridged version by Prince Kromaluang Isarasuntho'n.
3. *Bot Lakho'n Nai Unarut* written by King Rama I.
4. *"Krishnavatar"* in *Narai Sip Pang* of the Royal Press edition.
5. *"Krishnavatar"* in *Narai Yisip Pang* .
6. *"Krishna avatar"* in *Narai Sip Pang* of the Wacharin printing-house edition.
7. *Khlong Aniruddha* by Khun Pholakannuchit in the reig of King Rama V.
8. *"Krishnavatar"* in *Lilit Narai Sip Pang* written by King Rama VI.
9. *"Khlong Suphalak Watrup"*, a composition for a classical Thai dance written by King Rama VI.
10. *Bot Lakho'n Du'k Dam Ban "Unarut"*, a musical play.

---

[6] Known in Sanskrit literature as *"Vanaspati"*.

11. *Bot Lakho'n Du'k Dam Ban "Krung Phan Chom Thawip"*, a musical play.

12. *Bot Lakho'n No'k "Unarut"* in the *"Som Usa"* episode.

13. *"Unarut"*, a tableau vivant composition.

14. *"Unarut"*, a lullaby

It is notable that *Aniruddha kham chan* tells the story which is the closest to the Indian original. It is also the author's assumption that the poet wrote *Aniruddha kham chan* through inspiration from many Indian versions and that existing in earlier Thai literature. For this reason, its content does not correspond to any of the Indian versions. Besides, it has a characteristic episode of the banyan tree spirit acting as a matchmaker -taking Aniruddha to Usa's bedroom. The author presumes that the poet of *Aniruddha kham chan* based the banyan guardian spirit on Phra Sri Phromrak, the guardian god of the forest in the former version in order to suit Thai belief. This romantic match-making is the origin of the phrase "Um Som", a well-known phrase in Thai fairy tales.

It is also notable that though the story in *Aniruddha kham chan* is the closest to the Indian original, in that it retains the episode of the battle between the gods. It emphasizes the love between Aniruddha and Usa. This largely constitutes an easy tendency for the later Thai tales of Aniruddha to deviate from the original story as a Hindu myth to fairy tales focusing on the love affairs and adventures of the hero which are characteristic of Thai tales known as *"Nithan cak cak wong wong"*

The other versions found in the Central Region were mostly based on or developed from *Aniruddha kham chan*. Most of them appear in the form of performances all of which contain the episode of *"Um Som"* or the episode following *"Um Som"*.

In the South, the story of *Aniruddha* has been found in only one version in the style of *Bot Lakho'n Unarut* of Songkhla version. From its style of writing, wording and content, the author presumes it to originate from the Central Region's court plays of the same title.[7] The story may

---

7 It is found very often that the poet adds the word "Buddhabongsa" (พุทธพงษ์) after the name of Aniruddha though it should be the word (อนุพงษ์) which means the one who succeed the god Narayana who sleeps on the back of Sesa Naga. Besides, the type of the versification, *klo'n*, is not the one used in the characteristic versification types of the Southern literature.

have been passed down by oral narration before being written down afterwards.

In summary, it is likely that the Indian story of *Aniruddha* was introduced into Thailand by various ways, one being together with Hinduism that came with Indian immigrants, another by way of ancient Cambodia and the other via the ancient Laos or Lanchang Kingdom.

It is also apparent that the story of *Aniruddha* exists extensively in Thai society, being found in every part of the country and in a variety of styles and versions. Yet, all of them have a consistent theme - untraditional love between Aniruddha and Usa - which is the main cause of the conflict between Aniruddha and Usa's father that erupts into war some time later.

However, each version of the story contains different details which are in accordance with each writer's intention of putting it to use in the following ways.

THE PURPOSE OF WRITING THE THAI TALES OF *ANIRUDDHA*

A careful study of the the Thai tales of *Aniruddha* has enabled a classification of their purposes into four categories, as follows:

1. To extol the god Vishnu who was reincarnated as either Krishna or Aniruddha.

2. To glorify the heroic deeds of Aniruddha.

3. To relate one of the Lord Buddha's former lives and at the same time to teach the readers and the listeners about the consequences of doing good and bad deeds.

4. To explain the history of ancient remains found in the locality.

Despite the fact that all four categories retain the corresponding substance of the Thai story of *Aniruddha*, they have a variety of details which make the tales somewhat different. This will be further explained as follows:

THE DIFFERENT VARIATIONS OF THE THAI TALES OF *ANIRUDDHA*

As mentioned above, the Thai tales of *Aniruddha* may be classified as having four purposes for composition, each with particular details. The differences of detail are as follows:

1. The *Aniruddha* story was composed to extol the god Vishnu who was reincarnated in the human world to suppress the villain Banasura. This type of story gives significance to the details of Vishnu's godhood, his

suppression of Banasura who was Siva's disciple and the war between Vishnu and Siva's subordinates as well as between Vishnu and Siva himself. In the end, it cites Vishnu's great victory over Siva and his subordinates including Banasura. In some versions, there are descriptions about the cause of Vishnu's reincarnation and his return to his abode. However, based on a study of minor details, this type of *Aniruddha* story may be divided into two sub-groups, one with Vishnu reincarnated as Krishna, grandfather of Aniruddha and the other with Vishnu reincarnated as Aniruddha himself.

1.1 Vishnu reincarnated as Krishna - the story appears in *Aniruddha kham chan, Krishnavatar* in *Narai Sip Pang* of the Royal Press edition, in *Narai Yisip Pang,* and in *Lilit Narai Sip Pang, Krishna Avatar* in *Narai Sip Pang* of the Wacharin printing-house edition. In *Aniruddha kham chan* and in *Krishnavatar* of *Lilit Narai Sip Pang,* there are no accounts of the cause of Vishnu's reincarnation and his return to his abode. The remainder say that he is reincarnated to suppress Banasura at Siva's invitation and when he had finished this important task, he returns to his abode.

1.2 Vishnu reincarnated as Aniruddha - the story appears in *Bot Lakho'n Nai Unarut* by Prince Kromaluang Isarasuntho'n. It is obvious that Vishnu is reincarnated in order to suppress Banasura. Aniruddha kills Banasura by himself, despite the absence of a war between Vishnu and Siva. At the end of the story, Aniruddha returns to his abode, the Sea of Milk , after his death. The author presumes that the story in the second sub-group was written at a later date. This was to honour Aniruddha even more; he was promoted from the status of the god Vishnu's grandson to that of the god himself.

2. The Aniruddha story composed to glorify the heroic deeds of Aniruddha; the story appears in *Bot Lakho'n Nai Unarut* of King Rama I, in *Khlong Dan Ussabarot* of the National Library edition and in *Khlong Usabarot* of Pa Hin Temple version. In this category, Aniruddha is the killer while not being Vishnu reincarnation. Though certain versions, such as the *Bot Lakho'n Nai Unarut* of King Rama I refer to Aniruddha as the grandson of Vishnu's reincarnation, they show his general behaviour to be similar to those of fairy-tale heroes, which is to say that they mainly involve his love affairs and heroic deeds.

3. The *Aniruddha* story written to relate one of the Lord Buddha's former lives and to teach the readers and listeners about the consequences of doing good and bad deeds is found in only one version, namely the *Ussaparasa Jataka* with details of Anirut as Lord Buddha, Phra Khittarat or Phra Phan as Phya Sihanurat, Phra Phimasen as King Sutthothana, Phra Nangarasi as Phra Seribut, Banasura as Phra Supaphut, Suchada or Usa as Ubonwanna Theri. There is an emphasis on the consequences of the characters' deeds in their former lives. For instance, Banasura's secret seduction of Suchada, the god Indra's wife, stems from Indra's adultery with his wife in his former life. However, the revange Banasura takes against Indra by seducing Suchada creates his debt of misdeed against her. This makes her follow him into their present lives to make him pay for it by being killed because of her. This version also says that Barot and Usa are confined in a gold and in an iron pen for seven days because, in their former lives, they had caught and caged a pair of birds for seven days. So this cruel deed affects them in the same way in their present lives. It is notable that Usa in this version has the characteristics of women in some *jatakas*, e.g. the *Kakati Jataka* and *Sussondi Jataka*, being considered untrustworthy and dishonourable because of her disloyalty towards her husband. She loves her husband and another man at the same time. One part of the story describes how she falls in love with Khun Thai, Aniruddha's younger brother, the moment her eyes meet his. The *Ussaparasa Jataka* contains additional details, intended to teach the readers and listeners to refrain from committing sins, especially the five precepts. Anybody who disobeys will suffer in hell after death. By contrast, anyone who behaves well will enjoy a happy life in heaven.

The above-mentioned elements clearly reflect the influence of Budddhism on Thai society, to such an extent that a tale in Sanskrit literature was adapted into a jataka in imitation of a Buddhist jataka, the way the *Ramayana* was adapted into the *Phra Lak phra Lam jataka* by the Northeasterners.

4. The *Aniruddha* story made up to explain the history of ancient remains found in the locality and which is called a local tale exists in the Northeast only. This is because in the area of Phra Phuttabat Buabok Temple in the province of Udo'n Thani stand the ancient monuments that can be explained by the local people using the story's corresponding descriptions and details.

In *Lam Phra Kut Phra Phan* of the Ban Nong Paen Temple version, *Phra Kut Phra Phan* of the Khok Klang Temple version and Phra Ariyanuwat Khemmajari's Legend of *Phra Kut Phra Phan,* there are details about the desertion of Pakho town of Krishna and Sri Sattanaga Muang Phan town of Banasura. These towns were deserted due to a lack of rulers.

As for Pakho town, after Aniruddha had died of a broken heart like his beloved Usa, Krishna ruled it until the end of his life. But as there was no heir to the throne, it became deserted.

In the case of Sri Sattanaga Muang Phan town, after Banasura was killed by Aniruddha, his son who was also Usa's younger brother, succeeded him. But when Usa died of a broken heart, he died too. As the town had no ruler after him, it too was deserted like Pakho.

At the beginning of the story of *Phra Kut Phra Phan* in the *Legend of Urangkhathat,* there are some historical accounts of Nakho'n Phan, a town surrounded by mountains. They recount that it was created by the magical powers of Suwananak, whose town Siva wanted to give to Banasura, if Siva emerged the victor. Furthermore, he would use his magical powers to create a mountain range all around it. When he was finally defeated by Siva, he did what he had promised. Hence, the town of Banasura amid mountains.

The *Usa-Barot* story in the History of *Phra Phutthabat Buabok,* and the *Usa-Barot* story for children contain details about the origins of the ancient remains located in the area of Phra Phutthabat Buabok Temple in Tambon Muang Phan, Ban Phue District of Udo'n Thani Province, such as:

Ho' Nang Usa: A towering rock structure explained by the local people as the *Ho' Kham* built by Banasura for his daughter Usa to keep her away from men.

Khokma Barot: The Place where Barot let his horse rest after arrival on his search for Usa before he wandered off following the singing voice of Usa until they met.

Bo'nam Nang Usa: A well (not very big) believed by the local people to be Usa's bathing place while residing in Ho' Kham and also the place where the couple met for the first time after Barot had received Usa's garland floating along the Mekong River.

Wat Phota and Wat Lukkhoei: Two rock structures standing close to each other which, according to local belief, used to be two temples built in a competition between Barot and Banasura under one condition that each

180

must finish it within one night and the loser must die. As the story goes, Banasura was tricked by Barot and Usa and did not finish it in time. He died as he had promised and the two temples have remained to this day in the form of the two rock structures.

There is a point to be noted in this type of *Aniruddha* story, i.e. that the battle between Barot or in fact Aniruddha and Banasura was not a deployment of force but was a contest of acumen. It also shows Banasura's integrity in his dying to honour the rule.

This type of *Aniruddha* story is used to explain the history of the ancient remains located in the compound of Phra Phutthabat Buabok Temple in Udo'n Thani Province only. This is because their appearances may well be explained by the story which was suitably adapted for this purpose.

From what has been described, it may be seen that the four types of Aniruddha story contain strikingly different contents, in accordance with the individual purposes of composition.

A classification by content of the *Aniruddha* tales has revealed that the first type, with its detailed story of the reincarnation of Vishnu wielding his supreme powers, may be a myth. The second type which describes in detail Aniruddha's heroic deeds and his love affair, may be categorized as a fairy tale. The third type with detailed links between the former and present lives of the main characters as well as the consequences of their good and bad deeds may be classified as a jataka. As for the fourth and last type which is applied in the narration of the history of the ancient remains located in the compound of Phra Phutthabat Buabok Temple of Udo'n Thani Province may be termed a local tale.

However, it is notable that overlapping details can exist between the first and the second types of *Aniruddha* story because of the similar characteristics of myths and fairy tales.

A study of the *Bot Lakho'n Nai Unarut* of King Rama I has shown some reference to the reincarnating act of the god Vishnu, the bravery and great ability in battle as well as the love affair of Vishnu's reincarnation who was an ancestor of Aniruddha's. This is to emphasize the fact that Aniruddha was the descendant of a god.

Furthermore, the fairy tale type of the story may be adapted into a myth, i.e. the *Bot Lakho'n Nai Unarut* of Prince Kromaluang Isarasuntho'n which is an abridged version and promotes the status of

Aniruddha as the grandson of Vishnu's reincarnation to the reincarnation of Vishnu himself. This does not contradict with the story and even upgrades the status of the hero.

As mentioned earlier, the Indian story of *Aniruddha* spread to Thailand a long time ago, since the 20th century B.E. It either came directly from India or by way of other countries, namely the ancient Kingdoms of Cambodia and Laos (known as Lanchang). The Thai tale of *Aniruddha* closest to the Indian original is *Aniruddha kham chan*, a written version by a poet from the Central Region. The one presumed to have come by way of ancient Cambodia is the version prior to *Aniruddha kham chan*, from the early Ayutthaya Period. There is evidence of it in *Thawathotsamat Khlong Dan* and *Samutthakhot kham chan*. As for the version introduced through ancient Laos, it is found in the Northeast. Noteworthy is its tragic ending, with the death of both the hero and the heroine. Besides, there is evidence of the places claimed to originate from the story in this region as well.

The fact that the story of *Aniruddha* is found in dozens of versions in all parts of the country - the North, the Northeast, the South and the Central Region - clearly shows its popularity among the Thai people.

While of Indian origin, the adopted story has been altered and adapted in accordance with various purposes, based on the fashion of the Thai society of the period and locality. The version composed in the early Ayutthaya Period is very close to the original in Sanskrit literature, probably because of the great Sanskrit influence on Thai society at that time. This can be seen in the use of Sanskrit words in many important literary works of the period. Beliefs about Hindu gods are quite evident in the eulogy and contents of important literary works such as *Prakat Chaeng nam Khlong Ha* and *Lilit Yuan Phai*. Besides, many important characters in Sanskrit literature are mentioned in Thai literary works of that period too. Apart from these, Cambodian textbooks which Thais had brought from Cambodia after winning the great war over the Cambodians were counter-checked against those in Sanskrit. This shows the strong influence of Sanskrit on Thai culture. Later on, when the Thais liked to read and listen to the stories about romantic and adventurous heroes while their faith and belief in Hindu gods was waning, the*Aniruddha* story was then composed in the style of a fairy tale. When Thai society was under the strong influence of Buddhism, the story was adapted into a jataka. At the place with natural structures corresponding to the *Aniruddha* story's descriptions, it was remade into a suitable local tale.

The study of the prevalence and diversity of content of the *Aniruddha* story in Thai literature has revealed its popularity among the Thai as well as its other roles besides providing pleasure or emotional enjoyment for Thai society. It is also useful as a means of teaching appropriate and inappropriate social behaviour, which to follow and which to reject, by comparison of the characters' model conduct. Furthermore, it also serves as a narrative of the history of some ancient remains like those in the compound of Phra Phutthabat Buabok Temple in Tambon Muang Phan, Ban Phue District, Udon Thani Province, making the local people proud of the antiquity and importance of their locality.

REFERENCES

Cholada Ruengruglikit
  1992 Wannakhadi Thai ru'ang Anirut : kan su'ksa wikhro'
        (The Thai Texts of Aniruddha: An Analytical Study). A
        Thesis submitted for the degree of Doctor of Philosophy,
        Department of Thai, Graduate School, Chulalongkorn
        University.

Dowson John
  1961 *Classical Dictionary* , London : Routledge & Kegan Paul.

Jiraphat Praphanwittaya
  1990 Pratchaya khwamchu'a lae naeo khit mai nai mahabarata
        (*Beliefs and Concepts in the Mahabharata: Influence on Thai
        Culture),* Bangkok: Department of Eastern Languages,
        Faculty of Arts, Chulalongkorn University.

Langlois M.A.
  1834 *Harivansa ou Histoire de la Famille de Hari Tome seconde,*
        London : Parbury allen and Co.

Macdonell, A.A.

1971 *A History of Sanskrit Literature,* Delhi : Motilal Banarsidass.

Maneepin Phromsuthirak

1980 Hindu Myth in Thai Literature with Special Reference to the Narai Sip Pang A Thesis Submitted for the Ph.D. degree of the University of London, School of Oriental and African Studies.

Mani Vettem

1975 *Puranic Encyclopaedia,* Delhi: Motilal Banarsidass.

Narisa Photidej

1979 Rup khaorop phra kritsana nai esia akhane (The Krishna Idols in Southeast Asia). A Thesis submitted in Partial Fulfillment of the Requirements for the Degree of Bachalor of Liberal Arts, Department of Archaeology, Silpakorn University.

Phaithun Mikuson

1991 Isan nai prawattisat (Isarn in History). In *Isarn on the occasion of 55th Anniversary of Isdarn Association,* Bangkok: The Thanawit Press.

Phouvong Phimmasone

1959 *Literature, Kingdom of Laos,* Rene de Berval et al. Saigon: France-Asie.

Prakong Nimmanahaeminda

1992 Mahakap ru'ang Thao Ba Cu'ang: kan su'ksa choeng wikhro' (The Thao Ba Chueng Epic: An Analytical Study. AThesis Submitted for the Degree of Doctor of Philosophy, Department of Thai, Graduate School, Chulalongkorn University.

Prasert Na Nagara
   1960 *Khlong Nirat Haripunchai,*   Bangkok: The Satreesara Press.

Rene de Berval
   1959 *Kingdom of Laos The land of the million elephants and of
          the white parasol,* France : A. Bóntemps Co., Ltd.

Sahai Sachinand
   1978 *The Krsna Saga in Laos* , Delhi: B.R.Publishing Corporation.

Sanyal J.M. (trans.)
   N.D. *The Srimad-Bhagabatam of Krishna-Dwaipayana Vyasa
          Vol.V,* Calcutta : Oriental Publishing Co.

Shastri J.L.
   1990 *Ancient Tradition and Mythology Series,* Delhi : Motilal
          Banarsidass.

Singkha Wanasai.
   1976 *Ussabarot Lannathai literature in the Reign of King Kuena
          transliterated book No1,* The Lanna Study Programme
          Chiengmai: Chiengmai University.

Thompson Stith
   1997 *The Folktale,* California : University of California Press.

Wilson H.H. (trans.)
   1961 *The Vishnu Parana A System of Hindu Mythology and
          Tradition,* Calcutta: Punthi Pustak.

Winternitz M.
   1927 *History of Indian Literature Vol I,* Calcutta : University of
          Calcutta.

THREE PHRA MĀLAI MANUSCRIPTS AT HARVARD UNIVERSITY'S SACKLER MUSEUM : SHOULD THEY BE CONSIDERED CLASSICAL OR REGIONAL?

Priyawat Kuanpoonpol

Among the manuscripts (*samut thai*) collected by Philip Hofer in the 1960's, three Phra Mālai illustrated manuscripts are some of the most interesting. They date from the Ratanakosin era, probably in the mid-19th century.[1] The texts are written in Mul Khmer script, with polychromatic illustrations on some pages, flanking each side of the text. Two of these, numbered 1984.521 and 1984.522, are very similar in appearance, being of approximately the same size and width (5 1/2 by 25 5/8 in.), containing 48 folio pages. The contents of the pages are arranged in the same format: the first pages are devoted to an adoration of the three gems, followed by citations of canonical passages to be recited. According to a former monk, each citation leads into the bulk of the text which is then recited from memory. The monk who is the leading reciter reads from the book, and the assembled reciters join him. In the manuscripts, illustrations of monks chanting the canon accompany these recitative passages, capturing the scene in real life. After each lead-in passage, the name of the text is mentioned. The passages cited are in the book of the *Abhidhamma* , because the manuscripts are used for funerals when monks chant the *Abhidhamma* (*suat phra aphitham*). When the Pali passages end, Phra Mālai's story begins and continues to its completion some forty folio pages later. There is no colophon or dedication page, even though the manuscripts have obviously been carefully and artistically prepared.

The third text, 1984.440, is a small black book with undecorated covers. There is no scriptural passage. The book begins with pictures of soldiers and officials of various ranks spread across verso and recto sides of the

---

1. According to คุณก่องแก้ว วีระประจักษ์ of the National Library, and อาจารย์ ยศ สนสีมาตรั้ง of the Fine Arts University, the style of the script and colours of the illustrations definitely place the manuscripts in the early Ratanakosin era.

pages. The text begins unceremoniously in a quick hand that is often difficult to decipher. Bearing no apparent connection to the illustrations, the writing in the manuscript begins three quarters of the way into the text of the *Phra Mālai Klo'n Suat* (*PMKS*), at a passage describing three kinds of Bodhisattvas. While the nature and function of the first two texts are fairly clear, what sort of effort does the last manuscript represent? Is it for aiding memory? Is it simply a book of pictures with these verses added to increase auspiciousness? How can these texts help us understand the origin, production, and transmission of the *PMKS* , in so far as these factors are significant for determining their genre(s)?

The text begins with a short introduction of the monk Mālai, a divine *thera*. Illuminations show the monk going on his alms-begging round, being greeted and offered food by pious men and women. The story proceeds to descriptions of hell scenes accompanied by graphic illustrations of various kinds of torture. The story proper, i.e., that which is found in the *Māleyyadevattheravatthu* (*MDV*) begins with the offering of eight lotuses by a poor man. Phra Mālai, having received the flowers, soars through the upper realms to worship at the shrine of the Buddha's top-knot in Indra's heaven. His conversation with Indra concerning various gods and goddesses occasions a discussion of their good karmic rewards. Each god and goddess is mentioned with the name of his/her meritorious store (*sambhāra*), and the good things he/she, having been reborn in heaven, is receiving through these merits. After exhibiting a correspondence of good deeds with their respective meritorious acquisitions, the correspondence being a qualitative transference of the deed to its fruition, the thera finally speaks with the Metteyya Buddha. This Buddha of the future, also called Phra Si An (Skt. *Srī Āryamaitreya*), describes specific excellences of his kingdom that will come into existence: there will be no sickness, infirmity, hunger, hatred, enmity, or any other human weakness. Rather, there will be be peace and prosperity everywhere with a minimum amount of effort to cultivate them. The narrative closes with the frame story of the poor offerer of eight lotuses being reborn in Tusita heaven and living happily in the company of gods and goddesses.

Many excellent works in Thai, English, and French have been written on the subject of this text, the last and perhaps most comprehensive bing Bonnie Brereton's dissertation, the *Phra Mālai Legend in Thai Buddhist Literature: A Study of Three Texts*. In this paper, I will examine these

187

three manuscripts from the Hofer collection in regard to the problems assigning them to a genre. As Bonnie Brereton mentions in her dissertation, there are several Mālai versions in Thai. Indeed, every region has its own version, and even seems to use it in a different way (1992: 19-28).

Judging from the language, script, and orthography, the three manuscripts under discussion are from the central region. The *PMKS* texts of the central region are fairly uniform in all manuscripts I have seen, varying only in words or syllables. Although a large number of *PMKS* manuscripts deposited in temples have not been closely examined, edited texts based on several manuscripts are fairly uniform. An alleged Ayutthaya version edited and published by Mr. Jate preechanon from manuscripts in the National Library is much the same as the Sisakrabue (Thonburi) version compiled by Supaporn Makchang. The two complete *PMKS* in the Hofer collection do not differ significantly from these edited versions.

The origin of this text is still unclear. Despite the fact that all regions have their own versions, all clearly related to an original Pali version, and in spite of the fact that each local version is a uniform text, there is no mention of an author or authorship. We are ignorant not only of the provenance of the Pali text, but also of its rendition into regional versions in Thai. Scholars tacitly accept that the *Phra Mālai Klo'n Suat* is the work of a single unknown and unknowable author.

Mr. Jate Preechanon, introducing his 1992 edition, states that having asked Sri Lankan and Burmese monks and received the response from both that this text does not exist in Sri Lanka and Burma, he concludes that the vernacular and Pali versions must be of Thai origin. Jete believes that the Pali version was composed by a learned monk of Sukhothai named Vilasathera, and that the Ayutthaya vernacular version was composed in the latter part of the Ayutthaya period by a learned commoner, a monk or an official well-versed in Pali, after Prince Thammathibet composed the *Phra Mālai Kham Luang* (*PMKL*) in 2280 B.E. (1737 A.D.) according to the Prince's own statement in the introductory verses. Jete does not cite any evidence for his beliefs. Another Thai scholar, Supaporn na Bangchang, also believes that the Pali text was composed in Thailand while Supaporn Makchang thinks it originated in Burma. (See discussion in Brereton 1992: 50-60)

We may also consider the problem of a relationship between the Pali, the popular (*klo'n suat*) and the royal (*kham luang*) versions. Scholars disagree as to the time and place of origination of the *MDV* , but most date it between the 11th and 16th centuries, well before the 18th century (Brereton 1992: 50-60; Collins 1993: 9-11). The Pali text was probably well-known and popular among monks and intellectuals in Thailand when Prince Thammathibet composed the *PMKL* out of a desire to please the king and to increase his merits so as to see the Metteyya Buddha. The author made his creatorship and motive known in the composition itself. However, it is not clear whether the popular version was already in existence at that time? The *kham luang* and the *klo'n suat* differ sufficiently in style and compositional structure that it may be said that one was not a conscious imitation of the other, but one could have been composed independently because the other vernacular text was already very popular. The common people who wanted to hear a Phra Mālai recitation in Thai would not enjoy hearing the ornate royal version with its many Indic words. On the other hand, the royal circle probably required a version for its own use in the courtly ceremonies. What, then, is the difference between the two versions so that the royal version was signed and authored, but the popular one was not? Did both belong in the same genre of religious or secular literature? Do they today?

The soteriological benefits accruing from the composition and recitation of this text are evident, although the *PMKS* manuscripts are not often found to be dedicated by commissioners hoping to gain merits from them. Among the five manuscripts of the Sisakrabue Temple that Supaporn Makchang examined, she found one manuscript of the Ratanakosin era that was dated 2470 B.E; the colophon mentions that it was created as a memorial to a husband and wife and a means to promote faith in the religion. (Supaporn 1981: 6) An Ayutthaya manuscript has a colophon with the name of the "creator" who hopes the manuscript help him to nibbana, but this "creator" also specifically asks to be reborn in the time of Phra Si Ān. The meritorious benefits of the Mālai text seem not to arise primarily or purely from "creating," i.e., commissioning a text to be copied and preserved in the temple. Rather, they arise from hearing the text recited. This is particularly true of the *PMKS* , for the future Buddha, Phra Si Ān, sends a message via Phra Mālai exhorting those wishing to meet him to hear the entire Vessantara cycle in one day, to adore it with flowers, incense, food offerings, and festive decorations. (Supaporn 1981: 70) This approach to a sacred text is not different from Hindu and Mahāyāna devotionalism, in which whole texts or mantraic pasages, or syllables, are copied and recited as an efficacious means of transporting the reciter to the realm of that deity. This repetitive and recitative process is well known in several Mahāyāna Buddhist schools, such as the Pure Land, the Nichiren Shoshu, and so on. Vaiṣṇava devotionalism is also well known for the traditional practice of reciting and hearing: devotees are urged to love and worship Krishna through reciting and hearing the *Bhāgavatapurāṇa*. Hearing a recitation of the *Rāmāyaṇa* in one day also brings much grace and blessing from Rāma.

These devotional tendencies which are thought uncharacteristic of Theravāda Buddhism led Phaya Anuman Rajadhon to link Phra Mālai with the Bodhisattva Kṣitigarbha (Brereton 1992: 60). Furthermore, concerns on the part of the *PMKS* with the demise and resurgence of the religion, and the faith in a future Buddha's powers to bring about perfections in the world, recall the *Mahāyāna sūtras* such as, for example, the *Bhadrakalpa*, an oft-copied Tibetan text dedicated to the quick recovery of a sick person or to the smooth passage of a deceased person. The story of the Phra Mālai is also reminiscent of the Mahāyāna Boddhisattva's vow not to attain nirvana until all suffering creatures have been saved.

If these elements in the *PMKS* derive from Mahāyāna Buddhism, then they must have been present at some time and in some form in the Sinhalese Buddhism, if the Pali *Māleyyadevattheravatthu* was indeed composed in Sri Lanka. If it was composed in Southeast Asia, then the Mahayanistic elements must have been indigenous to Southeast Asia. Neither of these possibilities is out of the question. Many schools of Buddhism existed in Sri Lanka. It is also well known that Mahāyāna Sanskritic Buddhism flourished from early medieval period in Burma. (Ray 1936) However, these allusions to a future Buddha and his utopia exist in the *Cakkavattisīhanandasutta* of the *Dīghanikāya*, a fact that is also noted by Steve Collins in the introduction to his translation of the *MDV*. In this sutta, the Buddha foretells the coming of the Buddha Metteyya and the latter's perfect world. Conditions of Metteyya's utopia as they are described in the *MDV* and *PMKS* can also be found in the *Aggaññasutta* of the *Dīghanikāya*. Therefore, we can for the time being put the hypothesis of a Mahayanistic influence aside.

In considering whether the *PMKS* is religious or secular, we may look back to its posible Sri Lankan origin. The *MDV* has been much linked with the *Rasavāhinī* (*RV*) (Denis 1963: 19-46), a medieval Sinhalese collection of stories about people of various types who find refuge in Buddhism. The *RV* contains edifying tales that are, strictly speaking, not sacred literaturebut which promote greater faith in the religion. In genre and style, it is not different from similar medieval compositions in Sanskrit, such as the *Daśakumāracarita* of Daṇḍin or the *Kathāsaritsāgara* of Somadeva, except for the fact that works in Sanskrit are novelistic and secular; they are adventure stories involving a variety of people in different stations and circumstances. The *RV* , however, is distinguished by its religious overtone. It may give us a clue to an essential characteristic of the the Phra Mālai story as regards the question of genre.

While secular, novelistic works in Sanskrit are authored, and Pali compositions of the *vaṃsa* and biographical types even of the later periods, however, are authored by named, individual monks, the authorship of the *RV* is nebulous. It is said to have been originally composed by Mahindathera and subsequently edited and redacted by named monks, Raṭhapāla Thera and Vedeha Thera. A ṭikā called *Sārattha-dīpanī* was composed by Sirsiddhattha Mahāthera. (Saeng 1974: 1-2) The *RV* is in this respect akin to *purāṇa* s or the epics whose authorships are attributed to legendary sages, but its prose style, formal contents, and depictions of lives of ordinary people, set it apart from those genres. Thus, the *RV* seems to be a cross between the traditional Sanskritic *smṛti* and a medieval novelistic work. Perhaps for this reason, it is never considered a truly sacred religious text and belongs in a genre of semi-sacred literature that promotes, through the adventures of past believers, the zeal to practice the religion and its prescriptions.

The *MDV* and *PMKS* probably belong in this genre of semi-sacred literature. The reason for a lack of colophon, with the name and date of an author/scribe may be precisely that since the works are not considered sacred by the community of their users in the narrow sense of the word, the merits are gained not by commissioning and copying the texts; hence, there is no need to inscribe the names of the commissioner, the copier, those to whom the merits are dedicated, and the dedication. Since the text itself is not sacred, the purpose of copying is to preserve it for use rather than to earn merits by creating a piece of sacred literature. This hypothesis is supported by the fact that in the Northern and Northeastern traditions, the *PMKS* is a prelude to a religious, merit-making, event, namely the hearing of the *Vessantara jātaka* cycle. It is the hearing of the *Vessantara jātaka* , rather than the *PMKS* , that earns the worshipper a rebirth in the realm of Phra Si Ān. Phra Mālai helps to prepare them for the religious act by directing their mind to the essential means and ends of meritorious deeds.

In the central tradition, the recitations of the *PMKS* accompany wakes and funerals and often degenerate into comic performances. Thus, it seems evident that the *PMKS* and its performance are not religious in the strictest sense, but they support a religious act or occasion, such as the chanting of the *Abhidhamma* at funerals or the recitation of the *Vessantara* cycle at the Retreat of the Rainy Season. The *PMKS* is not recited for the sake of obtaining merit-accruing benefits, but rather for secular, aesthetic and emotional, benefits of the participants in funerals, marriage, and so on-- events that are dominated by their religious and ritual functions.

On the other hand, as regards authorship, since the *MDV* and the *PMKS* are semi-sacred and foretell the coming of the Metteyya Buddha, an ordinary composer could not have named his humble self as its author, any more than any one person may claim to have authored the *Rāmāyaṇa* or a *purāṇa*. For, such foretellings ccould be made only by an extraordinary person, namely, the Buddha himself. Once the prophecies have been recorded in the canon and fallen in the domain of transmission, a literary recounting of the Buddha's forecasts in a proper genre of 'history' (*vaṃsa*) or 'biography' (*carita*), can be appropriately authored with embellishments by individuals. It is in this type of literary genre that the works of Prince Thammathibet and other royal compositions fall; the *Phra Mālai Kham Luang* and similar compositions are properly considered court literature.

Eschatology and devotionalism are not considered characteristic of orthodox Theravāda Buddhism, but they are clearly present in the *MDV, RV,* and *PMKS*. The seed of devotionalism, furthermore, lies in the *Dighanikāya* itself in which the Buddha speaks of the fall and rise of the religion, foretelling the advent of the future Buddha who is the "Exalted One even as I am now." (Rhys- Davids 1965: *Dighanikāya* iii.76: 24-25) It seems only natural that "popular," vernacular texts grow out of scriptural passages. Moreover, works of semi-sacred literature may tell us a great deal about. popular Buddhism in its cultural milieu, a Buddhism rich in affective qualities and different from the straight and narrow doctrines of the orthodox and official religion. These texts may even give us clues, about changes in religious beliefs and attitudes, which are unavailable in other kinds of historical evidence.

The fact that it has been little altered seems to support the idea that people who use the *PMKS* recognize it as a unity of integrated parts that elicit certain responses from the audience. In theory, the Sinhalese *RV* was possibly composed or redacted in its final form with the aim of evoking the aesthetic sentiments, i.e., the *rasa*, prescribed by Indian Sanskrit poetics. Similarly, the *PMKS* was created with a view to stimulate and mix the audience's raw feelings with religious instructions. These emotive pleasures are aesthetic and literary, arising from the use of figurative language, versification, visceral descriptions of pains and delights, and finally the lofty portrayals of the utopia of Phra Si An. While descriptions of sins and tortures may be regional inventions, the serene delights of a perfect society are traced directly to canonical literture.

CLASSICAL OR REGIONAL

As a composed work, is it classical or regional? Here, if by the word 'classical' we mean, as we usually do, works that are commissioned, associated with, and recognized by the courtly circle, then *PMKS* is only marginally classical. Even with its varied literary and prosodic techniques--uses of figures of speech, rhymes and alliterations, metrical variations, and so on--our text is relatively unpolished. It is poetry to the ears of ordinary, perhaps country, folks. Compared to the more ornate and melliflous *PMKL* , the *PMKS* lacks a fine interweaving of Indic with Thai words and subtle allusions that are the mark of the royal version. The *PMKS* has several stock phrases, which are never found in the royal version, and these phrases betray a recitative nature that lends itself to extemporaneous, folk improvisation.

Today, with the recitative tradition fast disappearing, this text further eludes being typed as a classical work. We can consider it regional literature in the same way that we consider the *Phra Mālai* texts of Lanna or Isan regional. Here, we are faced with an inherent bias in our use of the word 'region,' with Central Thailand being the center relative to which all other areas are regional. Beneath the classificatory opposition of "classical" and "regional," the *PMKS* has the basic characteristics of popular traditional literature. We see reflected in it common people's joys and aspirations mingled with the religious tenets made accessible to them through the vernacularization of canonical and semi-sacred (perhaps "allegedly non-canonical" as coined by Somadasa and Hallisey) religious literatures.

Phra Mālai in Van Gennep's classificatory scheme is a liminal figure. Not only does he expedite transitions, but he also belongs to a group of Buddhist intermediary figures who embody passages. Popular religions and popular or 'regional' literary traditions are perhaps inextricable, because they coincide on highly emotional occasions at crucial passages in life.

Passages are consecrated by rites. In addition to religious rites performed by priests and monks, there are also lay rituals. By his liminal nature, Phra Mālai assists transitions such as in marriage and death. He embodies immanent changes--in life and death, in heaven and hell, from samsara to nibbana. In these transitional situations, a recitation's emotive contents mirror the feelings of individuals who may find themselves unable to verbalize them. In the case of death, for example, through fluid passages of Phra Mālai to various realms, a relative of the deceased perceives even in his/her grief that death is not an end, but only an end of a phase and a beginning of a new journey. With the monk as their messenger, the relationship of the relatives with the deceased also does not end but persists, through messages of admonition and hope brought back by the monk from another realm and through merits sent to relatives beyond.

Phra Mālai is an aesthetic and affective catalyst because he is approachable even as he approaches the august Indra and Metteyya whom ordinary mortals can only aspire to see in utopia. This humble monk has the power and wisdom to take a poor man's ordinary offering and make it a means to attain divine happiness. Thus, while Moggallāna Thera is a canonical figure known to have relieved sufferings of creatures in hell, it is rather to an ordinary, fictive figure of Phra Mālai that ordinary people seek for emotional refuge. The text takes care to identify the two theras by saying that they are of the same mold (กุจพิมพ์เกียว).

Phra Mālai, in other words, is made in the mold of Moggallāna Thera transposed to a local setting, a canonical personage becomes a cultural figure. The event of performing the *PMKS* , i.e., the context and use of its recitation, describes the religious cosmos for worshippers who even in their comic revelry traverse the whole ideational realm of the religion. Each hearer may identify himself/herself with a poor man who rises spiritually above his mean circumstance through a gift of eight lotuses picked while bathing and washing away the grimes of workaday life.

The elevation of a poor man to the realm of Indra and Metteyya surely means more than a change in social and material status. Or, to put it more bluntly, the *PMKS* is more than a story of getting the heavens for mere eight lotuses. A strain of devotionalism courses through the text: an adoration is made to the image of a Buddha's relic as a reminder of his renunciation that was the source and cause of liberating wisdom. This liberation ultimately gives justice to all unjust conditions against which a poor man is helpless. Their hopes are placed in a future Buddha, who has for sixteen epochs striven to build up perfections for the sake of creating a perfect world for weaker beings. Anybody's humble offering is a token of faith in that perfect society which will come about when all people have attained Buddha-like perfections. The *PMKS* implies that when people are perfect in morality and piety, the universe will also be perfect, and vice versa.

CONCLUSION

These three manuscripts in the Hofer collection invite a thorough study. They are beautifully copied and illustrated. Even without colophons and dedication pages, it is clear that their creators wished to create an aesthetically pleasing artifact. The small book, with its scrawled hand-writing, however, still escapes me as to its purpose and function. Thorough comparisons of these texts with others in various regions of Thailand will surely yield more knowledge about how these texts were copied and transmitted, and such studies will enable us to reconstruct a stemma leading to an "original" text, if there is such a thing.

Like the central figure's liminal character, the *PMKS* crosses boundaries of literary genres. Less than a religious text and more than a 'regional' literary composition, it combines religion with aesthetic sentiments. It is a communal text, for it is meant to be recited in an assembly of people rather than read in private by individuals. Because of its liminal nature, its central character expedites and ushers in changes, passages from one phase of being to another. The text moves from scenes of fear to sorrow to scenarios of ultimate bliss, from life to death, and finally to the realm transcending all transitions.

The lack of information concerning Phra Mālai texts invites us to further examine a genre of composed but authorless works. The questions of how these compositions came into being, how they retained their stable form through the centuries, and how they have been transmitted, are merely rough objectives for a serious investigation. If there was a single original Thai composition from which all others have been copied, where and how was it produced? Why are there no significant variations among extant manuscripts? The variants and idiosyncracies of these and other similar manuscripts, rather than their uniformity, will be most informative of their history and challenging to our reconstructive imagination.

REFERENCES

Brereton, Bonnie Pacala.
   1992   *The Phra Mālai Legend in Thai Buddhist Literature: A Study of Three Texts.* A Ph. D. dissertation. Ann Arbor, Michigan: University of Michigan.

Collins, Steve.
   1993   *"Braḥ Māleyyadevattheravatthum ".* Pali Text Society 1993: 1-96.

Denis, Eugene.
   1963   *Brah Maleyyadevattheravatthum: Légende bouddhiste du saint Thera Maleyya.* A Ph. D. dissertation. Paris: Sorbonne.

Dhaniniwat, Prince
   1944   *"'Phra Mālai, Royal Version, 'by Chaofa Kung, Prince Royal of Ayutthaya".* Journal of Siam Society, 32 (Oct.): 69-73.

Jate Preechanon (รองอำมาตย์ตรีเจษฎ์ ปรีชานนท์)
   1992   *Phra Mālai klo'n suat chabap Ayutthaya.* Bangkok: published by the author.

Ray, Nihar-Ranjan.

1936.   *Sanskrit Buddhism in Burma*. Amsterdam: S. J. Paris.

Rhys-Davids, T. W., and C. A. F. (trs.)

1965   *Dīghanikāya* , Vol. 3. London: Luzac & Co. Ltd. for the *PTS*.

Saeng Monwithun(tr.)

1974   *Rasavāhinī* . Amphawa, Samutsongkhram: Ministry of
        Education

Supaporn Makchang

1981   *Phra Mālai klo'n suat (Samnuan Wat Sisakrabue): Kan truat
        so'p chamra lae kan su'ksa priapthiap*. Thonburi: Centre for
        the Promotion of Cultural Development.

Thammathibet, Prince

1935   *Phra Mālai Kham Luang*. Reprint. Bangkok:
        Akso'nniphakhan Printers.

HEROISM AND EPIC VERSE-FORM : A STUDY FROM
LILIT YUAN PHAI AND THE EPIC OF *THAO CHEUNG*

Prakong Nimmanahaeminda

An important idea put forward by Jit Poumisak, an avant-garde scholar of the late 50s is vouched for by a study reported in this paper. If Thai literature is to be studied with the just benefits of scope and depth, the boundary which defines the traditional approach must be broadened to include the literary works of ethnic minorities as well as those rendered in the dialect branches of Thai language. Such literary contributions, as emphasized by Jit Poumisak would provide clues if not golden keys to many long standing literary questions, and enhance our appreciation of Thai classical literature (Jit 1981: 160). As a collary to Jit Poumisak's idea, the author of this paper proposes extension of the study to the literatures of Tai-speaking peoples in the neighbouring countries as well as in Thailand. The knowledge that comes out of such a study should form a significant basis for the understanding of the ways of living and thinking of our forbearers.

This paper is the result of a comparative study of two literary works; one is a master piece of Ayutthaya, *lilit Yuan Phai* and the other a master piece of Lanchang, *Thao Cheung*. Both belong to the epic genre. The study concentrates on comparing two main literary aspects i.e. 'Exaltation of heroism' and 'Verse Styles'.

In this study, the author chooses to adopt the definition of an epic along the line of the western theory of literature, i.e.

> "Epic or heroic poem is a long narrative poem on a great or serious subject, related in an elevated style, and centering on a heroic or quasi-divine figure on whose actions depend the fate of a tribe, a nation or the human race" (Abrams 1975: 49-51).

HISTORICAL ORIGIN OF *THAO CHEUNG* EPIC
The original copy of *Thao Cheung Epic* survives to the modern times in the form of palm leaves incribed in *Thai No'i* alphabets. In all, there are

553 leaves corresponding to 1105 pages. The archived records of Rama I concerning Wiangcan 1882 A.D. describe the presentation of *the book of Cheung* to King Rama I in accordance with the royal wish.[1] The author of this paper is inclined to believe that *the book of Cheung* is indeed the palm leaves of *Thao Cheung Epic*. The transcribing of *Thao Cheung Epic* was carried out during the reigns of King Rama V and King Rama VI. The last transcriber, Mr Sila Virawongse not only trancribed *Thao Cheung* but also gave it the *Khlong* form. *Thao Cheung Epic* was first published in Thai in 1943. Mr Sila later emigrated to Laos where he published *Thao Cheung Epic* in *Thai No'i* alphabet in *wanakhadi San* from 1950 to 1954. The latest publication in Thai was undertaken by Mr Pricha Phintho'ng, the owner of the Siritham Printing Company in Ubonratchathani province in the Northeast.

The original and transcribed copies of *Thao Cheung Epic* have been carefully read by the author of this paper. The literary devices, styles and rhythms suggest strongly that the author of *Thao Cheung Epic* is probably a court poet of Lanchang Kingdom and the composition date may be roughly placed between the end of the fifteenth century to the beginning of the sixteenth century A.D. (see Prakong 1981). It appears that there were other authors who addded their contribution to the *Thao Cheung Epic*. This later addition comes in two parts - one on the rice-growing activities of Thao Cheung and the other on the events following Thao Cheung's death. However the original part remains dominantly long and requires no less than 4,000 *Khlong* for the full narration. The term *"Thao Cheung Epic"* used in this paper applies to the original part only.

The epic was composed to praise Thao or Phya Cheung as a hero of great renown. The plot of *Thao Cheung Epic* is to be found in the oral and written literatures of the Lanna, Sipso'ng Panna, Chiangtung, Lanchang and the Tai Dam tribal group. A Comparative study of different versions has found that most versions refer to the epic hero as Phya Cheung. The versions of Lanna, Lanchang and Tai Dam depict Thao Cheung or Phya Cheung as King of Ngoen Yang city state, while the version of Sipso'ng Panna places Phya Cheung as the first King of Sipso'ng Panna kingdom (Tavee 1986). All versions are however consistent in portraying Thao or Phya Cheung as a king of great valour who was skilled in the art of warfare and whose influence was felt even in faraway lands. His great heroic act

---

[1] For more detail see Prakong 1981.

was manifested in the defeat of the Kaew (Vietnamese) who laid siege on the city of Ngoen Yang. Thao Cheung not only repulsed the enemy but pursued them to their city of Pagan which soon fell to his men. As a legendary hero, Thao Cheung won respect and tributes from neighbouring states. He died a heroic death on the battlefield. Most versions differ on the identity of the adversary in Thao Cheung's last battle.

OUTLINE OF *THAO CHEUNG EPIC*

Thao Cheung Epic was composed on a plot taken from the oral tradition on the legendary Phya or Thao Cheung. The epic begins with the life story of Thao Cheung. He is one of the sons of King of Nakong. Their father dies when Thao Cheung is still a small child. The throne is succeeded by his elder brother. Thao Cheung in his youth falls deeply in love with an older woman. She is Nang Ngom Muan, daughter of the King of neighbouring Chiangkua and is Thao Cheung's cousin. Before they are about to be married, the Kaew (Vietnamese) led by Angka, grandson of the Kaew King attacks the city of Ngoen Yang and spark off a great war. Angka had previously sent an emisary to the city of Ngoen Yang to propose marriage between himself and a daughter of King of Ngoen Yang. Angered by Ngoen Yang's refusal, Angka with the support of Thao Kwa, another Kaew King who rules over the city of Pagan decides to seek revenge on Ngoen Yang. As Ngoen Yang begins to crumble under the enemy attack, Thao Seum, King of Ngoen Yang summons his nephew, Thao Cheung, to help him repulse the enemy. Thao Cheung engages the Kaew in a fierce battle and slays Thao Kwa. The Kaew army is in disarray and retreats to the city of Pagan. Thao Cheung follows in hot pursuit and enters the city of Pagan as the victor. Thao Cheung marries a daughter of Thao Kwa and establishes himself as King of Pagan.

Later on, Thao Cheung decides to return to Ngoen Yang leaving the control of Pagan to one of his generals. In Ngoen Yang, Thao Cheung is married to the two daughters of King of Ngoen Yang in a royal wedding ceremony and is crowned as King of Ngoen Yang.

Thao Cheung never forgets his old flame, Nang Ngom Muan. He sends for her, and arranges for her to be brought to Ngoen Yang. The union between Thao Cheung and Nang Ngom Muan produces a son who is to be known as Thao Hung.

There are two important figures in the names of Hun Bang and Ai Hing. Both are grandsons of Thao Kwa and have fought on the side of Thao Kwa in the war against Ngoen Yang. Instead of fleeing to Pagan with the main body of the defeated army, both take refuge in the city of Tum Wang ruled by King Fah Huan. Hun Bang and Ai Hing have allowed themselves enough time to prepare a new army which they lead in the campaign to regain control of the city of Pagan. Once again Thao Cheung beats off the attack, forcing Hun Bang and Ai Hing to ensconce themselves again in Tum Wang. Thao Cheung sends a mission to Tum Wang asking King Fah Huan to hand over Hun Bang and Ai Hing to him. King Fah Huan's outright refusal to comply, sets off a war between the two sides. It is Thao Cheung who takes the initiative in the war, but the odds of the battle turn against him. Thao Cheung suffers a mortal wound and dies on the battle field.

HISTORICAL ORIGIN OF *LILIT YUAN PHAI*

Lilit Yuan Phai falls into the Thai genre of exaltation poetry. It consists of two *Rai* and 286 *Khlong* s. Of the *Khlong*, four are *Khlong Si Suphap* and the rest *Khlong Dan* most of which are *Khlong Dan Bat Kuncho'n* type. Considered to be the first Thai epic poem, *Lilit Yuan Phai* was composed to commemorate the heroic act of King Bo'rom Trailokanat who ruled Thailand from 1448 to 1488 A.D. The occasion was the captive of the city of Chiangchu'n or Chaliang from the control of King Tilokarat of the Lanna Thai Kingdom.

Thai scholars are at variance concerning its authorship and the date when the work was composed. H.R.H. Prince Damrong Rajanubhap wrote in the introduction of the first publication of *Lilit Yuan Phai*, suggesting that the most likely date is during the reign of King Bo'rom Trailokanat's son, Ramathibo'di II who ruled Ayutthaya from 1491 to 1529 A.D.. Po' Na Pramuanmak thought the work was written during the reign of King Trailokanat, probably some time between 1474 to 1488 A.D., and naturally after the victorious war, but definitely before King Bo'rom Trailokanat wrote *Mahachat Khamluang* (Thailand 1963). Dr Nida Laoasunthorn identified King Trailokanat's son, Bo'romaracha III as the author of *Lilit Yuan Phai* (Niyada 1981). M.R. Suphawatana Kasemsri shares his view on the date of the composition with Po' Na Pramuanmak and proposed that the author of *Lilit Yuan Phai* was a Buddhist monk in the rank title of

Panyaphisan. He bases his supposition on the third line of the 58th *Khlong* which may be translated as "*Panyaphisan* sets out to celebrate the royal might" (Suphawatana 1988).

OUTLINE OF *LILIT YUAN PHAI*

Lilit Yuan Phai opens with a poem praising the Lord Buddha followed by a poem in exaltation of King Bo'rom Trailokanat. It then proceeds to tell the life story of the great king. From this, we learn that he was born at Tung Phra Uthai Sub-district and was enthroned after the death of his father. The story tells of royal engagements particularly the nurturing and promoting of religious affairs. Then comes the heroic war which was triggered by *Phraya Yutthisathira*, the renegade Chief of Chaliang abandoning Ayutthaya to join King Tilokarat of Lanna. For this act, King Bo'rom Trailokanat led an army to regain the city of Chaliang. The sanguinary battle which is described in lucid poetical style concludes with a victory for King Bo'rom Trailokanat. The narration which follows relates important events which include King Trailokanat taking monkhood and ordering the construction of Wat Buddhaisavara, the departure of one of King Trailokanat's sons on a pilgrimage to Sri Lanka, the ensuring of the moral weaknesses of King Tilokarat who ordered the executions of his own son and another faithful nobleman of the realm. *Lilit Yuan Phai* ends with poems in exaltation to the might and glory of King Trailokanat who had secured the allegiance of many vassal states.

IMAGERY OF HERO IN *THAO CHEUNG EPIC* AND *LILIT YUAN PHAI*

Both *Thao Cheung Epic* and *Lilit Yuan Phai* run the stories on a unified plot. Their theme is glorification of a legendary hero, and the authors of both epics have succeeded in keeping to the main theme from the beginning to the end.

In glorifying heroism, the authors of *Lilit Yuan Phai* and *Thao Cheung Epic* not only praise victory in war and the valour of their victorious heroes, but also try to create an image of an heroic leader who is divinely endowed with grace and inner power. Both King Trailokanat and Thao Cheung are extraordinary bordering on divine personages practically from the moment of birth.

The authors have deliberately brought into play the social values and beliefs of the time for the purpose of raising heroism to further heights. "The beliefs of the Lanchang folk of those times were built around the Thaen god who was held to be the creator of all things on earth. King and leaders were thus sent by the Thaen god to rule kingdoms. The *Thao Cheung Epic* speaks of Thao Cheung as being sent to the world by the Thaen god in response to the supplication of Thao Jom, father of Thao Cheung. The celebration of Thao Cheung's birth has a familiar ring of the divine touch. Kings and princes from near and distant lands bring gifts of white and working elephants befitting a mighty king. Hilltribes from the depths of the hinterlands bring an assortment of weapons and musical instruments as tributes to the newly born prince. The glorification of Thao Cheung is said to be renowned throughout Jambu Davipa as well as in the heavenly abode of Brahma. It seems obvious that the Buddhist concept of the world has already formed a strong impression on the Lanchang mind and coexisted with the belief in the indigeneous Thaen god.

The narration on the execution of war forms an inevitable part of the heroic poem. The author describes Thao Cheung's army which defends Ngoen Yang as an mighty force of massive strength. It consists of well-trained war elephants and men who are skilled in the art of elephant warfare. The mere gleams of light from the blades of drawn weapons perpetrate fear into the hearts of the enemy. The author goes on to glorify Thao Cheung's triumph over the vanquished enemy and favourably compares Thao Cheung's heroic deeds and valour with those of Rama and Arajun, heroes of two great Hindu epics. It seems certain that Ramayana and Mahabharata were already well known to the Lanchang people of that time. We will note here that the author has employed a powerful comparative narration to present a highly credible image of his hero.

In the battle to subdue Hun Bang and Ai Hing once and for all, Thao Cheung breaks the enemy's ranks and leads his men past the enemy's front line before he finds himself overpowered. Missiles rain on him and his men. Blood spills and flows like a great water way. Wounded, Thao Cheung fights on valiantly until he succumbs to a mortal wound. Thao Cheung's death is mourned by angels who descend to earth to escort his soul back to heaven.

There are striking similarities between the imagery of a hero in *Thao Cheung Epic* and *Lilit Yuan Phai*. The author of *Lilit Yuan Phai* projects the majestic grandeur of King Trailokanat also by resorting to the Hindu-Buddhistic beliefs which already held a powerful sway over the Ayutthaya social system of that time. Eleven Hindu gods: Brahma, Isavara, Vishnu, Indra, Yama, Vayu, Varun, Agni, Kuvera, Aditya, Chandra are melted down and cast into King Trailokanat in flesh and blood. The author also alludes to the ten royal codes of conduct and other royal virtues upheld by King Trailokanat. Not only is he skilled in the use of arms, but also knowledgeable in various sciences. Blessed with lion-like physique, he radiates grace and inspires awe. King Trailokanat's army is strong in all departments, be it deft foot soldiers, speedy charging horses, combat-ready war elephants, or sleek armed boats. In battle, the army displays extraordinary martial prowess in cutting down the enemy's ranks with the swiftness of thunder and lightening. King Trailokanat is indeed an embodiment of supernatural achievements. The author proceeds to compare King Trailokanat with heroes of time-honoured epics. The reader is thus told: as a warrior, King Trailokanat is greater than Rama who vanquishes Totsakan (Ravana). In valour King Trailokanat excels Arajun who fights and destroys his kinsmen, and in military science King Trailokanat is wiser than Lord Krishna.

SOCIAL CONTEXTS OF THE TWO EPICS

Upon careful examination of the origins to the two epics, one major difference clearly reveals itself to the reader. *Thao Cheung Epic* borrows its plot from an oral literature which had been passed on by word of mouth for about 200 years before it is given the written form, while *Lilit Yuan Phai* bases its plot on an actual historical event and was composed while the actual hero of the epic was still living. The two epics, however, share one very important feature. Both authors of the two great epics had skillfully combined the tonal beauty and natural sweetness of the Tai language with some Pali and Sanskrit loan words to present a fantastic rendition of grandious glorification of their heroes. In view of the fact that the use of the court language to express sensitivities of interpersonal relationships between characters of different social stratification was employed with such precision and refiness, one may safely assume that the authors of these two epics were in the class of court poets and nothing less.

A question which may be asked is whether the two authors had any motives besides dedicating their works to heroic glorification. Historic events surrounding the period when the works were composed may guide us to an answer. Let us take the case of *Thao Cheung Epic* first. As mentioned earlier, *Thao Cheung Epic* by virtue of its content, style, and language is thought to be composed by a court poet of Lanchang before the end of the fifteenth century and the early sixteenth century. In those intervening years, Vietnam and Laos were known to be at a loggerheads. During the reign of King Lan Kamdaeng of Laos (1426-1428 A.D.), a certain Vietnamese king had sent an ambassadorial mission to the Loatian King requesting a Laotian army to fight the Chinese which were about to attack Vietnam. King Lan Kamdaeng thus dispatched a Laotian army of 30,000 men to Vietnam with the Vietnamese ambassador. For some reason which is still imperfectly understood, the Laotian went over to the Chinese side. The war ended with the defeat of the Chinese and a large number of Laotian fighting men were captured. The event had badly severed the good relationship between Laos and Vietnam. In 1479, during the reign of a Laotian King in the name of King Chai Cakraphat Phaenpaeo, a Vietnamese King had succeeded in annexing the whole region of Tai Phuan and with the support of the Phuan attacked the city of Luang Phrabang. King Chai Cakraphat was forced to flee to the city of Chiangkhan, while his Viceroy, Uparat Chianglo engaged the Vietnamese army to slow down the Vietnamese advance of King Lan Kamdaeng. As soon as it was learned that King Lan Kamdaeng was in safe territory, Uparat Chianglo and his troops retreated by attempting to cross the Mekong River to the western side. In the middle of the stream of the great river Uparat Chianglo and his elephant were swept away by the powerful current and drowned. Some of his troops were able to cross to the other side of the river and regrouped in the city of Chiangkhan. King Chai Cakrapat sent an army commanded by his son to engage the Vietnamese army at the estuary of the Phun River and finally beat off the Vietnamese invaders (Term: 1987). The author of this paper would like to propose that *Thao Cheung Epic* was composed and brought out during or after the time when Lanchang was at war with the Vietnamese. It is possible that the author of *Thao Cheung Epic* wanted to remind the people of Lanchang as a morale booster that the Vietnamese army had been beaten by the Tai people before and in any case the Vietnamese army was far from being invincible, especially in face to face combat with the likes of Thao Cheung's army.

The author of this paper would like to re-emphasize at the risk of being repetitive that *Thao Cheung Epic* was probably written between the end of the fifteenth century and the early sixteenth century and in any case before 1520, for in 1520 a royal editct was declared, forbidding the propitiation rites of the spirits and ordering all shrines for such rites to be demolished. In view of *Thao Cheung Epic*'s allusions the worship of the spirits, the Vietnamese seige on Luang Phrabang and the subsequent drive of the Vietnamese from Laos in 1477, the date of *Thao Cheung*'s authorship may be narrowed down to between 1477 to 1520. It is of particular interest to note that although Thao Cheung was king of Ngoen Yang and a hero who hailed from Lanna, no single Lanna poet had ever thought of composing the like of *Thao Cheung Epic*. In Lanchang, not only the account of Thao Cheung was put in the epic form, but also other forms of oral and written tradition. It simply shows how deep the Laotian's feeling were towards Thao Cheung. As an additional footnote, the Tai Dam (Black Thai) who constitute one of the ethnic minorities in Vietnam of today also have a strong oral as well as written tradition of Thao Cheung. The author of this presentation is in the process of studying one written Tai Dam version of Thao Cheung. The study is still in the early stage and it is too early to tell whether the version being studied is a Tai Dam creation or a Tai Dam inherit the tradition from Laos. In any case some Tai Dam still maintain the tradition of singing and dancing praises to Thao Cheung, the legendary hero from Lanna for his victory over the Vietnamese. It is possible that the Tai Dam as an ethnic minority in Vietnam have a strong determination to maintain their identity and are in need of a legendary hero to keep alive the memory of the heroic past of the Tai people.

The social context under which *Lilit Yuan Phai* was brought out present a somewhat different picture. The political situation of the Ayutthaya Kingdom prior to King Bo'rom Trailokanat's enthronement was less than secure. At the time when King Bo'rom Trailokanat was enthroned in 1448, King Tilokarat of Lanna was already 6 years on the throne. King Tilokarat's path to the Lanna's throne was by way of removing his own father from the throne and establishing himself king of Lanna. He gave up his old name of "*Lok*" meaning "six" and adopted the royal name of "Tilokarat" meaning "King of the Three Worlds". The words suggest that the Buddhist view of cosmology already flourished in Lanna and also imply his awe-inspiring power over his subjects and neighbouring kingdoms. During his reign his activities could be divided into two sharply defined areas : war on the one side and peace on the other. In the war department, King Tilokarat adopted the war policy either to expand his kingdom or to remove threat to his kingdom. In waging war, King Tilokarat either led his army or vested his power on his general to make war on his behalf. King Tilokarat already had a hold on Nan and Phrae before King Bo'rom Trailokanat was on the throne of Ayutthaya. In the reign of King Bo'rom Trailokanat, King Tilokarat had wrestled the control of Chaliang, and Chakangrao from Ayutthaya. When Luang Phrabang's army laid seige on the city of Nan, King Tilokarat sent an army led by the chief of the city of Prao to defend the seiged city and drove off the attackers. King Tilokarat had made several successful expeditions against Sipso'ng Panna Region and captured a string of cities which included Tun, Luang, Wing Banjae. He also invaded the cities of Pong and Nai now in Myanmar. In all he won the allegiance of eleven vassal kingdoms and captured a huge number of prisoners of war. With all these achievements, he failed to subdue Luang Phrabang. In the peace department, he ordained 500 Buddhist monks as well as being ordained himself. He had one Vihara built on the site where his mother was cremated. King Tilokarat also ordered the construction of the main vihara of Wat Cedi Luang and also the restoration of its main pagoda. King Tilokarat was the founder of Wat Photharam Mahavihara known as Wat Cet Yo't. His major achievement for the vital cause of Buddhism is the emendation of the Buddhist Text (Tripitaka) in 1477 (see Thailand 1971 and Prachakit 1973).

King Bo'rom Trailokanat gave up his old name of "Ramesuan" upon his enthronement in favour of the full name of King Bo'rom Trailokanat. The word "Tilokarat" and "Bo'rom Trailokanat" are similar in meaning and sound. "Bo'rom" is derived from a Pali and Sanskrit word "parama" meaning great; likewise "trai" meaning three; and "nat" meaning refuge, usually applied to the king. Thus "Bo'rom Trailokanat" should mean, "He who is the Great Refuge of the Three Worlds", or "He who is the Great King of the Three Worlds". The meaning of the two kings are practically the same except for the added word "great". King Bo'rom Trailokanat's early reign was marked by several eventful developments. In 1451 King Tilokarat seized Chakangrao and Sukhothai from Ayuddhya. In 1460, Phraya Chaliang rebelled against Ayutthaya and placed his city under the control of Chiangmai. In the following year, King Tilokarat attacked Phitsanulok but failed to take the city. In 1462, the ruler of the city of Nako'nthai and his family fled to Nan way out of the reach of Ayutthaya. King Bo'rom Trailokanat, having decided to reverse the tide of events established his royal residence in the city of Phitsanulok, leaving Ayutthaya under the rule of his son, Prince Bo'rom Racha. Within the same year, King Tilokarat launched a campaign on the city of Sukhothai. King Bo'rom Trailokanat drove off Phraya Yuthisathira and engaged Muen Nakorn in an elephant combat. Prince Intharacha sustained a serious wound to his face. In any case King Tilokarat withdrew his force to Chiengmai. In the year which followed, King Bo'rom Trailokanat turned his attention to religious activities. He built a vihara at Wat Culamani where he was ordained in the year of 1464 and remained in the monkhood for eight months. In 1474 King Bo'rom Trailokanat started a campaign on Chaliang and recovered the control of the city. It is victory which inspired the composition of *Lilit Yuan Phai*. In 1475, King Tilokarat sent a mission to King Bo'rom Trailokanat to establish peace between the two sides. As a result, there were no waring activities between the two kingdoms throughout the reign of King Bo'rom Trailokanat. King Bo'rom Trailokanat was said to have composed *Mahachat Kamluang* a Buddhist literature, in 1482.

Peace secured by the agreement between the two kings was an uneasy peace. King Bo'rom Trailokanat faced a difficult task of convincing the northern cities that King Tilokarat could be curtailed. Even though King Bo'rom Trailokanat could regain the city of Chaliang, King Tilokarat was not decisively beaten and was likely to resume an attack on any of the cities in the north at any time, considering that King Tilokarat had won many victories in Sipso'ng Panna and Chiangtung and could raise a strong army within a short time. The author of this paper would like to suggest the possibility that *Lilit Yuan Phai* is not merely a heroic poem inspired by the victory of King Bo'rom Trailokanat, it is also a work of "political pursuasion" based on the divine grace and power, and the Buddha-like virtues of King Bo'rom Trailokanat. If this is the case, we have a good example of the literary works which are created for the purpose of serving a political need.

VERSE-FORM

For a practical purpose, verse forms of the two epics will be discussed separately.

Verse Form of *Thao Cheung Epic*

Thao Cheung Epic in all consists of more than 4,000 stanzas. Of these, the majority are in *Khlong Dan* of the rhyming type. 22 are in *Khlong Si Suphap* which is not much different from the *Khlong Si Suphap* of our time. *Khlong Dan* of the non-rhyming type of *Khlong San* is also found. The poetry of this kind can be found in works such as *Khun Thung, Sangsilpachaya* and *Khulu-Nang-Ua.* This form of verse shows preference for consonant rhymes over vowel rhymes which appear in a very few places. The standard number of syllables in each line is 7, making a quartrain of 28 syllables. In *Khlong Dan* either of the rhyming or non-rhyming type, a group of words from 2 to 4 may be added and put either to the front or the end of each line. Usually there are six places of tone *"ek"* and five places of tone *"tho"*. The pattern is a little bit different from *Klong Dan* in Thailand. An example of *Khlong Dan* from *Thao Cheung* epic is given below:

Khlong Dan of non-rhyming type

ภูธร	โยเฉศเที้ยนประดับอยู่	เป็นถัน
	ทวนโสมงามอาบสี	สรงน้ำ
	ทงสบเสื้อผืนแดง	ง้อมฝาก
	ลอนเลือกแก้วสบนิ้ว	คู่ควร

Khlong Dan of rhyming type

	เมื่อนั้น ลมลวาดไม้ก้องกิ่ง	เหมือนฮ้วาย
	ฝูงครัวถาหาบคอน	แควนเข้า
	สองนายขึ้นลวาพอน	เลยล่วง
	ทางท่องเท้าเถิงห้วย	ตากผา

Khlong Dan of the rhyming type is in structure similar to *Khlong Dan* of the non-rhyming type, but contains a rhyming pattern within a quatrain and also links rhyme of rhyme between two consecutive quartrains i.e. *Khlong Dan Wiwit Mali* and *Khlong Dan Bat Kuncho'n.* The Rhyming rule one finds in *Thao Cheung Epic* is rather flexible, for instance the last word in the line may rhyme with the first, second, third, fourth or fifth word of the intended line in the quartrain. Another major difference between *Khlong Dan* in *Thao Cheung Epic* and *Khlong Dan* in thai literature is that in the former there may be only 2 lines from the quartrain. These two lines may be either the first and second lines or the third and the fourth lines.

The play on sound and word in *Thao Cheung Epic* has the effect of bringing out the full beauty in the sonorous nature of the language. Towards this end the author of *Thao Cheung Epic* employs various devices described in the following:

1. The play on the tone of the sound

The author puts the words which are built from the same consonant and the same vowel but carry different tones in the same line. This device increases the power as well as the beauty of intended sounds in the narration. An example is given in the following quartrain.

คืนแก่   นกฮ่ายไม้อิ่มไฮ่   กินไฮ
ภูเขาขวางอ่มฮัง   คอยฮั้ง
สูรย์ไคลคลล้อยเขาคำ   ใกล้คว้ำ
ประกับไพรยั้งนอนแล้ง   ลวดแลง

di kae² nok⁴ hai³ mai⁴ him <u>hai</u>³   kin <u>hai</u>

phukhao⁵ khwang⁵ hom <u>hang</u>   do'i <u>hang</u>⁴

sun⁵ khlai khlo'i⁴ khaw⁵ <u>kham</u>   Klai³ <u>Kham</u>³

pradap² phrai³ yang⁴ no'n <u>laeng</u>⁴   luat³ <u>laeng</u>

2. The play on repeated words

The device is to be found in many places in *Thao Cheung Epic*. The repeated word is used to emphasize and help project a clear picture of what is being described. The pattern of repeated words falls into three main categories i.e.

2.1 Repeated words introduced without a definite regularities as long as it serves to emphasize the point the poet wants to convey, as in

<u>สว่าๆ</u>ก้องเสียงแส่ง   สมคราม
<u>ยนๆ</u>ยอหลกแหลม   ไหลเข้า
<u>ฮวานๆ</u>เหลื้อมสูรย์ใส   เฮืองฮาก
เที้ยนสิ่งเหล้าฮันช้าง   ชุ่ภาย

<u>Sawa² sawa²</u> ko'ng³ siang⁵ saeng²   som⁵ khram

<u>yon yon</u> yo' ho'k² laem⁵   lai⁵ khao³

<u>hawan</u> <u>hawan</u> lu'am^3 sun^5 sai^5 hu'ang hat
thian^4 sing^2 lao^3 han chang^4 chu^3 phai

2.2 Repeated word is introduced at the beginning of each line in the quartrain as in

ผู้ว่า มรณาศล้มลคขั่ว   น่าๆ บ่นอ
ผู้ว่า ยังมีเสน่หาอ่วมสอง   สมชู้
ผู้ว่า ยังแสวงค้นคมอวล   อันอ่าว
ผู้ว่า หลงกลับก้าแกนฟ้า   ต่างหลิม บ่ผู้

hu^4 wa^3 mo'ranat^3 lom^4 lot^4 chua^3 na^3 du bo'^{2} no'
hu^4 wa^3 yang mi saneha^5 huam^3 so'ng^5 som^5 chu^4
hu^4 wa^3 yang sawaeng^5 dan^3 do'm uan   an ao^2
hu^4 wa^3 long^5 klip^2 kam^3 daen fa^4 tang^2 lu'm^5 bo'^{2} hu

2.3 Repeated word is introduced at the end of the first line and the beginning of the second line in the same quartrain, as in

เสือเพิ่งท้องแถวเถื่อน   <u>ไพรขวาง</u>
<u>ไพรขวาง</u>สุขสำราญ   ใบช้อง

su'a^5 phoeng^3 tho'ng^2 thaeo^5 thu'an^2 <u>phrai khwang^5</u>
<u>Phrai khwang^5</u> suk^2 sam^5 ran   bai song^4

3. Reversal of words

Two or three syllables at the beginning of the second line and so on until the completion of the quartrain. The reversal of words or "play-back" as in the audio-tape is accompanied with some slight modification in order to break the monotony as well as to give the reverse words new meanings, in

ประสงค์แนบข้อนสุคสวาท   <u>อรองค์</u>
<u>องค์อร</u>แอช่างชม   <u>ถนอมข้อน</u>
<u>ข้อนถนอม</u>อุ้มใจจง   <u>แม่นคิด</u>
คิด<u>แม่น</u>ช้องทวงท้าว   เย่งกระสัน

211

prasong^5 naep^3 so'n^4 sut^2 sawat^2 <u>o'n</u> <u>ong</u>

<u>ong</u> <u>o'n</u> ae chang^3 chom   <u>thano'm</u>^{5} <u>so'n</u>^{4}

<u>so'n</u>^{4} <u>thano'm</u>^{5} hu^4 mano cong   maen^3 <u>Khit</u>

<u>Khitmaen</u>^{3} kho'ng^3 thuang thuang^4 heng krasan^5

Verse Form of *Lilit Yuan Phai*

Since there is no officially amended version of *Lilit Yuan Phai* yet, *Lilit Yuan Phai* versions that have been published vary in length. In this study the version of Chanthit Krasaesin, published in 1970 will be used. Chanthit refers to this literary work as *Yuan Phai Klong Dan* instead of *Lilit Yuan Phai*. The supporting argument is that a *Lilit* should consist of *Rai, Khlong 4, Khlong 2 and Khlong 3* in rotating or cyclic order. Since this version contains only two *Rai* and the rest is *Khlong 4*, according to Chanthit it should not be classified as a *Lilit* (Chanthit 1970: 38). The author, however, is inclined towards retaining the title of *Lilit Yuan Phai* as it has been known as such for a long time. In Chanthit's version there are 2 *Rai Dan*, one of which is a poem in *Rai*, and the other is interspersed between the 264th and 265th stanzas of *Khlong si* which closely resemble *Khlong Si Suphap* i.e. 78th, 102th, 120th and 128th *Khlong* and the rest is 290 *Khlong Dan*. All verses, be they *Rai Dan, Khlong Si Suphap* or *Khlong Dan* are connected by a linking rhyme known in Thai as *"Ro'i Khlong"*. The major "linking rhymes" are *"Bat Kuncho'n"* type which is a special case of "linking rhyme" for *Khlong Dan Bat Kuncho'n* and is very difficult to concoct. It requires a rare kind of poetical adeptness, and an excellent knowledge of language for a poet to find rhyming words.

The linking rhyme of the *Bat Kuncho'n* type requires that the 7th syllable of the third line in the top quartrain rhymes with the 3rd or 4th syllable of the first line in the bottom quartrain, and so on. The verse form of *Khlong* is governed by the number of syllables in each line, rhymes and the number and position of "tone *ek*" and "tone *tho*".

Khlong Dan is considered to be abrupt and stern and suits a serious or solemnized occasion. There are two linking rhymes between two consecutive quartrain of *Khlong Dan Bat Kuncho'n*. If the two consecutive quartrains of *Khlong* are joined by one linking rhyme, they are known as *"Khlong Dan Wiwit Mali"*. The composition of *Khlong Dan Bat Kuncho'n* requires greater skills than that of *Khlong Dan Wiwit Mali*. In any case, linking rhymes are brought in to enhance the dignity of the literary style without any loss in literary content and meaning. the author of *Lilit Yuan Phai* demonstrates his mastery skills as an esoteric versifier by bringing in alliterations and verbal acrobatics of various kinds, some of which will be described here:

1. Repetition

In *Lilit Yuan Phai* repetition comes in various styles. The following quartrain repeats the same word in each of the four lines. The word *"eka"* meaning one or unique

เอกก๊ตวเอกาตมล้ำ เลอกษัตริย์ ท่านฤๅ
เอกทยาไศรยแสวง ชอบใช้
เอกาจลค่ารงรัช รองราษฎร์ ไส้แฮ
เอกส้ตว์เกื้อให้ สร่างศัลย์

<u>eka</u>tawa ekatama lam⁴   loe kasat² than³ lu'
<u>eka</u>thayasai⁵ sawaeng⁵   cho'p³ chai⁴
<u>eka</u>con damrong rat⁴   ro'ng rat³ sai³ hae
<u>eka</u>sat² ku'a³ hai³   sang² san⁵

There are quite a number of quartrain which resort to powerful repetitions using words such as *Tawi, Tri, Benca, Sata, Asta, Nopha, Thosa, Phra, Kon, Luang, Sia* and so on.

Besides repetition in word, the author also introduces repetition in sound such as the sound of "r" or "b" in the following quartrain.

ระบินระเบียบเท้า เบาราณ
ระบอบระบับยล ยิ่งผู้
ระเบียนระบิกานต์ เกลากาพย์ ก็ดี
ระเบอศระบัศรุ์ รอบสรรพ์

rabin rabiap² thao⁴   bao ran
rabop² rabap² yon   ying3 phu
rabian rabi kan   klao kap² ko'3 di
raboet² rabat² ru⁴   ro'p³ san⁵

2. The play of "krathu"

When a word or groups of words of the same number usually no more than three, are used to lead each line in the quartrain form or column, and the reading of words from the top to the bottom of the column may form either a proverb, a riddle, a narration or even a slogan. The quartrain is said to be *Khlong Krathu*. One such quartrain appears.

พิศณุพระกร แกว่นส้าย สงคราม
พรพระกรรณ ไกรกล วากไว้
พรรณพระเกตุ เงื่อนงาม โสภาศ
เพศพระกาล ควรไท้ แทบองค์

phisanu phrako'n kwaen^2 sai^3 song^5 khram
pho'n phrakan krai kon   wat^3 wai^4
phan phraket^2 ngu'an^3 ngam   so^5 phat^3
phet^3 phrakan khuan thai^4 thaep^3 ong

The comparision of the narration styles between the two epics show that both authors are given to employing *Khlong Dan* of *Bat Kuncho'n* as the medium of delivery. Their common choice is probably based on the distinguised nature of the *Khlong* particularly of the *Bat Kuncho'n* type in conveying power and dignity. It also allows the authors to give displays of all kinds of verbal acrobatic act with all its beauty and pleasant sound befitting heroic poems such as *Lilit Yuan Phai* and *Thao Cheung Epic*. The rhyming pattern and the position of "ek" and "tho" are more formal and consistent in *Lilit Yuan Phai* than in *Thao Cheung Epic*, while alliteration is found almost in every quartrain in the two epics.

CONCLUSION

The comparative study of *Lilit Yuan Phai* and *Thao Cheung Epic* is anchored at two aspects i.e. heroic exaltation and verse forms. The two epics are found to exhibit some similarities as well as differences. *Lilit Yuan Phai* was composed to celebrate the heroic victory of King Bo'rom Trailokanat of Ayutthaya Kingdom over King Tilokarat of Lanna and was written while the hero was still living. In view of the fact that King Tilokarat was also a great warrior king who had snatched control of many cities in the North from Ayutthaya, and dominated a chain of cities in

Chiangtung and Sipso'ng Panna regions, the author of this paper suggests the possibilities that *Lilit Yuan Phai* besides being a heroic exaltation poetry was also conceived as a means to convince the chiefs and bureaucrats of the cities particularily in the North of King Bo'rom Trailokanat's abilities and might in order to subdue King Tilokarat of Lanna and thus win their confidence and loyalty to fight the enemy.

Thao Cheung Epic was likewise composed to glorify Thao Cheung's victory over the *Kaew* and was written almost two hundred years after the actual event. The poet was from Lanchang while the hero came from Lanna. Both belong to the *Taik* family group. The author of *Thao Cheung Epic* had at his heart the desire to arouse patriotism in the Laotian people and a readiness to take up arms to fight the Vietnamese which defeated the enemy of that historical period.

The manners in which the heroes of both epics are projected are strikingly similar. Both heroes were presented as super human-beings and endowed with royal virtues and grace. King Bo'rom Trailokanat was a combination of the divine qualities of Lord Buddha and Hindu gods, while Thao Cheung was indeed sent to this world by the Thaen god.

The verse forms employed by the authors of the two epics are equally alike with both authors showing a strong preference of *Khlong Dan* of *Bat Kuncho'n* type. Their choice is readily understandable for this type of verse allows only the poets of exceptional skills to bring out the dignity, sweetness, and beauty of the language to the full. The plays on words, sounds and alliterations were also exploited to their full effects by both authors. *Lilit Yuan Phai,* appears to be strict in rhyming and form pattern, while *Thao Cheung Epic* gives the appearance of being flexible. This is probably due to the former being in all likelihood written for recitation in a ceremony and the later having been developed from an oral tradition.

After having examined quite a few early literary works of Ayutthaya, Lanna, and Lanchang, the author of this paper reached the same conclusion as Jit Poumisak, namely that *Khlong* of early periods are governed only by the number of words, rhythm and the position of *"ek"* and *"Tho"*. *Lilit Yuan Phai* and *Thao Cheung Epic* are poems distinguished by elegant "internal" and "external" rhymes and a multitude of verbal aerobatic devices points to a high state of *Khlong* development long achieved before the time of both authors. This is evidence suggesting close interaction between Ayutthaya and Lanchang and it is of little surprise that there are similarities in the literary composition of both kingdoms.

A Study of both the contents and verse forms of the two epics, *Lilit Yuan Phai* and *Thao Cheung* has shown that Ayutthaya and Lanchang during the 15th century had already achieved a high level of literary development, and the two great Hindu epics, *Ramayana* and *Mahabharata* were already well known in both kingdoms. In expressing religious ideas, Ayutthaya seemed to be firmly influenced by both Buddhism and Hinduism, while Lanchang appeared to be superficial and was in effect well grounded in animism and beliefs in the spirits and the *Thaen* god.

REFERENCES

Abrams, M.H.
   1975   *A Glossary of Literary Terms.* Bangkok.

Chanthit Krasaesin
   1970   *Yuan Phai Khlong Dan.* Bangkok: Mit Sayam.

Jit Poumisak
   1981   *Ongkan Chaeng Nam lae Kho' khit Mai Nai Prawattisat Thai Lum Nam Cao Phraya.* Bangkok : Mai Ngam.

Niyada Lausoonthorn.
   1992   "Yuanphai Khlong Dan: Kho' Sanoe Mai" (A New Approach to Yuanphai Khlong Dan). In *Phinit Wannakam: Ruam Botkhwam Thang Wichakan Dan Wannakhadi Lae Phasa (Su'ksa Cak Ton Chabap Tua Khian)* (Collection of Academic Essays Based on Manuscripts), Niyada Lausoonthorn. Bangkok: Samnak Phim Mae Kham Phang, 34-41.

Prachakit Koracak (Chaem Bunnak), Phraya
1973   *Phongsawadan Yonok*. Bangkok: Khlang Witthaya.

Prakong Nimmanahaeminda
1981   "Mahakap Ru'ang Thao Ba Chueng : Kansu'ksa Choeng
Wikhro'" (The Thao Ba Chueng Epic: An Analytical Study).
Ph.D Thesis, Chulalongkorn University.

Suphawatana Kasemsri, Mo'm Ratchawong
1988   A lecture given at the seminar on "500 years of King Bo'rom
Trailokkanat", Silapakorn University.

Tavee Sawangpanyangkul.
1986   *Tamnan Phu'n Mu'ang Sipso'ng Panna*. Bangkok: Mitnara
Kanphim.

Term Vibhakphochanakich.
1987   *Prawattisat Lao*. Bangkok: Social Science and Humanity Text
Book Foundation.

Thailand
1963   *Prachum Phongsawadan Vol. 1*, Bangkok: Ongkan Kha
Khurusapha.

1971   *Tamnan Phu'n Mu'ang Chiang Mai*. Bangkok: Khana
Kamakan Cat Phim Ekasan Thang Prawattisat, Office of the
Prime Minister.

LOCAL LITERATURE OF SOUTHERN THAILAND

Suthiwong Pongpaiboon

BACKGROUND ABOUT SOUTHERN THAILAND

The South of Thailand denotes 14 provinces: Chumpho'n, Rano'ng, Suratthani, Krabi, Phang-nga, Phuket, Trang, Nako'nsithammarat, Phatthalung, Songkhla, Satun, Yala, Pattani, and Narathiwat. It is a region distinguised from the rest of the country by language, custom, and other aspects of culture.

By geographical delimitation, the South is located between the latitudes of 11 degrees 42 minutes north and 5 degrees 37 minutes north, and is 592 kilometres in length. Its width lies between the longtitudes of 98 and 102 degrees east, about 232 kilometres at its widest and about 50 kilometres at its narrowest at the Kra Isthmus. The land stretches lengthwise from north to south, flanked by the seas, whose coasts total 1,672 kilometres in length. In area, the entire soughern region is approximately 70,189 square kilometres.

By historical evidence, the southern region in about 100-200 B.E. (444-343 B.C.) was called *Malayathawip* or *Yommathawip*, as well as *Suwanthawip* in the great epic *Ramayana* of India. In *Mahanithet* and *Chulanithet*, it is *Suwannaphum*. Pomponius Mela's book of geography written in B.E. 586 (43 A.D.) called it *Chrys Insula* 'golden island', while in a geography book by Ptolemy, the Greek geographer, it was *Chryse Chresonese* 'golden peninsula, Ptolemy's book having been written between 670-684 B.E. (127-141 A.D.) *Milintha Panha*, written in 943 B.E. (400 A.D.) called it *Suwannapum*. In *Mahawong*, a historical account of Lanka written in the 11th. century B.E., the southern region appeared as *Suwannapum*. The travel journal of a Chinese monk named E-Ching who made a journey through the southern region to India during the period of 1214-1238 B.E. (671-695 A.D.) called the area of what is now Southern Thailand *Chin Chow* 'golden island'. A royal decree of the Ayuthya period (1084 B.E. or 541 A.D.) called it ปากใต้. The Luang Prasert version of Ayuthya historical accounts used ปักใต้. The spelling ปักษ์ใต้ was found in the Brahman Legend of Nakornsrithammaraj, whose year of completion was indicated as 2277 B.E. (1734 A.D.) As for the designation ภาคใต้, it was probably used initially in public administration in the reign of Rama VI in an announcement about the Vicerey's duties and power dated December 13, 2458 B.E. (1915 A.D.), while earlier the southern region had been labelled ภาคปักษ์ใต้ with the title of Viceroy having been inaugurated as อุปราชปักษ์ใต้ 'the Viceroy of the southern region'. The title of ข้าหลวงยุติธรรมภาคใต้ 'His Majesty's Chief Justice for the southern region' was found in an announcement of court regulation in 2478 B.E. (1935 A.D.) (Institute of Southern Thai Studies 1986: 7: 2577-2588).

The inhabitants of the southern region of Thailand consists of 4 major groups, namely, the Tai-Kadai group: malay people whose language is Malay; the Moken of Orang Laut group: boat dwellers along the sea coasts and near river mouths; and the Austro-Asistic group: Negritos, the Semang whom the Thai call เงาะ or เงาะป่า, i.e. Negritos.

By archaeological evidence, it was found that in the pre-historic days there were 2 groups of inhabitants of the southern region: the cave dwellers and the sea coast dwellers. The former made their appearance in the region no less than 20,000 years ago, and 6,500-5,000 years ago attained a certain degree of development with an ability to make and use metal tools, for example, in producing clothes or cloth fabric from tree barks. They lived the life of a hunters' community by hunting off the forest lands around them. The sea coast dwellers inhabited the coastlines, for instance, around the *Kalok Phi* 'skulls of the dead' Cave or the *Phi Hua To* "oversize-head ghost' Cave in Krabi Province, and the islands and sea coasts of Trang and Puket Province. They caught marine animals for a living.

The southern region of Thailand, along with Malaysia, Indonesia, and the islands nearby are similar in climate and natural resources. Close and long-time intermingling are thus their manners of basic livelihood and systems of thought and belief generated in conformance with their social contexts which make up the roots of their cultures. Examples are their nomenclatures for plant and fish species, their wisdom in harvesting rice with their unique harvesting knife called *kae*, their cultural aspects about eating and food preservation, and their wisdom in architecture. Because of the location of the region at the cultural crossroads of the Arabs, Persia, India, China, the Cham, and the Khmer, for several successive centuries the intermingling of the people and cultures thereof in the region ensued with continuity and in a complex way. For example, the Hindu cultural aspect related to Sivaism of the Brahman religion may be noted whose presence has not only been confirmed by the evidence of Shiva and Uma lingams, but has also been found embedded in the *Nang Talung* shadow play, where homage must be paid to Ishavara or Shiva, and in the funeral *Kalo* musical performance which accompanies the rite of conducting the spirit of the dead to obeisance before the god *Kala* (i.e. Shiva) and the goddess *Kali* (i.e. Uma). So also is the cultural aspect about the *Kris*, which as legend has it is a creation of the Hindu trinity: Shiva, Vishnu, and Brahma, thereby causing the Shiva and Uma lingams to be intricately woven into the makeup of the traditional *Kris* of Java, Malaysia, and Pattani. Mahayana Buddhism has especially diffused and deepened through the region so as to become the trait of the Srivijaya cultural group, as found in Java and at the archaeological sites of Pattani, the Ranote and Satingphra Districts of Songkhla, Kakornsrithammaraj, and Chiya, either as ancient sites or as pronouncements of belief. These things have all permeated southern Thai literature in a complex way. The 19th century B.E. was Islam spreading into the region and causing those who worshipped it to abandon the traditional Hindu and Buddhist views, beliefs, and cultrual aspects which were in violation of the commandments of Islam. Thus did a part of the population of the southern region come to profess themselves adherents of Islam, called Muslim Thai, who have heretofore densely congregated in the southern border provinces. As for the Central Thai or Metropolotan culture, its connection with the southern Thai culture only began in earnest during the final stage of Ayuthya,but has accelerated since. They entry of the Chinese and their culture into the southern region was substantial during the Bangkok period, especially in the reign of Rama V. Most of the Chinese are related to those in Malaysia and Singapore. Their marked cultural aspects in this connection have to do with architecture, food, and business, among others.

It should be noted that the aspects of culture related to Buddhism were presented in great variety in the local literature, from parts of the Principles, the Sutras, the Explications, the Jatakas, and romantic tales in forms of outline, plot, or dialogue. Numerous were those works with purely Buddhist elements, while into others wuch as medicine formulas, law texts, fortune-telling manuals called *Sastra* some Buddhist flavour was blended. Few works dealt with the Hundu culture exclusively, such as the

Brahman Legend of Nako'nsrithammarat, Tri-Narayana. Fragments were present, however, such as those about Hindu gods, the garuda, the hansa 'noble swan', the four guardian gods. Linguistically, Pali and Sanskrit elements have profoundly blended into southern Thai dialects, in spoken language and written literature alike, with modifications in form, sound and meaning in varying degrees, such as *athan* from *adhama, borithiw* from *perathiw, khotai* from *akkhohini, saddi* from *svasti, thana* from *than, sapde* or *somdi* from *somrueti, thiamda* from *devata, hunman* from *hanuman.*

THE SCOPE OF SOUTHERN THAI LITERATURE

Southern Thai literature means the literary works composed, adapted, or translated principally for southern Thai people to chant, read, and listen to. The diction and manner of speech of Southern Thai were favoured as the medium of transmission, with southern Thai cultural contexts interwoven in such works in a profound and complex way. Any reproduction of non-southern Thai literature in all its original diction is not considered part of southern Thai literature.

TERMS FOR WRITTEN LITERATURE

The southerners call written literature by the kind of material on which a work is written and by the process of production of the material. If the material is palm leaf, the work would be called 'bound volume" according to the way in which the leaves are bound together. If the material is tree bark, call *samut kho'i* literature in Central Thai, the South calls it *bud*. In some localities, the *prisna* vine is favoured, so the literature is called *prisna* volumes.

The word *bud* has probably weakened from the word *pusta* or *pustaka* in sankrit, which means 'book', 'writen work', or 'manuscript', which corresponds to the Pali word *potthaka* for palm leaf. There are many words of Sanskrit origin which have entered Southern Thai with a slight shift in form and sound, and it is possible that the Pali and Sanskrit *pustaka,* the Southern Thai *bud,* and the Central Thai *samut* are the same word, which in Central Thai means book, such as *samut Thai* 'Thai book (volume)' or *hao samut* 'book hall' and hence 'library'. Further, it should be noted that in Malay the word for 'bookshop' is *pustakan.*

There are some localities where a *bud* volume is called *kritna* or *prisan,* as Pattalung Province.

Thai reference in *Subin Kham Kap:*[1]

> "I the owner had long contemplated and then went
> searching for some *pritna* vine to make into inscrib-
> ing leaflets on which to record tales for the young
> who in honing their intelligence may chant these....."

which shows that even a volume made with paper from the *pritna* vine may be called *bud* too.

There are two kinds of bud literature in the South, namely, *bud khao* 'white *bud*' made of whitish paper and its letters written in black ink, and the other kind of *bud dam* 'black *bud*' made of black paper of which the blackening material is obtained by first charring coconut or betel nut leaf base and then mixing the charred material or soot therefrom with rice stock, after which the misture is painted onto ordinary paper, and is polished when dry. The writing on the *bud dam* is done in white or yellow. Most southern literature is *bud khao*. What remains of *bud dam* is sparse and is often a reproduction of Central Thai literature of the Ayuthya period.

The literature about history or legend is what Southern Thai people put in a group by itself called *plau;* for example, *Plau Muang Pattalung* means a history or legend of Pattalung, or *Plau Nang Luat Khao* refers to a legend of the woman of that name.[2]

The literature for setting auspicious moments is given the name of *nangsu' huang* because it contains some tables of eyelet shape to classify various moments by their worth for astrological purposes. Some also call *bud* type by the name of *huang*.

One other kind of local literature is for fortune-telling by lot. Each section points out a fortune, often with an illustration. A person wanting his fortune told would hold it up overhead, think out a request, and draw his lot. This kind of literature is called *sastra*.

---

[1] Kapya is a form of Thai verse

[2] The origin of the word *plau* may relate to the name of a kind of tough paper like the *khoi* paper but thinner on which pencil was used for writing, the kind of paper being called *plau* paper, which in the South refers to volume made with sheets of such paper.

THE ALPHABETS

There are two kinds of alphabet in the writing of southern literature: the *Kho'm* alphabet and the Thai alphabet. The *Kho'm* alphabet was widely used to record Buddhism-related literature in Pali language. Some writings of substance held in as high an esteem as the Scripture or something exalted such as the work *Kalapana*, were written in Thai with the *Kho'm* alphabet. This kind of recording is called *Thai Kho'm*. Tales and other kinds of literature such as writings about beliefs, medicine formulas, and *sastras* were recorded with the Thai alphabet, but when some spell or induction of faith was desired in some parts of such writings the *Kho'm* alphabet was frequently used in the parts concerned; in romance tales, for example, the parts announcing types of literary composition were registered with the *Kho'm* alphabet.

The *Kho'm* alphabet was called tua poch in some localities, as seen in the inventory of items sent by Chao Phraya Wichienkiri (Men an Songkhla) to Bangkok in B.E. 2424 (1881 A.D.) for display at the centennial celebration of Bangkok (B.E. 2425): "This volume in *tua poch* of old, translation of the Buddhist principles book 2. This volume "in *tua poch* of old, *Suwannasam,* book1. This volume in *tua poch* of old, *Thampu,* book1." The term *tua poch* was probably derived from *Kampuch,* which refers to Cambodia or Kampuchea.

The use of the *Kho'm* alphabet and the Thai alphabet for the South was similar to the way in which the *Lanna* alphabet was used for the North and the *Dharma* alphabet for the Northeast. To be worthy of the status of scholar, a southerner was required to master Pali, *Kho'm,* and *Thai Kho'm,* as seen in the verse at the end of *Maharaj in Chantha* (*Chantha* is a form of Thai verse), also indicating somewhat the composer's modesty: "I though not a scholar am using *Kho'm* words in this versification on record."

A southern Thai expression reproaching an illiterate person runs thus: " *Ko'* (the name of the first letter of the Thai alphabet), *Kho'* (the second letter), or *Namo* (the beginning word of Buddhist prayers signifying reverence), he knows none."

Professor Dr Prasert na Nagara was of the opinion that the southern region, unlike the North and the Northeast, had no alphabet of its own because the *Kho'm* alphabet always seerved as the alphabet of the South without any problems about recording the sounds of the Southern dialects.

The use of the *Kho'm* alphabet in the South continued until the reign of Rama VI of the Bangkok period, after which there was a decline in the number of those literate in the *Kho'm* alphabet. At present, a reader of Pali *Kho'm* or Thai *Kho'm* is a rarity. The literature inscribed in the alphabet is therefore left with hardly a connoisseur.

CERTAIN CIRCUMSTANCES
1) Quantity, condition, and repository
From this writer's direct experience, it may be estimated that 50 years ago over 95 per cent of the wxisting southern Thai literature could still be found, for at the time any monastery not without monks would have a library where palm leaf and bud volumes, from 100 to 1,000 or more in number, of local literature were kept. But nowadays even 10-20 such volumes would be hard to find among 50-100 monasteries.

Because almost all the literature was created by charity-minded individuals to serve the Buddhist faith, to keep any work of the literature at one's home would have been wrong and damaging to oneself. The library of a monastery was thus a communal library, usually situated in a building on stilts in water to prevent to ravage of termites. At least 3x4 m2 in area, such a library housed volumes of material in at least half or more of its space, with more material in the *Kho'm* script than in the Thai script.

In the past 50 years, the number of connoissueurs of this kind of literature has dwindled. Part of the material has been destroyed by rain and humidity. Some has been taken for burial under a newly-built pagoda in the belief that it would bring merit to the people concerned. Some was burned for smoke to cure nasal bleeding, or was used for pasting around an infected earfor effective cure as dictated by the folk belief involved. Not a small amount of the material was burned as waste paper. some other amount was moved from monasteeery to home, especially the material about medicine formulas, guikdlines for setting auspicious moments, formulas for assessing the worth of domestic animals, as there were still some people who believe in these and put them to use. Few of the younger generations keep up the maintenance.

The writer's interest in collecting southern literature material began about 2510 B.E. (1976 A.D.) It was then discovered that the repositories of the material at most monasteries were not being cared for, and that over 95 percent had decayed or had been ravaged by rats and termites beyond repair.

Only after 2510 B.E. did the southern literature manuscripts gain the attention of the higher education institutions of the region. Those which serve as important repositories are the Institute for Southern Thgai Studies and the teachers colleges of the South. Some individuals and organisations in the private sector have also taken part. Based upon some past data, these repositories contain altogether about 8,000 volumes of the *bud* manuscripts. Palm leaf volumes are very few. None of the institutions has seriously undertaken collection of such manuscripts.

2) The status of study and research

Of the said number of about 8,000 volumes that still remain, only about one per cent altogether has been subjected to textual editing, studied as parts of graduate programmes, and treated by research methodology. Most of the treatment has been oriented towards belles-lettres. There has been little treatment of any other aspects.

In sum, the situation of the study of southern Thai literature is similar to taking but a few tress from a vast forest that has disintegrated in a complex way. What is left connot be a comprehensive body of knowledge; only as a microcosm of particular volumes and titles can it at best be enjoyed.

ABOUT THE AUTHORS

Because most works of southern Thai literature were composed in worship of the Buddha, principally for merit making, fame was not sought by the authors, who usually remained anonymous.

The three terms referring to the coming into existence of a work are **compose, write,** and **make.** All the three may designate authorship, but write may signify a scribe, and **make** could mean the person who employed or entrusted someone else to compose a piece or to copy from some original work, as mentioned in the *Maha Jatakas* of Wat Machimawas in Songkhla:

"A learned one I am not, nor am I of scholarly bent well drilled
in verse making. Having long heard stories of old, and distorted
I may have the original form of the Scripture, my conscience is

clear, as in blissful faith I compose the *Maha Jatakas* based on
the Scripture, as much as may intellect allows, for there is no
original to rely on."

This means authorship.

From an older version of *Subin* :

"I invented and added to the story brought from outside,
having thought out words with which to mend and insert
in the original. Low of intellect am I, finish it I can but
by no means very well."

This indicates an authorship based on some original plot from some
other locality, with some more elements added as the writer's talent would
permit.

In *Manohranibat:* "........Finish writing on........" The term 'write'
should mean 'copy' rather than a claim to authorship.

The story *Chalawan*, of which the original manuscript extant was
obtained from Kradang-nga Village, Satingphra District, Songkhla
Province, sated: Khun Iam had this made for the Buddist faith. Old Man
Kerd was the scribe. Please help correct any errors which I, old as I am, may
have made." Here, Old Man Kerd did the copying, which Khun Iam caused
the copying to be carried out.

It may be concluded that in the creation of local literature, the
creators, meaning either authors or ones causing works to be done by
hiring or begging someone capable to compose a new piece, or having a
scribe copy from an existing text, resolved to achieve the following benefits:

1) To show reverence to the Buddha

In the early days of local literature, the southerners who were literate
enough to compse and read had received their literacy training and the rest
of education at a Buddhist monastery. Their knowledge and faith were
grounded in Buddhism with the belief that creation of Buddhist-based
literature was a merit of gift of knowledge that would bring nothing but
happiness to oneself and the reader--a truly great deed of helping others, as
seen in *Sinnuraj Kham Kap:* "To the creator of a work of reference goes an

intense merit, and one who completes one reading earns an eternity of merit." It was believed also that such a deed would liberate one from hell and usher him heavenwards, and that it would make possible a rebirth into the perfect world of the *Sri Ariya Mettraya* Buddha, as well as a path for the happiness of *Nibbana*, as found in *Subin Kham Kap*:

> "I the owner contemplated for a long time and then went searching for some *pritna* vine to make into inscribing leaflets on which to record tales for the young who in honing their intelligence may chant these, so that I may be saved from evils present and future. May I be kept off hell and on course towards heaven upon expiring, together with all my kinsmen and parents. May I transcend suffering to reach a sage's happiness. Of low intellect in this life, may I be endowed with a quick mind in the next one to master the Buddha's teachings and to be gifted with keen intelligence like the learned Phra Buddha Kosa. May it be said that evil desires never touch me. I hereby make wish to be reborn in time for the coming of the Sri Araya Buddha and to attain Nibbana , achieving that knowledge transcending the worldly realm."

From *Nok Cap:*

> "I, Promsuwan, have contributed to the Faith by having created the tale *Nok Chap.* May I mind the precepts and never misstep in my acts and thoughts, and be endowed with skill in all. May I be reborn in time for the ominscient and just Sri Ariya Buddha."

From *Phra Lakana Kham Kap:*

> "I offer the tale *Phra Lakana* to the sacred Faith. In this life and next may I be endowed with an intelligence greater than Phra Mahosot's, and master all the Dharma, from this moment onwards."

2) For specific purposes

A certain amount of local literature of the southern region was what the authors had faith in as a collection of knowledge and rules of practice. It was created for accuracy and precision of utilisation. There was some which was created to transmit the wisdom and beliefs involved to beloved and trusted pupils. The substance of this kind of literature covers both popular wisdom and things arising from ignorance, i.e. beliefs born out of lack of thorough knowledge, namely, the literature about folk medicine formulas, ways of interpreting human and animal attributes, the setting of auspicious signs and moments, astrology, magic incantations for good or evil, occultism, and lottery fortune-telling.

This kind of literature has been used by the faithful up to the present, such as the examination manual of herbal medicine (medicine formulas) which C. Chuachanchai wrote in verse with the following stated as his purpose.

> "A text written about medicine, complied as written messages in verse, from medicine fromulas of old successfully applied by masters. Ilinesses may be relieved and diseases driven away with the Thai medicine formulas from the collection to save lives in time of need."

3) To promote faith in specific things

In some works of southern literature, the authors aimed at honouring things which they valued, in order to spread their popularity. One such example is the *Written Gesture of Homage*, which is a chant in praise of the Buddha's footprint and composed in *Kap* verse. It describes all the symbols that make up the footprint and invokes participation in the worship by chanting the verse twice daily, at bedtime and early in the morning, as follow:

> "All women and men, every evening and at rooster's crow, for enternity, do pray, Whoever pays respect to this record will achieve great merit, all the 84,000 chapters of the *Tri-pitaka*, as if to encounter the Buddha in person. Mark well this written record of Dharma and the Buddha's footprint."

Some further examples of the literature along this line are the *Legend of the Buddha's Relic,* the *Brahman Legend of Nakornsrithammaraj, Plau Nang Luad Khao.* In verse there are such works as the *Boat Celebrating Chant,* the *Rice Celebrating Chant,* and the *Chant to Invoke Saftely and Happiness.*

4) Chanting to enhance the reading skill

King Chulalongkorn made a royal order of November 11, 2441 B.E. (1898 A.D.) appointing the Supreme Patriarch Krom Phraya Vajirayana Varoros Director of Education of the Provinces throughout the Kingdom. This resulted in the composition and reproduction of southern Thai literature in Thai alphabet, to such a great extent that this period may be called one of prosperity for local literature, for the literature was used in part for chanting practice to sharpen the reading skill, as exemplified in the work *Khobut Kham Kap*: "This story *Khobut* has been created for the Faith so that adherents may practice reading by chanting it." And in *Pathom Ko' Ka,* it is stated: "Done in verse, this is all meant for boys' reading practice in mastering all the sections of syllable-forming combinations."

5) For instruction

A considerable part of southern literature was aimed at instructing its audience so that they would be well apprised of affairs of life, and grounded in ethics and humane qualities to make themselves useful members of society. This is didactic literature, such as *The ABC Proverbs* by pantha Satitsomboon of Songkla Province:

> "*Kaw Kai* [3] is beautiful because of its plumage, like a properly dressed person. Be misled not by outward beauty. Rather, admire the beauty within.
>
> *No'Nu* [4] realises its misdeed and fears punishment, so it resorts to dwelling in a hole to hide its ears and head. A wrongdoer who does not turn a new leaf is bound to go on being depraved to the point of demise."

---

[3] The first letter of the Thai alphabet with which the word 'rooster' is spelled in Thai.
[4] The letter of the Thai alphabet in the word for 'mouse'.

As a parable:

> "Our body organic changes through time, mornings and
> evenings, days and nights. Entertain not the idea that one always
> stays young. Reflect upon impermanence. Be not vile or rude.
> Our lifetime is hardly long, so hasten to climb up out of reach of
> things evil."

Three kinds of purposeful poets normally found in the literature of
the capital or the royal court is not manifest in southern literature:

(a) To dedicate to or glorifify a king, as in *Lilit Phra Law:* "In
dedication to the well situated great king."

(b) To create some work of literary merit, such as *Lilit Yuan Phai:* "A
message in Siamese of melodious verse. Equal it is to a pliant bouquet of
heavenly flowers."

(c) To demonstrate one's own literary acumen, such as *Nirat Narin:*
"To compose these words as a comprehensive record of so exalted a poet of
splendid diction worthy of praise of one learned once it is persued.

Modesty probably accounts for the absence of the three kinds of
purpose in southern literature. To state the said purposes would have been
aspiring beyond one's true station. A show of humility was often the rule,
as in *Maha Jataka*, version of Wat Matchimawat:

> "Learned I am not , nor am I of the class of scholars wise in the
> way of verse. I am but one who have long heard tales of old.
> Should there be any deviation from the original Scripture, may
> my good and glad intention in writing this *Maha Chat* based on
> the Scripture make up for it."

SOUTHERN LITERATURE AS A REFLECTION OF THE WORLDVIEW AND SOCIAL CONTEXT OF THE SOUTH

An analysis of the substance of southern literature would bring out some
points about the worldview and social context of the southern region,
including traditional beliefs, faith in Buddhism, expectations about life and
society, as well as unavoidable circumstances of necessity, which may be
categorised as follows:

1) Buddhism-related literature

Because the learned of the southern region of such intellect as would be capable of literary composition during the reign of Rama V of the Bangkok period and farther back into the past were all educated at Buddhist institutions, with absorption and comprehension of Buddhist affairs, be they teh teachings, places, personages, and rites of Buddhism. Concomitant was the fact that the Buddhist laity of the time had faith in achieving merit and great deed of charity through knowing and practising the Dharma and worshipping the *Tri Ratana* 'Triple Gem'. This explains the dominant presence of Buddhist elements in southern literature. Some outstanding examples are:

(a) About the Supreme Laws and the Scripture. These were mostly inscribed in Pali through the *Kho'm* script.

(b) About the Buddha's life. There are such stories as *The Five Buddhas, the White Crow, the Buddha's Predictions, Tri-lokavithan.*

(c) About Buddhist precepts. For example, the *Sawasdiraksa* (in verse) version of Wat Hongsaram, Panarae District, Pattani Province, explaining concepts such as *bun* 'merit', *bap* 'wrongdoing', *Nibbana; Dharma* (in verse); and *Phra Chamna Marn* 'the Subjugator of *Mara*' (in verse)

(d) About Buddhist places. Such as *The Legend of the Great Buddha's Relic of Nakornsrithammaraj, A historical Account of Hansawati* (about the Buddhist places in Hansawati), and *The Buddha's Relic of Rangoon.*

(e) About the *Jataka* (Buddha's incarnation), both from and outside of the Scripture. Such as *Maha Chat, Vessantara, Maharaj, Manohranobat,* and *Ho'i Sang,* all in verse.

In particular, allusions to consequences of *Karma*, regarding hell and heaven alike, may be found in almost all works of local literature. Notably one such as *Phra Malai*, which is a literary creation of utmost refinement, made with a special kind of paper and binding design, all its letters (of the *Kho'm* script) inscribed with care, its illustrations depicting the domains of hell, heaven, and Buddhist salvation in all their complexity, as well as supplementary pictures of artistic distinction throughout the volume. It has been reproduced far and wide.

In substance the literature related to Buddhism is more marked for personification than for abstraction about the Dharma, more oriented towards Mahayana Buddhism than towards Hinayana Buddhism, with greater emphasis on cultivating faith for adherence to the precepts (verbal and bodily acts) and to the Dharma (spiritual training) than on intellectual development.

2) Beliefs

The inhabitants of the South made their living from low-land and highland farming, fishing, selling products of the forest, and catching land and water animals. High risk was involved in life and property, with security and certainty hard to come by. They naturally lacked self-confidence, and had to resort for morale boosting to what they believed to be cupernatural capable of benefiting or punishing them. Their system of thinking was full of beliefs not consistent with scientific principles and religious essence. It was born out of ignorance and not empirically verifiable.

These beliefs were transmitted through the local literature at the time of uninquisitive conviction, in order to enforce rigorous observance. Sometimes such literature was regarded as a body of prescriptions serving as rules, customs, and mores of society, which may be categorised thus:

(a) Beliefs about invocation of good fortune and prevention of misforturne

Such as formulas to invoke well-being, to determine auspicious moments, to assess the attributes of pet animals such as dogs and cats, to apraise amulets such as the Kris, and formulas of incantation.

(b) Beliefs about promoting favourable means of livelihood

Such as formulas for the ploughing ceremony, about the attributes of the Kris with which to convey lustral water to rice seeds prepared for planting; formulas for setting auspicious moments of departure for hunting or business trips, and for assessing cattle of burden; formulas for rice celebration and boat celebration.

(c) Beliefs about safety of life and property

Such as formulas for choosing weapons superior to those of one's enemy, for assessing animals or objects to prevent a fire or theft, for counteracting conditioned poison, and for incantations to alleviate a misfortune.

(d) Beliefs about fortune in general

This has to do with fortune as source of honour, fame, power, opportunities of gaining slaves and followers, wealth, and women. For this there are formulas for auspicious moments for travel, for appraising personality, and for interpreting signs of omen, as well as for fortune telling by lot, or *sastra*.

The beliefs mentioned in (a) - (d) above maintain that a right choice would bring benefit and a wrong choice harm. Under each topic benefits and harms were presented side by side to choose from as desired.

(e) Beliefs about magic

This was an expectation of benefit for oneself and harm for one's enemy, such as making an infatuation-inducing charm, setting incantations for the purpose of harming others, and voodoism. This kind of literature usually offers guidelines for rituals along with related incantations. It was transmitted by rote and was rarely recorded in writing.

3) Knowledge

Most knowledge is gained from experience and wisdom accumulated in a group of people. the more widely known the group's wisdom is, the more peace it brings to the group, with no harm attached. Wisdom is usually transmitted with nothing held back. But some kind of wisdom if not properly applied may be harmful to its user and others, or give its user some unfair advantage, in which case the wisdom would be kept secret. If written, so as to prevent a trick of memory, a false lead was usually given through some misinformation, causing some literature related to wisdom to look more like a nonsensical belief than some piece of knowledge.

The literature with knowledge substance is as follows:

(a) Folk medicine

This is most numerous of all the literature about knowledge. some was done in verse, such as the heart stimulant from the medicine formulas in verse by a herbalist, C. Chuachanchai of N-yong Village, Muang District, Trang Province: "This heart stimulant is a mixture of flower petals and vegetables of exquisite flavour and fragrance to uplift the heart, all the ingredients put together in a concoction pot, and once taken it helps to refresh."

It has been observed that the ingredients of some formulas became more numerous as the formulas underwent further and further reproduction. This may be due to the fact that either those who copied them at later dates had increasing knowledge about medicine, or the subsequent generations, to compensate for lack of thorough knowledge and self-confidence, brought in some more ingredients for experiment, in effect to obtain a cure-all medicine. Such is one reason why this branch of knowledge turned from wisdom to ignorance and gradually declined in popularity.

(b) Instructional texts

Texts such as *Pathom Ko' Ka* (a primary reader), *Sirivibulkit*, served as reading primers, in Pali, *Kho'm*, and Thai.

This is an excerpt from the autobiography of Phra Ratanatachamuni (Chu Thihparaksaphan) born in 2415 B.E. (1872 A.D.):

> "At the age of 11 my father sent me to study the *Kho'm* script at Wat Ty-yao under Acharn Khui's tutelage. He taught me the *Kho'm* script both of Pali variety and the kind used in sermon volumes, and then sent me on to learn some primer with Acharn Pan at Wat Koakbiao. When I finished memorising the Sondhi formula, I went to learn under Acharn Rod.....who taught me several arithmetic formulas and further arithmetic for astrology. I was about to embark upon arithmetic for horoscope casting when he told me I was too young and should wait until I grew up. At the time, I was fully 15 years old."

(c) Law

An example is *Folk Law*, some of it composed in verse, such as: "If a rape is committed against an unmarried woman, a fine must be levied on the culprit, but should the victim is married, let the fine be reduced."

(d) Specific knowledge

Such as a drawing text dealing with methods of drawing, for example, Thai designs, animals of the Himavanta Forest. Besides, there were works of *Plau* (history and legend) category, such as the *Brahman Legend of Nakho'nsithammarat*. There were also food recipes, which were usually inserted in some left-over space at the end of other writings, such as one recipe about the secret of mixing certain kinds of curry ingredients:

> "less fish paste in *Kaeng Bo'n* (a curry made with a kind of vegetable), and more fish paste in *Kaeng Yuak* (a curry made with shreds of banana tree trunk)."

Which means that if the *Khun* or *Au* plant (a kind of long-stem plant) is used for curry, the fish paste must be toned down in the curry, while in a curry with shreds of banana tree trunk more fish paste is needed. This kind of knowledge was probably oral to start with, and was later written down for further knowledge sharing.

4) Instructive literature

The instructive literature of the South reflects the people's expectations about cultivation in the young such attributes as would be appropriate to the sex, age, and status of each individual. Besides adherence to Buddist principles, a man must be brave, fair-minded, and wise in the way of the world, for a man must be strong and able to protech his honour as a man as family honour. Bravery is a sign of manliness. A brave man is considered to possess a minimum for survival. A man must also be fair-minded, and stout-hearted to boot in the spirit of giv-and-take, not taking advantage of others, and generous in cultivating kin and friends. As for girls, the emphasis of the instrumtion was upon composure and humility, obedience to seniors, patience and restraint, diligence, refinement and, most of all, preservation of chastity, for premarital loss of virginity or an illicit love affair was considered a curse on the family and not merely a personal fault.

Examples of such literature are *A Verse to Instruct Boys and Girls, Proverbs of Pali*[5] *Instructing His Younger Brother* (in verse), *Mind-Training Proverbs* (in Kap and in prose), *Khlong Proverbs.*[6]

5) Romances

This kind of literature was created for emotional sustenance, chiefly for entertainment. It was based upon the *Jatakas,* some folk tales, as well as newly composed tales. Most was written in *Kap* verse, such as *Wan Kan, Nai Dan, Sappradon, Cet Wa,* all in *Kap* verse.

VALUE OF SOUTHERN LITERATURE

Of altogether over 100 works on southern literature as literary analyses, undergraduate and graduate theses and dissertations at various

---

[5] A monkey chief in the epic Ramayana.
[6] Khlong is a form of Thai verse.

universities, and reviews published in the *Encyclopaedia of Southern Thai Culture,* those related to value are as follows:

1) Literary value

Suthiwong Pongpaiboon did a literary analysis and critique of *Manohra Nibat,* version of Wat Matchimawat, Songkhla, held to be the first work of southern literature to be so treated, and summed up its literary value thus: "The style of composition, diction, and language was all poetic," and "It is complete in literary value, in substance as well as in flavour."

The same scholar did a literary analysis of *Sutikam Kham Kap* and pointed out:

> "The movement of the plot shows a high artistic calibre so that the story is concise and clear in the right places--concise where appropriate and detailed where elaboration is needed. The diction is simple and yet outstanding of sense, not densely packed with teminology, but with manifest evidence of scholarship on the part of its author."

Prapon Ruangnarong analysed *Phra Wo'rawong,* a literary work of Suratthani Province, in his M.A. Thesis at Silpakorn University, and in appraising the aesthetic value of this work, concluded that the art of language in the work indicates an ability to choose words of simplicity to suit the readers; the words were well chosen for their sounding effect to be evocative of emotion; repetitions were used to accentuate feelings and intensify figures of speech; the use of symbols, rhetoric of comparison, and witty exchanges sparkled; there is an orderly way of repetition of words and positions similar in quality of *Samutthakot Kham Chan* and *Anirut Kham Chan;* the narration and description are moving and complete with the nine literary flavours consistent with the principles of literary composition of *Alangkarnsastra.*

Suebpong Thammachat, analysing the *Jataka* literature of the South as part of doctoral study in the Faculty of Arts, Chulalongkorn University, ranging over 20 works, summed up the literary value:

> "The literary value analysed involved choice of words. In the work, there were several ways in which words werre chosen

236

for composition: the use of words for melody and beauty, changes in word form for rhyme and melody, ornamental use of words both in sound and sense, the use of simple, concise, and communicative words. Of figure of speech there were several kinds: simile, metaphor, symbol, personification, hyperbole, onomatopoeia, allegory, pun, rhetorical cuestion, and imagery. From the analysis, each *Jataka* episode was found to contain all ingredients blended the aesthetics of belles-lettres into the contents, making the work readable.

From the literary analyses of over 100 scholarly titles, the conclusion was unanimous that in all southern literature the presence of attributes of literary value is evident, both in versification and in the art of diction rich in quality of uterances and individual words alike, no less than what has been found in Central Thai literature or in the literature of any other region.

2) Social and Cultural value

Southern literature depended upon the contexts of agricultural and Buddhist society to mould the authors' worldviews and values. The authors attempted to translate their worldviews and values into images of ideas and expectations for transmission to society, both in a straightforward way and through techniques of presentation. The expectations have permeated and have been anchored profoundly to the way of life of the people, to the extent that they have become folk culture, which embraces several distinctive attributes of common personality of the southern society, such as:

2.1 To cultivate human worth as part of personality

The attributes of a good person ideal to the people of the South as reflected in the local literature are:

2.1.1 Personal attributes

Southern literature reflects expectations about human qualities in individuals in the following ways:

(a) To be morally proper, knowing right and wrong by the Buddhist principles, as staated in *Swatdiraksa Kham Kap*:

237

"On a l,ong journey, what companion have you?
Verily your personal merit and sin will as
your constant attendant serve you.

.....Never tire of earning your livelihood.
Merit you hasten to make. Practice discipline
and charity. Navigate you boat floating
midstream; mend its mast; steer straight."

Subin, older version, describes how Supaki, Subin's mother, was
divested of her soul by a messenger of hell who led her soul to the nether-
world, where she was subjected to interrogation by the guardian of that
domain about her past deeds:

"So, into specifics, the interrogation went.
'Tarry not, you lowly one, name whatever sins
you committed, or whatever merits you made.
Say the truth and fear not. 'Her palms joined
overhead, her lips quaking, no merit could she
recall. 'I, an indigent old woman, only collect
firewood mornings and evenings and sell it for
bare subsistence. Sin and merit I understand
not. Beg your mercy. This is my truth.'"

Here answer confessing her ignorance of sin and merit led to the
following: "The powerful guardian god became enraged, his eyes blazing:
'You wicked woman, in vain were you born with a human nose and
mouth, not knowing any deed of merit whatever. Why should you be
counted as a human being? Stay you not on earty, for useless you are. Ho!
Guardian of the world, make haste and seize this wicked woman; hurl her,
then, into the pit of eternal fire.'"

(b) To encourage people to be hardworking and frugal, as in
The Proverbs for Maidens:

"As our ancestors said: a maiden with but some rag cloth
and a needle wandered into the jungle and ended up staying with
a grandma on a sesame farm. Crocheting and sewing, she turned

the cloth into one product or another for grandpa to take to market. Their finance improved, so they bought silk thread to make into more cloth. Sell it they did for a goodly sum, a fine product it was which fetched a high price. Slaves, elephants, and horses they owned, from the worth of her needlework invested. The maiden thus acquired riches which filled the house. So could the value of rag and needle help sustain and save one from degeneration."

(c) To instruct a maiden on being ladylike and disciplined in manner, and a man on being motivated towards learning, as in The Proverbs for Maidens:

"Properly would you speak or inquire, or laugh;
overdo it not beyond the bound of etiquette.
Hurry not through a meal, nor fidget monkeylike.
Should you walk, stay calm and collected. Wander
not like cattle."

From Suthikam Jataka: "A lady is well-mannered and adheres to truth as her integral part."

From Subin, older version: "One who is diligent is like a candle flame lighting up the Faith, glorifying it far and wide the world over."

2.1.2 Behaviour towards society

(a) To be merit-minded, with a sense of generosity, sharing, hospitality, and compassion, as stated in *Suthikam Jataka*, for example: "Once rich, hasten to give, and the giving shall bear fruit in your favour and deliver you from the four vices."

(b) To have a sense of gratitude, and not to return evil for good done, To practice honest, as in the story *Nok Cap*: "One who contemplates evil for his master will himself face misfortune in no time at all." From *Subin*, older version: "Show gratitude to your parents; serve them well, and never be rough or insulting. What the senior monks or the elders advise, heed that. Keep your greed and envy in check."

(c) To be respectful towards the elders:

"Gentle beauty, be you humble. Mind your
own mother, brothers and sisters, uncles
and aunts, maternal grandfather, and kinsmen.
Whatever they caution about, treat it not
with hauteur; be not unruly, and defer to
your own paternal grandparents."

In sum, a good person as expected by the concept expressed in southern literature is one who must make merit and perform useful deeds for oneself and kinsfolk, and who does not do evil to impair oneself and others, rather than one with keen intelligence or riches of good fortune, rank and of material possessions but devoid of happiness.

2.2 Source values of the system of beliefs and traditions

Numerous values in southern literature have contributed to the emergence of the system of beliefs and traditions, as referred to in the following:

Prapon Ruangnarong, in an analysis for his graduate thesis about *Phra Worawong,* a literary work of Suratthani, categorised beliefs into those about occult, astrology, Buddhism, and various traditions.

Sompong Thammachat did an analysis for his dissertation about the *Jataka* literature of *bud* volums, and identified beliefs about the following: the Triple Gem, causation, good and evil as well as hell and heaven, nest life, merit-making by putting food into the monk's bowl for the merit to be transmitted to the deceased, the supernatural and magic; it also presented some reflections of practices related to Buddhist ordination, wedding celebration, Songkran festival, oath-taking by partaking of sacred water, funeral rite, and festival to mark the end of the tenth lunar month.

Ubonsri Atthapanthu, in her analysis of *Nok Cap,* a *bud* volume, dealt with topics such as types of entertainment for celebrations at rites and ceremonies, beliefs about the cycle of existence and *nibbana,* among others.

Here the writer wishes to discuss the ramifications of the roots of those ideas and beliefs, and shall focus upon only 3 points for illustrationl

2.2.1 Emergence of beliefs about the cause and effect of one's deed, hell and heaven.

The literature resulted in making people evil-shunning and merit-making, as in *Kintakinara jataka:*

"My beloved I think of. Die or bear
with hardship would I. as my deeds of
old catch up with me" My hope is to
say good-bye and depart for heaven.

Should I think now of roistering in
town, and of deeds involved I have caused,
hell would my growth retard. Eternally
would a fire of desire burn, thousands and
thousands of years."

2.2.2 Rise of the custom of entry into Buddhis monkhood and preference for a male heir

The literary work, *Subin,* of which there several versions, particularly gave rise to the belief that every man must spend part of his life in monkhood, for the ordination of a son would give the parents a hold onto their monk son's hem of yellow robe so that the parents would be saved from hell and allowed entry into heaven, as in the case of Subin in the story who, even only after his ordination as a novice, was able to save his mother who was undergoing punishment in hell from the need to serve any more time there:

"Oh, guardian of the world, make haste and seize the
wicked woman; hurl her, then, into the pit of eternal fire.'
dragged her away by the hands. Hurt and weeping, she saw the
flames and was horrified as if about to die. Said she, 'Ah, the
gentle flames, so like the hem of my son's robe, a novice he is.
Serve and care for senior monks does he, and mastered the
Dharma he has. May his merit save his mother now...
    The force of her ordained son's merit sprang a lotus amidst
the flames. The golden lotus, blossoming to receive the mother,
spread its petals of comforting fragrance. A heavenly rain fell all
a sudden in huge drops breaking the pit asunder. The glowing
ceal was extinguished. All hell turned cool much like a river."

Also, the incluence of such beliefs has extended in such a way that southern Thai people learned to expect a son rather than a daughter, for a son would be the one to enter Buddhist monkhood so that his parents and kinsfolk would be privileged to hold on to the hem of his yellow robe for entry into heaven as earlier mentioned.

2.2.3 Source of the cultural aspect of caring for one's parents

Both local and folk literature of the South have complemented each other in stressing to southern Thai people the obligation of caring for their own parents, so that the parents could depend upon their children or grandchildren to look after them in illness and death. This caused the family to be closely knit, with its kinsfolk enjoying the security of assisting and caring for one another, as exemplified in *Subin* when *Subin* was reproved by his mother for having deserted her to take up the life of a Buddhist novice:

"Woe, my Subin, I have given you sustenance for seven years and four months. Oh, the love of a mother for her son! Who else would possess a love so dear? A mother I am, keeping watch over the house, and entrusting myself to you should illness or death befall me.

Sedulously have I preserved you like the pupils of my eyes; not even a slight cause of irritation have I allowed to come near you. No matter what hardship, a hunddedfold extraordinary, and even if I had to do without food until late each morning, surely a sight of you quenches all pangs of hunger."

It can be seen that the reason why a mother has nurtured a son amidst much hardship and with great loving care is the mother's hope in her evening of life to entrust herself, in illness and upon demise, to the care of the son. Such was the source of this distinctive cultural aspect oof southern Thai life: the obligation of children and grandchildren to do their utmost to care for their parents, or else to suffer social condemnation as an ingrate.

THE WISDOM AS SEEN IN SOUTHERN LITERATURE

The Literature reflects elements of southern Thai people's wisdom as follows:

1) The knack of inculcating in the reader a sense of appreciation and preservation of books

It is considered a cultural aspect of southern people to instill in the reader a sense of appreciation and preservation of books for utmost benefit to others, with this admonition: anyone who reads while lying down, who fails to keep books in a proper place, who causes a book to be torn or damage, who regards a book as plain sheets of paper, is bound to be visited by misfortune and some kind of punishment to the extent that a point of emphasis was made about the ill fate of such a one to be reborn an animal or to be slated for hell, as exemplified in the following:

From *Mahajataka*

"Whoever borrows this be apprised: Chant not the words of Dharma while lying down, for a sanke you would become as a consequence; nor should you while lying down listen to the words of Dharma; thoroughly would I advise you; rush not through chanting and, too, put your volume our of harm's way.

From *Ka-khao in Kap*

"Hark you, those chanting and those listening, of faith worthy of praise: Whoever prays at bedtime should sit erect, palms joined overhead in reverence of the sacred five; focus the mind, and then exercise it reading. Those listening: respectful be they, and a gesture of homage proffer."

From *Chantakat*

"Unmindful be you not; and let it not be torn, take care. Through ache and pain did I labour to yield this creation. Let no harm come to it. Should you have it on loan, read it not while lying down. This *Jataka Nibat* about the Great Teacher would

243

subject one who treats it carelessly and coarsely to abysmal punishment."

It was indeed a subtle way of wisdom to promote conservation of literature by employing the concept of a sinner being punished for his sin to admonish those who subscribed to the concept. It was more effective than straightforward words of prohibition or rebuke, as found in *Phra Mahosot*, version of Wat Choenglae Tai, Ranote District, Songkhla Province, written by the copying scribe thus:

"I have done this for our common monastery. When you are through using it, don't ever treat it carelessly. It hurt a lot at my waist while I was doing the copying. If you are careless with it, then you are dogs, the whole lot of you!"

2) The wisdom that accentuates the value of worthy human resource

A work of southern literature, *Phya Chatthan*, contains an aspect of wisdom to inspire the reader to praise and protection of human resource, in proportaion to the worth of such resource. Scholars, especially, must be exalted and protected by society, as pointed out in a scale of comparative severity of wrong deeds whereby even killing as many as 1,000 abbots would not be so severe a sin as taking the life of only one scholar:

"One thousand novices, if you killed them, your sin would equal that of killing one monk, who lives by discipline. One thousand monks, should one cause their lives to be taken, this would be a sin equal to that of killing on abbot, who ives by strict self-control. Killing abbots, truth to tell, even as many as one thousand, would be killing one scholar."

3) The aspect of wisdom indicative of southern people's religious scholarship

The people of southern Thailand were praised for their religious scholarship by the Sukhothai Kingdom to the effect that the religious scholars of the time who had mastered the whole of the *Tripitaka* all hailed from Nakonsithammarat, and that the southern region was once the centre of religious brilliance, so that it was called the land of *Dharma*.

Some trace of the Buddhist scholarship is visible in such works as *Swasdiraksa in Kap,* version of Wat Bangsarm, Panarae District, Pattani Province, which deals with *nibbana* and heaven in a diffenent way from what is found in the *Jatakas* of traditional accounts, and which is close to the Scripture, actually, in the concept of *nibbana* and heaven, as in the following:

> "*Nibbana* and enjoyment of happiness, peaceful in cherishing sacredones. *Nibbana* exciting, rays of a brilliant gem, glittering and bright. Tha path is near. Seek, then, the way of *nibbana*. Should one find it, verily he is an heir of Lord Sri-ariya, and is born to the circle of those not to be long under any spell of illusion, and soon to come upon the path of realisaion of true existenc."

The wisdom in southern literature is characterised by versatility. For example, the wisdom about development of manpower of high quality, which in substance may be grouped into 4 categories:

(a) The wisdom about knowledge and working technique for careers.

(b) the wisdom absout Buddhist meritocracy and about the ethics to suit the sex, age, and staatus of the individual.

(c) The wisdom about worldly affairs and human behaviour.

(d) The wisdom about mental and physical health.

SOME POINTS OF OBSERVATION

This writer has some points of observation about southern literature as follows:

1) As deduced from the writer's own direct experience, it can be estimated that five decades ago more than 95 per cent of southern literature records still remained, whereas at present there are approximately 10,000 volumes (only of the *bud* kind) extant in the collections at various educational institutions and cultural centres, not even one per cent of what has been wasted away, ruined, or lost.

2) Of the records which have been preserved, less than one per cent has been subjected to study and analysis, mostly for literary significance. There has been little critical work about any other aspects of the literature, thus presenting too scaarce a sum of reliable body of knowledge either in developmental or functional sense.

3) The works of southern Thai literature are mainly anonymous, without definite dates of production and deviod of the authers' addresses and of the places where the writing of the works was undertaken. So there are problems about analysis of social contexts and people as mirrors of the periods of time involved.

REFERENCES

Institute for Southern Thai Studies
    1984 *Southern Thai Worldview*. Songkhla.

    1986a *Saranukrom Watthanatham Phak Tai* (Southern Thai Culture Encyclopaedia) 3.

    1986b *Saranukrom Watthanatham Phak Tai* (Southern Thai Culture Encyclopaedia) 7.

    1986c *Saranukrom Watthanatham Phak Tai* (Southern Thai Culture Encyclopaedia) 10.

Prapon Ruangnarong
    1980 Phra Wo'rawong, M.A. Thesis, Silpakorn University.

Prateep Chumphon
    1976 *Southern Literature*, Department of Oriental Languages, Faculty of Archaeology, Silpakorn University.

Ratanatachanmuni (Joo Tiparaksapanthu), Phra
    1962 *Itsarayan Thetsana,* Cremation Volume for Phra
        Ratanatachamuni.

Seubpong Thammachat
    1991 An anlytical Study of Southern Thailand's Jatakas, Bud
        Volumes, Ph.D. Thesis, Chulalongkorn University. Bangkok.

Suthiwong Pongpaiboon
    1970 *Manora Nibat Chabap Wat Matchimawat, Songkhla,* The
        College of Education, Songkhla.

    1974 *Sutthikam Chadok Kham Kap Maharat Kham Chan*
        Srinakharinwirot University, Songkhla.

    1976 'Local Southern Thai Literature,' *Journal of the national
        Research Commission,* 8: 1.

    1985 *'List of Items Sent by Chao Phraya Wichienkiri (Maen Na
        Songkhla) to Bangkok in 2424 B.E. (1881 A.D.)',* Cremation
        Volume for Suchat Ratanaprakarn.

Ubonsri Atthapanthu
    1991 *Textual Reconstruction of Bud Literary Work: Nok Cap,*
        Institute for Southern Thai Studies, Songkhla.

A COMPARATIVE STUDY OF
ISAN AND LANNA THAI LITERATURE
Dhawat Poonotoke

From a study of the literatures of the various regions of Thailand, one finds that the literatures of the north and northeastern regions share great similiarities. They share similarities in their plots, perspective, major themes, as well as their style of writing and the type of alphabets that they use. From a geographical perspective, one would not expect to find such similarities between the two cultures, as they are separated by a mountain range which makes communication and cultural contact difficult. One would expect that the cultures of these two regions would originate in the royal capitals of Sukhothai, Ayutthaya, and Bangkok, which have been the political and cultural centres of Thailand. This, however, is not the case. The people of north and northeastern Thailand have distinctions in their culture specific to their particular regions, although their overall societal structure is similar to that of the various Tai cultures throughout Thailand. Differences include language, literature, values, and life style, etc.

ISAN -- NORTH-EAST THAILAND

According to archeological evidence, the people of Isan have had a long cultural tradition. The beginning of their history appears to be in the 6th century. However, we are not able to establish whether the people in Isan during this time were Tai, as the inscriptions that have been found during this period are written in southern Indian characters from the reign of the Pallawa dynasty, and the language of the inscriptions is Sanskrit and ancient *Mo'n*. During the 10th through 12th centuries, the characters began to evolve into ancient *Kho'm* characters, and the language that was used was Sanskrit mixed with *Kho'm*. Therefore, Isan culture during the 10th through 12th centuries was that of the *Kho'm*. Even though there is evidence that Tai people began to play a historical role in Southeast Asia by the 10th century, there is no evidence to support the belief that the culture in Isan during this time was that of the Tai[1]. During the 12th through 13th centuries, we have found no inscriptions or archeological sites, which raises the question of what happened to the people living in Isan in the previous time. We should consider the great corvee of labour to build religious sites and fight wars during the reign of the *Kho'm* King Chaiyawaraman VII (1181-1218). The people of Isan were probably a major source of this labour. After the corvee, the people who remained were probably few in number and without leaders active in the building of monuments. The type of culture that is observable in Isan during the following period is not related to or developed from the culture in the same region during the previous centuries. The new culture can be referred to as that of the people of the Mekong river valley. The art is different from the previous period. For example, the Buddhist figures from this appearance have Lao faces, and the shape of the script is influenced by ancient *Mo'n* (i.e.*Tham*) and Sukhothai (i.e. *Thai No'i*) script. The content of the inscriptions is also different from inscriptions of the previous period. Therefore, one is led to believe that a new ethnic group immigrated into the region. The new group, the Tai people of the Mekong river valley, known as the Lao, established their culture in Isan from the 15th century onwards.

The history of the Tai of the Mekong river valley began during the era of King Fa Ngum in 1353[2]. Before this time, although Tai people existed in this area, they had not yet created an independent state. The Kingdom of Sukhothai during the time of King Ramkhamhaeng claimed much of the Mekong river valley as part of its territory, as follows: "To the east, up to the banks of the Mekong, up to Wiangcan (i.e. Vientiane). Wiangkham, is ours" (Thailand 1972: 10). According to the historian John F. Cady, "The Lao built a secure Kingdom during the year 1353. King Fa Ngum took advantage of Sukhothai's weakness in strength, and the fact that Ayutthaya was a great distance away, and that Vietnam had been

---

[1] The Champa inscription at Bonakar temple in the city of Yatrang in the year 1593 writes of Cham king named Chai Paramesuan Wannathep who restored a religious site and donated 55 slaves, which included the ethnic groups Cham, Khmer, Chinese, Burmese and Siamese (see Subhadradis 1979: 225).

[2] The history of the Tai people in the Mekong river valley probably began before this date but we have no evidence other than in various chronacles, such as Khun Burom, and Thao Hung Thao Cheung.

invaded by the Chinese Meng dynasty. The Kingdom of Lanchang reached its height during the reign of Samsaen Thai (1373-1416). The Kingdom of Lanchang was important from this time onwards, and became commonly known as Lao" (Charnvit 1977: 160)

During the time of the early Ayutthaya period, communities in Isan appear to have been small in size and therefore Ayutthaya did not regard them with the same importance as it did the Kingdom of Lanchang. Therefore Thai historical chronicles include much information about Vientiane but do not mention the various towns in Isan. Such towns were probably not large communities, and were under the influence of Lanchang. Towns in Isan are continously mentioned in the Lao historical chronicles, for example: Khotabo'ng (Khotabun), Bak Huai Luang (Phongphisai district, No'ng Khai), No'ng Han (Sakon Nakho'n), and Lom and Loei, which shows that these towns were under the political influence of Lanchang. However, towns deeper inside of Isan such as Phimai, Khorat, and the old city of Chaiyaphum are infrequently mentioned in Lao historical chronicles, indicating that they were beyond the political influence of Lanchang.

From the time of King Narai, Thai chronicles began to mention Isan, specifically Khorat and the neighbouring regions. Prince Damrong wrote that: "King U-Thong sent his troops to fight the *Kho'm* kingdom. At that time *Kho'm* power had weakened considerably. The army of Ayutthaya took control of the *Kho'm* kingdom and its various towns in Isan, such as Khorat. During this period, the population of Khorat appeared to have largely been Khmer. However, the *Kho'm* Kingdom was not completely defeated, and during the following reigns the Thai had to send their army to fight the *Kho'm* several times. It appears that during this period the Thai controlled only Khorat in Isan (specifically the subdistrict of Sung Noen). Therefore, Thai historical chronicles do not describe events in Khorat until the reign of King Narai" (Damrong 1968: 8-9). The fact that the king sent a governor, Phraya Yomarat, to govern Khorat during the reign of King Narai, shows that the area had begun to be considered important by the Thai. From this time onwards there were attempts to control the various towns within Isan, using Khorat as the central headquarters. Internal conflicts within the Vientiane dynasty during the latter period of Ayutthaya caused an increasingly large migration of people to settle in Isan, including Campasak (the group of Phra Khru Phon Samet),

Ubon (Phra Wo' Phra Ta), Kalasin, etc. During the Rattanakosin era, by the year 1779, the Lao Kingdoms of Vientiane, Campasak, and Luang Phrabang were under the control of the Thai.[3] During the latter period of Thonburi, regional nobles were encouraged to have their people settle and establish towns within Isan. This caused Isan communities to increase in size and number, and caused many of the people who fled into the forest during the war with Vientiane in 1779 and during the rebellion of Chao Anu in 1836 to return (Phaithun 1975: appendix K) An anthropologist has concluded: "The people of Isan are closer ethnically to the people of Lanchang (Lao) than to the people of the Chao Phraya river valley" (Suthep 1968: 230). The history and culture of Isan and Lanchang are very closely related. The governing of the various towns in Isan before 1897 was based upon traditional Lanchang practices, known as the Anya system (Phaithun 1975: 10).[4] Therefore, Isan society up until this period was similar to that of Lanchang.

Isan literature is descended from the literary tradition of the Kingdom of Lanchang. The beliefs and values in the literature are expressions of the way of life of the people of the societies of Lanchang and Isan. The scripts used in the literatures of the two societies are also the same, i.e. the *Tham* script for religious works such as scriptures and *Jataka* tales, and the the *Thai No'i* script for worldly matters such as religion for entertainment, etc.

THE TRANSMISSION OF CULTURE BETWEEN NORTHERN AND NORTH-EASTERN THAILAND

The people of northern and northeastern Thailand and only began to have close contact with the people of the Cao Phraya valley during the Rattanakosin period. During the early Rattankosin period, the Thai ruled the various towns in the region in the feudal style of 'Cao Khro'ng Nakho'n'. Therefore the power of the Thai kingdom in the regions was restricted to that of the nobles who were sent to govern the towns. The majority of the regional people were not influenced by central Thailand. The culture and way of life of the people of Isan and northern Thailand was still based upon traditional practices. Central Thai culture did not

---

[3] Phongsawadan Yo' Mu'ang Wiangcan "sakarat 141 (B.E. 2322) 'kat kai' year (i.e. Pi Kun - year of the 'Pig') 11th month, third night of the waxing moon, Monday fell to the Thai" (see Thailand 1941: 189).

[4] In the fifth reign, the traditional method of governing in Isan was abolished.

become an important influence until the reign of King Rama V, who introduced the Centralized Administrative System of Reforms in the regions during the years of 1893-1910. This resulted in the introduction of Thai culture into the various regions of Thailand, which became prominent when compulsory primary education was introduced during the reign of King Rama VI. This was a major factor that caused the deterioration of the traditional transmission of culture in the regions. Compulsory education brought in new values, language, and literature from central Thailand. It also caused the abandonment of the use of the regional alphabets. Regional literature was replaced in importance by central Thai literature taught in the classroom.

1) The transmission of culture from north to northeast Thailand.

During the beginning of the Mangrai dynasty in Chiang Mai, the rulers of Lanna and Lanchang shared a close relationship. The rulers of the two kingdoms were related by blood. King Phothisarat (1520-1550)[5] took the daughter of the Lanna King Phra Mu'a ng Ket Kaeo as his queen. He also sent a diplomatic mission to Chiang Mai asking for the Buddhist Scriptures, the Tripitaka, and the monk Phra Thep Mongkhon Thera during the year 1517, to help spread Buddhism in Lanchang. Earlier, during the reign of King Wisunrat (1500-1520) (Laos 1957: 99) there was an important religious revival. At this time, although there is no evidence that monks were invited from Chiang Mai, many important monks received their religious education form Chiang Mai and other cities in Lanna. During the reign of King Wisunrat, there were many Buddhist scholars, for example, the Supreme Patriach Wisun Maha Rachathibo'di, who translated the *Pancatantra,* and Phra Maha Thep Luang and Phra Mongkhon Sithi, who wrote the chronicle Khun Burom with other scholars (Laos 1957: 101). During the reign of King Phothisarat, the revival of Sri Lankan style Buddhism continued. Lanna literature reached its height during the reign of King Phra Mu'a ng Kaew. The transmission of religion from Lanna to Lanchang was an important factor in the spreading of Lanna literature from the former kingdom into the latter. Therefore, one finds that the majority of literature that one finds in Isan (which was influenced by Lanchang) has similar plots to the literature of the north, for

---

[5] The dates of various reigns in northern chronicles and Lanchang chronicles have minor differences. The correct dates have yet to be established.

example, *Thao Kam Ka Dam, Nang Phom Ho'm, Lin Tho'ng* (known in the north as *Suwanna Sio Ha Lin Kham)*, etc. The *Vesantara Jataka,* an important literary work, is especially similar in both regions, with minor differences.

2) The spreading of Buddhism and Buddhist literature.

The spreading of Buddhism and Buddhist literature was an important factor in the transmission of *Yuan* (i.e. *Tua Mu'a ng)* and *Fak Kham* characters from Lanna into Lanchang. The people of Lanna originally adapted the ancient *Mo'n* script to be suitable to record their own language. The adapted script was known as *Yuan,* or *Tua Mu'a ng.* The people of Lanchang borrowed the script from Lanna and transformed it into the *Tham* script. Through years of usage, the shape of the letters used in Lanchang and Isan was gradually transformed from that of the *Yuan* script. At the same time, the shape of Yuan characters evolved from the time in which they were borrowed by the Lao during the Mangrai dynasty. Therefore, at present the Yuan characters used in the north and the *Tham* characters used in Isan have considerable differences.

The *Thai No'i* script of the Lao is likely to have been developed from the *Fak Kham* script of Lanna.[6] It is note-worthy that during the reign of King Lithai of Sukhothai, Buddhism was spread into neighboring kingdoms. Phra Sumana Thera was invited to introduce his religious reforms into Lanna during the reign of King Ku' Na. Phra Suwanna Khiri similarly brought Buddhist to the city of Chawa (Luang Phrabang). Religious missions were sent to various other cities, for example, Nan (led by Phra Wessaphu), Ayutthaya (led by Phra Piyatassi), and Pa Mai Mamuang in Sukhothai (led by Phra Anan in place of Phra Sumana Thera) (Thailand 1976: 194). When Phra Sumana Thera led his religious mission to Chiamg Mai, he introduced into Lanna the *Fak Kham* script of Sukhothai. It is likely that the script was similarly introduced into Lanchang during Phra Suwwana Khiri's mission to Luang Phrabang. However, no inscriptions have been in Luang Phrabang from this time. Regardless of their exact origins, there is no doubt that the *Fak Kham,*

---

[6] Scripts of the various Tai groups including Thai No'i, Thai Tangkia, and Thai Dam, are considered to have been derived from a Thai script which was developed at a similar time as the ancient Khom and Mon alphabets. We have found no inscriptions written in a Tai script that are older than the inscription of King Ramkhamhaeng of Sukhothai. Therefore it is generally accepted that Thai No'i was derived from the script of Sukhothai.

Sukhothai, and *Thai No'i* scripts are related, and descended from the same proto-type.

CHARACTERISTICS OF THE LITERATURE OF THE NORTHERN AND NORTH-EASTERN REGIONS OF THAILAND

1) The centre of literary development

The northern and northeastern regions of Thailand are similar in that religious institutions are of greater importance in the creation and development of literature than the monarchy. This is a major difference between the literature of these two regions and that of central Thailand. The great majority of the literature is religious in content, for example: *Jataka* tales, didactic literature that teaches moral behavior, various chronicles tracing the spread of Buddhism in Southeast Asia (for example, *Munla Satsana* and *Chinakalamalipako'n* in the north, and *Urangkathat* in the northeast), and various chronicles which are related to Buddhist prophecies or history, for example, *Chamthewiwong, Tamnan Singhanawa Kuman, Tamnan Suwanna Khom Kham* in the north, and *Khun Burom* in Isan, etc. Considering that the temple was the traditional centre of literary development, it is not surprising hat the content of the literature is based upon Buddhist philosophy. In many cases, (for example the *Pannasa Jataka),* local folk-tales have been transformed into *Jataka* tales. These stories are used to instill·the local people with Buddhist religious values. At the same time, Buddhism is diluted with local beliefs in spirits and the supernatural.

There are two major sectors involved in the creation of literature:

2) The temple as the centre of literary creation

In northern Thailand during the Mangrai dynasty, the monkhood played an important role in the creation of literature. Lanna literature during this period included religious and didactic literature as well as apocryphal *Jataka* tales created from local folk-lore. Folk tales that were transformed into *Jataka* tales were endowed with various religious conventions such as the use of the Pali language. In such a manner they were given a sacred status, highly respected by their audience. The use of the Pali language also added to a work's artistic beauty and increased its literary value. The temple was traditionally the centre of scholarly knowledge in society. The creators of literary works were almost entirely derived from the monkhood.

Therefore, conventions and values of Lanna and Isan society during this period (i.e. the 15th to 17th centuries) were largely dictated by the temple.

Isan was influenced by the literature of the Mekong river valley of which Lanchang was the cultural centre. Therefore, its literature is similar to that of Lanna. The literature of Lanchang (and Isan) was adapted to a certain extent from the literature of Lanna to fit the differing values and ways of life of the Lao. During the reign of King Suriyawong in 1633-1680, Lanchang literature reached its golden age (Laos 1957: 155). During this time, Buddhist religious thought and conventions exerted great influence on the literature. Examples can be seen in *Sang Sinsai* by Thao Pangkham and *Pu So'n Lan* by Supreme Patriarch Siri Jantho.

In contrast to Ayutthaya, during the time that religious literature was of importance in north and northeast Thailand, there was no definite code of laws to govern the two societies. There was only a set of customary laws developed from local traditions, such as *Mangraisat* in the north and *Hit Sip So'ng Kho'ng Sip Si* and *Kho'ng Khun Burom* in Isan. Therefore, the temple played an important role in supervising people's behavior. During the Mangrai dynasty in Lanna and the reigns of Kings Wisunrat, Photisarat, etc., in Lanchang, the religious and royal institutions shared a close relationship. Religious and didactic literature performed the role of societal control. Values were taught through the insertion of Buddhist philosophy in the literature. Literature taught people to hope for a future life which depended on their present actions, and instilled in them the hope to be born to see the future Buddha, *Phra Si An*. It also taught people to accept their station in life through the belief that their status was the result of their karma. In such a manner, Buddhist philosophy as presented in the literature created legitimacy for the ruling class. Thus the temple helped the monarchy to govern the people in the absence of a strict code of law.

3) The creation of non-religious literature

Non-religious literature is relatively scarce in north and northeastern Thailand. Examples are *Nirat Hariphunchai* in the north and *Khunlu Nang Ua* in the northeast. As previously stated, the vast majority of the literature, regardless of actual origins, was presented as life tales of the Buddha.

The subject and conventions of non-religious literature is considerably different from that of the counterpart literature of central Thailand. In central Thailand, the majority literature was created in close relationship with the monarchy, and was intended to be presented to the king. Central Thai works of this type were not greatly influenced by Buddhist philosophy. Although some owe their origins to *Jataka* tales, they were transformed in a manner that stressed their entertainment rather than religious values. An example is *Su'a Kho Kham Chan*, which was based on an apocryphal *Jataka* tale. Other central Thai works were written with the purpose of extolling the monarchy, such as *Lilit Yuan Phai*, and various Khlong works.

4) The use of literature in northern and northeast Thailand

Literature was traditionally performed before the public in Lanna and Isan. Literary performances served a role as entertainment and as a teacher of societal values.

(a) The reading of literature during funerals in Isan.

In the past, it was traditional in Isan that literature would be read during funerals which were known as *Ngan Hu'a n Di*. Stories that were commonly read include: *Sang Sin Sai, Champa Si Ton, Thao Kam Ka Dam, Kalaket, Thao Busaba (Pla Daek Pla Samo'), Suphrom Mokha, Thao Lin Tho'ng, Thao Khatthanam*, etc. The majority of these works share a similar plot with works in the Pannasa *Jataka* in the north. People of all ages enjoyed listening to literature during funerals. The works would generally be read to a type of melodious chant known as *Lam Phu'n* or *Lam Ru'a ng*. It is worthy of note that many works read during funerals are also preached by monks on auspicious occasions. Sometimes the same version of the work is read both inside and outside of the temple. Other works are converted to '*Jataka* Tales' when they are used as sermons. The reading of literature during funerals is an important factor that have made Isan people knowledgable of their own literature. People who are illiterate have a chance to hear the various stories. Reading literature at funerals also serves the purpose of uplifting peoples' spirits because of the beauty of its sound, the rhythm of the reading, and the exciting content of the story. In the past, other forms of entertainment, such as cinema and music, had yet to reach rural Isan society, and the reading of literature served an important function as entertainment.

(b) The reading of *Khao So'* literature in northern Thailand.

In northern Thailand, *Khao So'* literature was traditionally performed in public as entertainment. The reading of *Khao So'* literature, known as *'Lao Khao'*, occured during auspicious occasions such as ordination and marriage, as well as during funerals and merit-making ceremonies for deceased relatives. In the past, the host of an event would search for a person with a good voice to read the literature to a melodious chant. (At times, the *So'* instrument, which is similar to a violin, would be performed in accompaniment.) There were various styles of melodies that were used in the performance of *Khao So'*, depending on the mood of the work. Types of chants included the melodies of Chiang Mai, Mu'ang Thoen, Lampang, Chiang Saen, or the melodic styles of *Kong Hiao Bong, Ma Yam Fai, Wingwo'n*, etc. (Saneha 1976: 9-20). These type of performances made the people of the north familiar with their regional literature. Thus the values and philosophy expressed in the literature had an important effect on the people of Lanna.

It is note-worthy that the majority of the literary works performed before the community in the north are believed to be *Jataka* tales. Almost all of the stories are similar to those also performed as *Tham Khao* (i.e. religious works intended to be preached in the temple.) However, the style in which they are written differs from *Tham Khao*. The style of *Tham Khao* works generally differs from *Khao So'* in that they retain more of the conventions that one finds in scriptural *Jataka* tales such as the use of Pali, etc.

The *Sepha* melody was traditionally used in the public performances of in central Thailand. The story *Khun Chang Khun Phaen* was commonly read. Other central Thai works were generally performed as plays known as *Lakho'n No'k*. The staging of *Lakho'n No'k* plays required great expense. Therefore, the common people of central Thailand had less opportunity to hear their own literature than did the people of north and northeastern Thailand. One type of central Thai literature performed before the public was *'Suat O E Wihan Rai'*, which consisted of stories known as *'Cak Cak Wong Wong'* which were generally written in the *Klo'n Suat* form (*Kap Yani, Chabang,* and *Surangkhanang*).

5) The role of literature in governing behavior in society (didactic literature)

The literature of northern and northeastern Thailand not only played a role as entertainment, but also was used as a method of controlling people's ethical behavior in society, whether or not this was the original intention of its composers. Generally the people who listened to the literature had little choice in chosing the story to be read. Such a choice rested with the performer. Literature performed in the temple was generally chosen by the monks who performed the works rather than the laymen who listened to them.

As previously stated, the creators of the literature were generally monks rather than laymen. Therefore, Buddhist religious values were prominent in the literature, mixed with regional values and beliefs in the supernatural. Therefore, through the creation and performance of literature, the temple played an important role as a teracher of moral values, thoughts, and beliefs.

The governing of traditional Lanna and Lanchang society was facilitated by the temple's role as a teacher of moral behavior. This role was largely accomplished through the use of literature. Buddhist philosophy was adapted to fit in with local beliefs, customs, and way of life. Customary law, known in Lanchang as 'Hit Sip Saung Khaung Sip Si', was taught through the literature. The teaching of this code of behavior benefited those who governed the kingdom. At the same time the audience of the literature enjoyed the entertainment that was provided by the performance. They also believed that by listening to the literature they were making merit that would be beneficial to them in the future. People believed that it was their duty to follow the moral code presented in the literature. This was the result of their belief in karma in which they believed that they would be rewarded for their good behavior and punished for their bad behavior. The literature told of the happiness that they could attain in their next life-time. For example as a result of the merit that they made in their present life, they might be born again in the time of the future Buddha. Therefore, people were taught to accept the hardship that they endured in their present life and believe that it was the result of their *karma*. At the same time, they were taught to follow society's code of behavior in the hope of a better future life. One observes that religious literature frequently describes myterious phenomenon such as the universe, the era of the future Buddha and frightening scenarios for the world after the disappearance of Buddhism. Such descriptions helped to instill faith in Buddhism and make people fearful of committing bad deeds. In the popular Buddhism of Lanna and Lanchang, people were more concerned with attaining a future life in the presence of the future Buddha than they were with actual enlightenment and the attainment of *nirvana.*

An examination of didactic literature helps to illuminate the role of monkhood in the traditional societies of north and northeastern Thailand. Didactal literature in both regions not only taught a general code of behavior but also the proper role of the monarchy towards the people that they governed. Literary composers generally justified their instructions on the proper role of the monarchy by claiming that they were the teachings of the Buddha. an example of a work of this type is *Thammada So'n Lok* in Isan, which stresses that the king must follow the Buddhist Dharma and local customs, and be compassionate towards his subjects. Similar values are taught in northern Thai works such as *Kham So'n Phraya Mangrai,* which states that.

"The monk Tissa Thera, who was free from earthly desire, taught King Mangrai the way in which Haripunchai and Chiang Mai should be governed."

The work explains how a kingdom should be ruled in order that it will be filled with happiness and contentment.

Didactic literature of northern and northeastern Thailand also teaches general roles of people in society. It teaches, for example, how commoners should act before the king, and how the various members of a household should interact with one another. Didactic work in northern Thailand such as *Pu So'n Lan, Phra Lo' So'n Lok, Cao Withun So'n Lan,* and *Thammada So'n Lok,* are fairly similar in content. Didactic works in Isan, such as *Kala Nap Mu' Suai* teach people to fear the disappearance of Buddhism from the world. Other works in Isan include: *Pu So'n Lan, Lan So'n Pu, Inthiyan So'n Luk* (which teaches women's behavior) *Phraya Kham Ko'ng So'n Phrai* (which teaches how various classes should interact in society), *Siri Canthowat Kham So'n* (which teaches ethical behavior), *Thao Kham So'n* (which teaches how to choose a proper mate) etc.

The didactic literature of northern and northeastern Thailand teaches not only individual behavior, but also the proper role that various classes should play for the benefit of society. Traditional regioanl customes and values are the basis for such teachings. These works played an important role in controlling societal behavior.

It is note-worthy that in northern and northeastern Thai literature, there are many works that teach in a straight forward manner the proper role of the monarchy. In contrast, didactic works in central Thailand would necessarily be indirect in their teaching of the monarchy. For example, the central Thai work *Phali So'n No'ng* teaches the monarchy but it does so indirectly, and does not stress the duty of the king towards the citizenry. In fact, the teaching is interpreted merely as philosophy and morals of a general nature. Other central Thai didactic works teach moral behavior rather than duties within society (With the exception of *Suphasit So'n Ying* written by Suntho'n Phu.) Therefore, one can conclude that the monarchy in central Thailand could not be given advice or teaching because of its great power. Even the monkhood was fearful of its power. Although the monarchy had to respect the monkhood, the king with his semi-divine status (during the periods of Ayudhaya and Rattanakosin) was in too high a position for the monkhood to be able to criticise. If one examines the societal regulations created by the monarchy in Ayudhaya, for example *kot Monthian ban* (Palatine Law) *Kotmai Laksana That* (Slavary law) and *Kotmai Laskana Aya* (Criminal Law), One can see the clearcut division of the various classes within society. Incontrast, if one examines the structure of the societies of northern and northeastern Thailand, one observes that social rules dividing the various classes were relatively flexible. The population of the various cities in these regions was not very great, and thus the governing of society was as if that of a father and son. The temple acted as the dictater of societal values and conventions. Therefore, the interaction between the monarchy the temple and the common people was as if a triangle. The social contract between the relers and the ruled was created in the temple. The monarch and the common people had obligations to one another as supervised by the temple. Religious and didactic literature played a special rele in teaching how the common people should interact with the king. Such teaching facilitaated the governing of society by creating unity and order. At the same time, the literature gave the king legitimacy in the eyes of the common people by its portrayal of the monarch as on of great merit.

6) Themes in northern and northeastern Thai literature.

The themes of the literature of the two regions are very similar. In the following explanation, I will restrict my use of examples to works of Isan literature. Northern Thai literature has minor differences from the literature of Isan which at present are impossible summarize. Students of northern Thai literature should make a comparatrive study to reveal themajor differences between the two literatures.

As literature is a reflection of society throug a literary study one can learn much about a society's set of values and way of life, By studying the characteristics of literary heroes, for example, one con learn about the type of male and female the society wishes to present as role models. The philosophy of the society can be seen through the behavior of various characters, ideal moral values etc., as shown in the literature. If the values and beliefs within a given story are not generally accepted by the society in which the work is written, the story will not be popular. It will not be commonly read or transcribed. As stories need to be transcribedand to survive, if a story lacks sufficient popularity, it will disappear within a short period of time. Although certain stories in Isan were composed several centuries ago, the fact that they are still commonly read and performed at funerals is proof that the values presented in the stories are accepted to contemporary society. A thematic study of Isan literature reveals the following major points:

(a) Philosophy of life as shown in Isan literature.

Although the plot of Isan literature shares similarities with the 'Cak Cak Wong Wong' stories of central Thailand there are distinctions reflecting values specific to northeastern Thailand. For example, stories describe the conflict between characters who perform good deeds and characters who perform bad deeds (the latter including Yaksa, Queens, astrologer, etc.) Such stories teach that one will be rewarded for performing meritorious acts. Another major theme is the separation of a character from his home and for the people that he loves. Mysteries also play a major role in the literature, building up the religious faith of the audience and teaching them to be fearful of committing bad deeds. Literary composers attempt to instill values and religious teaching in a story's audience through the use of plot and through the description of heroes and heroines, as follows:

Religious Teaching:
Literary composers emphasise the consequences of performing good and evil acts. Characters are divided into two major groups by the type of their actions. The evil characters attempt in various ways to destroy the hero and other good characters. They make use of spells, bribes to astrologers, their influence on the king, etc. in an attempt to convince society that their evil actions are justified. Their evil acts and the consequences build up the suspense throughout the society. However, their evil actions are not ultimately successful as the hero is protected by supernatural forces. The invincibility of the hero teaches the audience of the power of people who have made great merit in previous life-times. Although the hero suffers hardships through his past accumulation of good deeds he ultimately attains happiness. At the sametime, the people who perform bad deeds ultimately suffer. Although the evil doers may possess high status and honors, this will not provide them with true happiness.

Separation:
The composer attempts to show the law of pharma and to create the belief that one's actions in a previous life will have an effect on one's condition in the present. Therefore, the hero (and characters in general who perform good deeds) are caused to suffer to pay for bad acts that they committed in previous life-times. However, they eventually achieve happiness due to their greater accumulation of good deeds than bad. Therefore, in Isan literature one commonly observes the separation of the hero from the one that he loves. Although the immediate cause behind the separation may differ in individual works, in all cases the suffering of separation is ultimately the result of the hero's *karma*.

Societal Beliefs and Values:
Mysterious events, lands beyond our realm, and unearthly beings play an important part in Isan literature. Examples include Himmaphan Forest, the land of *Yaksa*, *Garuda*, *Naga* etc., and various miracles and supernatural mysteries. Many stories describe the interaction of humans

with non-humans. For example: *Thaw Phadaeng Nang Ai Thaw Sithon* (i.e. *Phra Suthòn Manora*), *Thaw Khathanam, Phayakhankhak* (where a toad fights a battle with the king of *Thaen*), etc. These stories reflect the traditional world view of the Isan people in which there was no separation between the actual world and the world of myth and imagination. Isan stories emphasis the use of miracles (such as the ability to fly) and supernatural objects as means by which the hero gains power and defeats his enemies.

(b) Heroes-Ideal Role Models of Society:
An analysis of the concept of what a hero should be like in Isan society, as reflected in the literature.

An analysis of heroes in Isan society, as reflected in the literature shows that the Isan concept of an ideal ruler differs greatly from that of central Thailand. Isan people, for example value people of high morals as heroes, rather than those with a good figure. Important attributes of Isan heroes include intelligence, and the consideration of the general good of society rather than personal happiness.

REFERENCES

Charnvit Kasetsiri et al. (trans.)
  1977   *Thai Phama Lao Lae Kamphucha.* Bangkok: Phikhanet.

Chiangmai University
  1967   *Satsana Phraya Mangrai (Phak Pariwat Lamdap Thi Nu'ng).*
         Chiangmai: Department of Social Anthropology, Chiangmai
         University.

Damrong Rajanubhap, Somdet Krom Phraya
  1968   *Thiaw Tam Thang Rot Fai.* Bangkok: Pracakwit.

Laos
      1957   Phongsawadan Lao Chabap Kasuang Su'ksathikan Lao.
             Publisher Unkhown.

Phaithun Mikuson
      1975   *Kan Patirup Kan Pokkhro'ng Monthon Isan 2436-2453.*
             Bangkok: Khurusapha.

Saneha Bunyarak
      1976   Wannakam Khao Kho'ng Phak Nu'a. Bangkok: Khurusapha.

Subhadradis Disakul, Mo'm Cao
      1979   *Prawattisat Esia Akhane Thu'ng Po' So' 2000.* Bangkok:
             Samnak Lekhathikan Khana Ratthamontri.

Suthep Sunthornphesat
      1968   *SangkhomWithaya Mu Ban Phak Tawan O'k Chiang Nu'a.*
             Bangkok: Samakhom Sangkhomsat.

Thailand
      1941   *Prachum Phongsawadan Phak Thi 70.* Bangkok: Phracan.
      1972   *Prachum Sila Caru'k Phak thi 1 Lak Thi 1.* Bangkok:

Khurusupha.
      1976   *Tamnan Munla Satsana.* Bangkok: Phracan.

WHISPERED SO SOFTLY IT RESOUNDS THROUGH THE FOREST, SPOKEN SO LOUDLY IT CAN HARDLY BE HEARD : THE ART OF PARALLELISM IN TRADITIONAL LAO LITERATURE[1]

Peter Koret

1) INTRODUCTION

The intention of this paper is to suggest a new direction in the study of Lao literature. At present, the major weakness with Lao literary scholarship is not in what has been analyzed, but rather in what has been ignored. The original work on Lao versification, written in the 1940s by Maha Sila Wirawong, was heavily influenced by previous Thai literary scholarship. Such scholarship applies to a very different type of literature than Lao poetry and as such is not always an appropriate model. Thai literature was

---

[1] There has been much debate in recent years in Thailand over an appropriate name for the literature. There is a hesitation about calling the literature Lao because more of the ethnic Lao (who are the composers, transcribers, and performers of such works) live at present in the political boundaries of the Thai state than do in Laos. I myself, however, consider Lao the most appropriate label for the literature because the one common bond that links together its practitioners is that they are either ethnic Lao or have borrowed the tradition from the Lao. (Certain ethnic groups with strong Lao cultural influence, such as the Phuthai, or the Tai Aet of northeastern Laos also maintain a similar literary tradition.) Many Thai books written on the topic refer to the literature as belonging to Isan, Isan being the Thai name for the region of northeastern Thailand where the majority of the ethnic Lao live. The literature described in these books was traditionally recorded in Lao scripts by ethnically Lao people both in northeastern Thailand and throughout Laos. To label it as the literature of Isan, a region of Thailand, is to place modern political boundaries on a cultural tradition that was in its prime before such boundaries were in existence. Another common label for the literature is 'The Literature of the Kingdom of Lanchang.' Lanchang was an ancient Lao kingdom whose territory included both present-day Laos and much of present-day northeastern Thailand. The Lao literary tradition began and many of its classic works were composed during the time of this kingdom. However the kingdom disintegrated in the seventeenth century whereas the literary tradition did not. A large percentage of Lao literature and in particular Lao poetic works are distributed exclusively outside of the traditional cultural centers of Lanchang, and were probably composed after its demise. Several works, such as Thaw Lao Kham, Pheun Viangjan, etc., are known to have originated considerably after the time of Lanchang, even centuries afterwards. The literary tradition was quite active up until the earliest twentieth century, and exists at present. (For example, the important center of Lao literature, Naung Lam Jan temple in Suwannakhet province, where several literary works appear to have been composed, reached its peak after French colonization in the year 1893.) Therefore, although the tradition had its origins in the literature of Lanchang, the label is misleading.

traditionally composed, transcribed, and performed by and for a small circle of nobles in the royal court. In contrast, the majority of Lao literature was intended for all levels of Lao society and was centered around the village temple. As a result, there are important differences between the two literatures' form and content. Contemporary Thai scholars have in many ways improved upon Maha Sila's rules. Most importantly, a few scholars, such as Jit Phoumisak and Prakong Nimmanahaeminda, have begun to question the standards of Thai literary scholarship that have formed the basis behind the classification of Lao versification (Jit 1981: 161-209 and Prakong 198-290).[2] However, up until the present, the perspective from which Lao poetry has been studied has essentially remained the same. Versification rules that were originally written half a century ago are examined and reexamined while no new avenues of research are explored. It is time to reconsider what it is that makes Lao poetry 'poetry'. The study of Lao literature especially needs to be given a wider perspective in light of findings concerning similar types of narrative traditions throughout the world.[3]

The contention of this paper is that the major principle in the composition of Lao literature has been over-looked. In studies of *Kaun An*, the poetic form in which the majority of Lao literature is composed, previous scholars have concentrated soley on examining rhyme of sound. The most significant rhyme in *Kaun An*, however, is not a rhyme of sound but rather a rhyme of meaning. The fundamental characteristic of Lao literature, both prose and poetry, is the consistent use of repetition and parallelism. Upon reading Lao stories, it is noticable that after a certain event has occurred or an idea has been stated, that the same event or idea, expressed in slightly different form, will be repeated continuously. This element of the literature has led people to observe, generally in not so favorable terms, that it is repetitive and not overly original. However, upon examination of exactly how and why Lao literature repeats itself, one

---

[2] The same problem can be seen in the study of specific works of Lao poetry. One notices that as time passes by, more and more books, papers, and theses are being written on a very small number of Lao stories that were cited by Maha Sila Wirawong for their excellence. There is no doubt that such works are worthy of interest. At the same time, the great majority of works of Lao literature are literally ignored. Similarly, one finds that a few Lao stories, such as *'Sang Sinsai'* and *'Thaw Kam Ka Dam'*, are repeatedly transcribed and published. The large majority of stories, however, have yet to be transcribed.

[3] Several relevant books are listed in the bibliography that provide descriptions of narrative traditions that are intended for a listening audience in societies throughout the world.

sees that rather than being haphazard or the sign of lack of skill on the part of a composer, the repetition is ordered very systematically. What has been dismissed as an inconsequential and, if anything, negative aspect of the literature, is, in fact, its basic structural principle. The plot of Lao literature on every level is composed of an intricate and symmetrical layering of parallel pairs.

My examination of parallelism in traditional Lao literature has grown out of the realization that the medium in which Lao literature has been recorded and performed is foreign to contemporary scholars, and only if this foreignness is taken into account can a balanced study be made. An understanding of parallelism is an important step towards the 'decoding' of the literature that is necessary before an appreciation of its contents can truly be gained.

The study of parallelism as a rhetorical device in literature began in the eighteenth century. Professor Lowth of Oxford University observed that a fundamental characteristic of the poetry of the Old Testament was a 'carefully contrived pairing of line, phrase, and verse' (Fox 1977: 60). In 1778, in an introduction to a translation of Isaiah, he provided a description of parallelism:

When a proposition is delivered, and a second is subjoined to it, or drawn under it, equivalent, or contrasted with it in sense, or similar to it in the form of grammatical construction, these I call parallel lines; and the words or phrases, answering one to another in the corresponding lines, parallel terms (Fox 1977: 61).   Lowth's study of parallelism in the Old Testament proved useful in the nineteenth century to linguists and literary scholars who discovered that it was a similarly significant characteristic in narrative traditions throughout the world. It was observed to be particularly prevalent in story-telling traditions that are either composed orally or intended for a listening audience. According to Roman Jakobson, parallelism may be considered 'canonical' in traditions in which 'certain similarities between successive verbal sequences are compulsory or enjoy a high preference' ((Fox 1977: 77). Canonical parallelism has been observed in narrative traditions in the Austronesian, Polynesian, Mongolian, Dravidian, Turkic, Finnic-Ugraic, and several Central American Indian languages (Fox 1977: 63-65, 68-69). In Southeast Asia, parallelism has been studied in the literature of the Vietnamese and the oral poetic traditions of various ethnic groups throughout Indonesia (Fox 1977: 63-64, 76-77). It has also been the subject of comment in studies of the Garo, Shan, Burmese, and Thai languages (Fox 1977: 63).

It should not be surprising, therefore, that parallelism is a fundamental characteristic of Lao literature. Lao parallelism is unusual, however, in the complexity of the form that it takes. The symmetry of the placement of parallels in Lao poetry appears to be without parallel in previously studied narrative traditions. To illustrate the intricacy of Lao parallelism, this paper traces its evolution, beginning with its origins in the spoken language, and then continuing step by step from its smallest to largest manifestations in Lao poetic literature.

2) THE BEGINNING OF PARALLELISM IN LAO LANGUAGE AND LITERATURE

2.1 Parallelism in Spoken Lao

Parallelism in Lao literature has its origins in the spoken language. A common characteristic of spoken Lao is the use of parallel pairs, the pairing of two words of analogous meaning, for example: *ban heu'an* 'house > home', and *muan seun* 'happy > cheerful'. One explanation for the use of parallel pairs is that individual words in monosyllabic languages such as Lao tend to have many possible meanings. By pairing together two words of similar meaning, the specific meaning intended is clarified by placing the word in proper context. A second reason for the pairing of words is that pairs tend to have a greater breadth of meaning than either of the words would have individually. This is due to the fact that the words, while similar in meaning, are often not identical, and the meaning of one tends to complement the other. A third explanation is a poetic one. Paired words are frequently alliterated or assonant, adding to the harmony of the spoken language. For any or all of these reasons, using pairs is considered to make ones' speech more formal and graceful. Thao Nhouy Abhay in an article on Lao versification sums up their use by saying: 'The effect produced seems to me a happy one' (Abhay 1959: 349 fn.2).

The parallel pair is the most basic form of parallelism in Lao. It may be called the mother of all parallelism. In Lao spoken and written expression, parallel structures, no matter how complicated their form, are generated from the parallel pair. To understand the nature of parallelism, one must study this process of generation, the way, step-by-step, in which smaller pairs replicate into larger ones. The first step is where a two syllable pair duplicates into a pair of four syllables. In a single pair of monosyllabic words, there is the simple balance of two syllables facing one another, each parallel in meaning and frequently matched in sound:

$$O \ / \ O$$

When pairs are doubled, the symmetry is enhanced. Two pairs are joined together, each consisting of two syllables:

$$OO \ / \ OO$$

Doubled word pairs are common both in the written and spoken language. They are frequently referred to as *kham nyap* or *kham nyauy*, which can be translated as 'ornamental words'.[4]

While there are a wide variety of types of doubled pairs, there are two that should be considered in the context of Lao literature. The first type is the doubled pair with identical initial words. It consists of two phrases, each composed of identical initial words followed by words of parallel meaning. For example, we have previously mentioned the pair *ban heuan* 'house > home'. If one wishes to say 'I will go home', instead of simply stating 'I will go *ban* ', or 'I will go *heuan* ', one can add to the rhythm of one's speech by joining the two phrases together saying, 'I will go *ban* , I will go *heuan* , as follows: pai **ban** / pai **heuan** literally, 'Go **house** / Go **home**'.[5] This type of doubled pair, simple in its structure, is the most frequent type that one finds in spoken Lao and Lao 'prose' literature, known as *Nitsay*.[6] It is, however, relatively uncommon in poetic literature.

The second type of doubled pair is the doubled pair without identical initial words. It consists of two parallel pairs with no shared words. In its most basic form the two pairs are parallel to one another but there are no parallels between words in individual pairs. For example: ban keut >

---

[4] Each of these two phrases is composed of the identical word *kham* word', followed by *nyap* or *nyauy*, which are specific types of Lao oranaments. Joined together, the phrases in and of themselves form an alliterated doubled pair: *kham nyap kham nyauy.*

[5] The importance of pairing phrases in adding rhythm to Lao spoken expression is ilustrated by the fact that when an analogous partner for a word can not be found, an alliterated syllable will frequently be invented (according to certain formulas) to serve the same purpose.

[6] Works of prose literature (which are generally believed to be Lao translations of Pali texts) are commonly referred to as *Nitsay* in Laos. The word *Nitsay* is derived from the Pali word *Nissay*, which means 'foundation, reliance on, support'. People who do not understand the original Pali text can 'rely on' the Lao translation. The term *Nitsay* is not commonly used among the people of northeastern Thailand.

meuang naun or literally, 'village of birth, country of sleep'. Typical of doubled pairs of this type, the first words of the respective pairs, *ban* 'village', and *meuang* 'country', are also commonly joined together to form a single parallel word pair. In the most complex form of doubled pair without identical initial words, not only are the pairs parallel to one another but each pair in and of itself is composed of two parallel words:

$$a1 > a2 \quad > \quad a3 > a4$$
$$\text{O} \quad \text{O} \qquad \text{O} \quad \text{O}$$

For example: *pa dong phong phai* 'forest' (All four words share the same meaning.) Because of its added complexity, the doubled pair without identical initial words gives the language a more elevated and literary style than does the previous kind. It is correspondingly the most frequent type of doubled pair in Lao poetic literature.

2.2 Parallel Pairs and Doubled Pairs in Literary Lao

Parallelism is a stylistic device in the spoken and written Lao language. The higher the level of the language's style, the greater the amount and complexity of its parallels. The amount and complexity of parallels steadily increases from spoken Lao to *Nitsay* prose to *Kaun An*, the poetic form in which the majority of Lao story-length literature is composed.[7] It is interesting to note, however, that upon reading the prose and poetic forms of literature, the prose appears to be the more repetitive. This is due to the fact that poetic style involves both raising the level of parallelism and at the same time making the parallels less noticeable by increasing their subtlety. This can be seen, for example, in our previous observation that in contrast to *Nitsay*, Lao poetic literature favors the use of doubled pairs without identical words in which there is no repetition of actual words.[8]

An important characteristic of Lao poetry (in contrast to prose or spoken Lao) is the symmetrical placement of parallels. Using the word 'symmetrical' to describe a literature that was meant to be heard rather than read may be seen as a mixing of metaphors. There is, however, no denying

---

[7] In a study of six thousand word samples of *Nitsay* and *Kaun An*, I counted 57 parallel pairs and 16 doubled pairs in the prose form, and 177 parallel pairs and 62 doubled pairs in the poetic form.

[8] Other types of repetition found in *Nitsay* and lacking in *Kaun An* include a) the continual repetition of large 'chunks' of information throughout a piece of text, and b) the tendency for the first half of a sentence to consist of a repetition of information included in the previous sentence. These types of repetition are much more obvious than their counterparts in *Kaun An*.

the role of symmetry in the placement of parallels in *Kaun An*. Consider the structure of *Kaun An* and the effect that it has on the form of its parallels:[9]

1. *Kaun An* is made up of poetic lines which are divided into two hemistichs of respectively three and four syllables.[10]

OOO OOOO

As analogous words are commonly joined together in a parallel pair, analogous hemistichs are frequently paired in a poetic line.

A1   >   A2

OOO   OOOO

For example:

maen si	*thuk meu san*	*nyak nying nak na*
'Even if it is	ten thousand layers of hardship	the greatest>heaviest of difficulties'

(Kai Kaew)

We have observed that in the most complex type of doubled pair each individual pair is composed of two parallel words. Similarly, in the most symmetrical type of poetic line composed of two parallel hemistichs, each of the individual hemistichs is further divided into two parallel words or phrases.

A1   A2

a1 > a2 >   a3 > a4

O   O   O   O   O   OO

---

[9] It should be noted that the visual structure of Kaun An is only a recent invention. Traditionally, words in Lao poetry were written together without separation. There were no divisions marking different hemistichs, lines, or verse. The Lao scholar Maha Sila Wirawong, whose earliest work on Lao versification, *'Baep Taeng Klau Thaiy Wiangjan Lae Baep Taeng Kap San Wilasini'* 'Methods Of Composition Of The Poetry Of The Vientiane Thai And *Kap San Wilsini*,' was printed in 1942, was the first person who analyzed Lao verse, set down its rules, and organized it on a printed page according to those rules. It was Maha Sila Wirawong, for example, who first marked a separation between the left and right hemistichs in a poetic line. One must bear in mind, however, that such a division was not created arbitrarily but rather reflects the traditional rhythm of reading where there is, in fact, a pause between hemistichs (See Prakhaung 1981: 247, 249-251). Similarly, the division of poetry into verses and quatrains, whether or not traditionally labeled as such, is a characteristic clearly observable from ancient manuscripts.

[10] There are also optional initial and final phrases which are each generally of two syllables in length but may be longer.

For example:

an neung   *phit bau saup thae*   *long khwam bau khaung kau di*
(If I am)   wrong/not correct   astray/ not fitting
(Thaw Kam Ka Dam)

2. As one line is formed of two hemistichs, one verse is formed of two lines. The two lines in a verse are frequently statements of parallel meaning:

A1

OOO OOOO

>

A2

OOO OOOO

For example:

1) *Di kae   lom thip taung   saphao ten laen pai*
The wind struck; The ships travelled quickly
2) *nyap nyap nyay   saphao laen tam lom   phun nyeu*
Together the ships travelled quickly following the wind
(Thaw Bae)

In the most complex type of doubled pair and poetic line composed of parallel hemistichs, a larger pair replicates into two smaller parallels. Similarly, in the most symmetrical type of verse, not only are the individual lines parallel to one another, but each hemistich is also parallel. For example:

1) *ba kau   nae kau jai wai*   *ling kabuan thuk thi*
   He   surveyed   looked over its appearance every place
2) *thaw kam   liaw phun phi*   *liaw kai sua kai*
   He   looked there>here   looked near>far
(Thaw Kam Ka Dam)

Notice that each hemistich in the second line further breaks down into a smaller parallel pair, respectively *phun > phi* 'there > here' and *kai sua kai* 'near > far'.

3) As one verse is consists of two lines, one quatrain is formed of two verses of two lines. Frequently quatrains are composed of two parallel verses:[11]

A1

OOO OOOO

OOO OOOO

A2

OOO OOOO

OOO OOOO

Similar to the smaller parallels preceding it, the most symmetrical type of quatrain consists of a doubling of doubles. Each of the verses is comprised of two parallel lines. The following example describes the great noise made by the troops of King Thaen on their journey from the sky to the earth in answer to the call of the hero.

A1) First Verse (Consisting Of Two Parallel Lines):

1) *kheun kheun kaung*   *siang sanan phay bon*   *phun nyeu*
'Kheun Kheun' resounding noise up above--- over in the distance

2) *kheng kheng siang*   *thua bon phay fa*
'Kheng Kheng' noise everywhere up above in the sky

A2) Second Verse (Consisting Of Two Parallel Lines):

1)   *kheun kheun kaung*   *phon mak phranya thaen*   *phun nyeu*
'Kheun Kheun' resounding noise of the great troops of King Thaen-- over in the distance

2)   *kheng kheng siang* *mi nan khung fa*
'Kheng Kheng' noise clamorous up to the sky

   (Thaw Kam Ka Dam)

The structure of the quatrain can be described simply as :
A1)

   a1) *'Kheun Kheun'* resounding noise   great noise up in the sky
                                               over in the distance

---

11 According to Maha Sila Wirawong in his book *'Santhalaksana'* 'Versification,' a complete quatrain in *Kaun An* consists of two different types of alternating verse. However, *Kaun An* is more frequently composed of the same type of verse occurring consecutively throughout large sections of a text. Regardless of whether a quatrain is made up of the same type of verse repeated twice or two alternate types, there is frequently a parallel relationship between the two verses.

a2) *'Kheng Kheng'* noise   up above in the sky
A2)
a1) *khuen khuen* resounding noise of the troops of King Thaen
     over in the distance
a2) *Kheng Kheng* noise   great noise up to the sky

Verses A1 and A2 are parallel to one another both in their meaning and structure. Both describe the great noise of the troops. The left hemistich of the initial line of verse A1 is identical to the left hemistich of the initial line of verse two (*Kheun Kheun* resounding noise). The left hemistich of the second line of Verse A1 is similarly identical to its counterpart hemistich in the second line of Verse A2 *Kheng Kheng* noise). The initial lines in both verses share an identical final phrase, 'over in the distance' whereas final phrases are absent in the second lines of both verses.

The two lines in an individual verse (whether A1 or A2) are also parallel in meaning and structure. Both describe great noise. The left hemistichs of the first and second lines in a verse each consist of onomatopoeic phrases (alternately *Kheun Kheun* and *Kheng Kheng*), both of which begin with identical initial consonants.

One could speculate that the *Kaun An* was originally created to enhance parallels, both of sound and meaning, that already existed in the spoken language. However, regardless of origin, the structure of *Kaun An* gives poets a multitude of opportunities to create symmetrical parallels, and in so doing encourages the use of parallelism as a poetic tool.

3) THE AAB PATTERN: THE BUILDING BLOCK OF LAO NARRATIVE
3.1 The AAB Pattern: A General Introduction
Small parallels such as the pairing of words and phrases and the matching of poetic hemistichs, lines, and verses are significant not merely in and of themselves, but in that they form an important part of a larger parallel unit, a pattern that is fundamental in the building of a story's plot. Before describing this pattern, however, there is one point that should be taken into account. To appreciate the form that parallelism takes in Lao literature one should first consider the significence of the number three both in Lao literature and culture in general. The number three is held to be auspicious by the Lao. When asked the reason behind its auspiciousness, most Lao point to the Buddhist religion. In Buddhism, the greatest

significence of the number three is that it represents the sacred trinity, the Triple Gems: the Buddha, the Dharma, and the Priesthood. The number three plays a similarly important role in the Hindu religion, another important influence on the Lao.[12] Whether or not these are the reasons behind the number's literary significence, however, is debatable, for the number three is also a common characteristic in folk traditions throughout the world, and is typically predominant in folk tales.[13] However its origins, there is no question of the importance of the number three in Lao literature. It is immediately noticable for example, that lead characters, events, and beautiful princesses tend to occur in threes or in multiples of three. Similarly, journeys frequently last for three days, three months, or three years.[14]

The basic building block of Lao literature is a pattern of three which will be referred to as an AAB pattern. Stated in simplest terms, an AAB pattern consists of two parallel statements (A1 and A2) followed by a third statement (B) that is a conclusion or result of the previous statements. This pattern, of no fixed length, has been traditionally used by Lao (and other Tai) poets to narrate a progression of ideas, time, or events, for example, the passage of time from night until dawn, or a sequence of actions that transform a character from a despised beggar to the world's most powerful monarch. The English expression 'Ready, Set, Go' is a good example of this pattern:

A1) Ready

A2) Set

B) Go

---

[12] The number three is important in the symbolism of both the Buddhist and Hindu religions. Buddhist prayers are generally repeated three times, one makes three prostrations in front of a Buddha image, and one circles three times around a Buddhist temple on religious holidays in respect to the sacred trinity. There are three realms of being: heaven, earth, and hell, three sections in the Buddhist scriptures, known as the Triple Baskets, etc. In the Hindu religion there is a trinity of major Gods, Brahma, Vishnu, and Shiva. The sacred scriptures are similarly divided into three sections, etc.

[13] Several writers, such as Alan Dundes, Emory B. Lease, etc. have described the number's significance in western culture. 'When a folklorist comes upon a three,' writes Axel Olrik in *Epic Laws of Folk Narrative* , 'he thinks, as does the Swiss who catches sight of his Alps again, "Now I am home"' (1965: 133).

[14] Another frequently occurring number is seven, which is also auspicious in Lao culture, the Buddhist religion, and folk traditions throughout the world.

The first two words are parallel in meaning, which result in the action, 'to go'. Typically, a pattern concludes with an idea or action that furthers the plot, as in this example the third word starts the race.

AAB patterns are a basic characteristic of various types of oral and written Lao narrative. They are observable in many examples of Phanya, Lao oral poetry. They are fundamental to both *Nitsay* (prose) and *Kaun An* (poetic) literature. Their characteristics in the two types of literature are generally similar with a difference in detail caused by the varying possibilities afforded by the different styles. This paper is devoted exclusively to a study of patterns in *Kaun An* literature. Due to the structure of Lao poetry, the pattern attains levels of complexity and subtlety that is greater than in other forms of Lao narrative.

3.2 Types of Progression in an AAB Pattern

The AAB pattern is a device that Lao composers have traditionally used to organize plot in Lao literature. It is a format in which to organize a progression of events, ideas or time. We can distinguish between different types of patterns according to the kind of progression that is involved:

1: The progression from a character's wish to its fulfillment (or failure) through a series of actions

This is the most prevalent type of pattern. It begins with the statement of a problem which is generally expressed as the wish of a character in the story. It ends with the problem's resolution (or ultimate lack of resolution). Although the problem is usually that of one specific character, the actions that carry it through to its resolution frequently involve two or three different groups of people. In the following pattern the king's servants bring the hero before the king.

A1)

1   *tae nan*   *phranya luang jao*   *mi kham owat*
Then the king spoke words of command
2   *hip than ma*   *su hong ku thae*
"Hurry and bring Little Crow to my palace"

A2)

3   *tae nan*   *tai dek nauy*   *pai hip hew phalan*
Then the young ones went in great hurry
4   *kau jing*   *theung*   *thaw kam nauy ja tan bauk ba*

276

And thus came to the Little Dark One and spoke to him:

5   *an wa   rasa jao   than ma hew hip   jing day*

"The king (orders you) brought before him in a hurry"

B)

6   *tae nan   khao kau   pha jaem jao   ba thaw su hong*

Then they brought him to the palace

7   *khao kau   uan ba kheun   hau luang nao nang*

They led him up to the royal palace (where he) sat

8   *khao kau kom khap wai   thun jao su khon*

Everyone prostrated and paid respect before the king

   (Thaw Kam Ka Dam)

In Section A1 of the above pattern the king orders his servants to go and bring Little Crow before him. In Section A2 the king's servants travel to Little Crow and tell him in parallel terms that the king wishes to have Little Crow brought before him. Finally, in Section B, the conclusion, Little Crow is brought before the king.

2: The progression of actions or events to the completion of their role in the text

This type of progression differs from the previous category in that the actions or events are not directed towards an intended goal. Their completion, however, has a role in furthering the plot in a story. In the following pattern the hero returns home from work to find a delicious-looking meal spread out on his dinner table. Initially he is suspicious and afraid to eat it. However he eventually succumbs to his curiosity and hunger and overcomes his reservations.

A1)

1   *ba kau   bay ao khao   ma kin kham neung*

He took the food, and ate one mouthful

2   *phau ham wai   jai jao yu khang*

He held himself back; his heart was upset

3   *du aun aun   haum thua thang khanaung*

(The food) looked soft; It was fragrant all over

A2)

4   *bakhan leuy   teum saung kham khao*

He thus ate an additional second mouthful of food

5   *du saep thae   lai long bau hu meua*

It was truly delicious and went down without a thought

B)

6   *ba teum sam   kham khao haut sam*

    He ate in addition another mouthful of food, his third

7   *leuy nya bau day   kep sai lay kham*

    Then he could not stop himself, taking many mouthfuls

8   *mam mam kin   su an nyau mian*

    Eating greedily without stop, he put away every bit

   (Thaw Kampha Phi Nauy)

The conclusion of this pattern is the hero's decision to eat all of the food on the table. This leads to the following scene where he meets the woman who is secretly providing him with food and takes her as his wife. (This is a standard sequence in the plot of one type of Lao story.)

3: The progression of an idea (stated either by the narrator or a character in the story) to its conclusion or fullest expression

The progression of ideas is commonly organized as:

    a: Expresses the same idea in greater detail

    b: Two parallel statements followed by a conclusion

    c: Two parallel statements followed by a third statement which is a question or a call for action based upon the previous statements

In the following example, the hero, with the outward appearance of a small and ugly child, courts the village women. One of the women reprimands him, telling him that he is too young to court them:

A1)   *an wa   dek nauy nauy   ma ja kae leua to   thae nau*

    "A small small child speaking older than his age

A2)   *hua bau   phiang kok kha   wa si ao mia saun*

    Your head does not reach up to my leg and you say that you will take a wife to love

B)   *meung bau ling   du kabuan na   phau   huan   som   hup meung nan*

    You do not look at your own face to see what is fitting for one of your   shape"

   (Thaw Kam Ka Dam)

The first two statements, expressed in Sections A1 and A2, are parallel observations. The reference to the hero as 'A small small child' in the left hemistich of Section A1 is echoed in the left half of Section A2 in the statement 'Your head does not reach up to my leg'. The statement that he speaks older than his age in the second hemistich of Section A1 is similarly parallel to the statement in its counterpart hemistich in Section A2 that he (i.e. one whose head does not reach up to the woman's waist) says that he will take a wife to love. The two observations lead to the conclusion, a general statement admonishing the hero for his behavior.

4: The progression of time

There are two types of progression in this category: a) the progression of time from one interval to another, and b) the progression of time that leads to an event. In the following example the concluding event in Section B is the result of the passage of time as described in the previous two sections.

A1)   *lay wan dai   lay deuan thaem thay   ma laew*
      Many days and many months passed by

A2)   *lay khuab meu   radu dai khuab pi*
      Many days, seasons, and years

B)   *nang kau thong khap nauy   buttarat kumman*
      She became pregnant with the king's son

(*Thaw Bae*)

3.3: Mimic Patterns

In addition to actual patterns, there are also passages that can be referred to as mimic patterns. Mimic patterns are sequences of narrative that lack one fundamental attribute of AAB patterns. They mimic actual patterns in that:

a: Outside of the attribute in which they are lacking, their structure is identical to AAB patterns in all aspects.

b: Frequently the patterns are phrased to mimic the attribute that they are missing. They do so by partially fulfilling the requirements needed for its presence. The attribute, therefore, at a superficial glance may appear to be included.

There are two basic types of mimic patterns:

1: Mimic Patterns In Which There Is No Progression Of Events

In this type of mimic pattern, there is no progression from a beginning to an end. There is no conclusion. Frequently patterns in this category consist of lists, for example, a description of the activities of three different groups of people, or the qualities of three different types of objects.

1. The following example describes the journey of three separate characters.

1)

1   *meua nan*   *in kau*   *nyaeng meua kam*   *dawadeungsa thewalok*

    Then Indra headed for Dawadeungsa, the celestial world

2   *khao su haung wisayonkaew thi sathian*

    He entered his precious eternal Wisayon palace

2)

3   *meua nan*   *thaen luang jao*   *phranya meuang fa kheun*

    Then the Thaen King, Fa Kheun

4   *sadet su haung*   *wisayon kaew haeng ton)*

    Returned to his precious Wisayon palace

3)

5   *an wa*   *nako jao*   *phranya luang nak nyai*

    As for the great King of the Nagas

6   *kau lao*   *meua su nam*   *wang kwang haeng ton*

    He returned into the water to his great palace

(Thaw Kam Ka Dam)

This example describes the journey of three different characters in parallel terms. The third section is not a conclusion but merely one among three journeys depicted in the passage. Although not an actual pattern, this sequence mimics a fundamental characteristic of patterns that is described in Section 3.4.3 on page 20: Section B is distinguished in detail from Sections A1 and A2. The third character, for example, descends into the water in contrast to the previous two, who ascend to their palaces in the sky. The third section is further differentiated in its use of minor phrasing.

2: Mimic Patterns In Which The First Section Is Not Parallel With The Second

In the story *Thaw Kam Ka Dam*, the hero, Little Crow, is born with a hideous outer 'shell'. In the following example, Little Crow takes off his ugly shell and secretly enters the princess's palace.

1)

a1)   *tae nan*   *ba baw phu*   *ka dam nauy thaut kajom*

    Then Little Black Crow **took off his outer layer**

a2)   *thaw kau*   *thaut khap wai*   *da di mian jaep*
      He **took off his costume,** put it away well > stored it carefully

2)

a1)   *si jaem jao*   *ba thaw khao pai*
      He **entered** (the palace)

a2)   *thaw kau*   *nyap khao kai*   *li yu mi ting*
      He **entered closer** (i.e. moved close to the princess), hiding motionless

3)

1   *ba kau*   *fang siang nang*   *sapsing gan kham len*
      He listened to the sound of the servants whispering playful words
   (Thaw Kam Ka Dam)

The first two sections of this passage are both composed of parallel pairs. However, whereas the lines are parallel in their individual sections they are not parallel between them.

The two lines in the first section describe Little Crow taking off his ugly outer 'shell'. The verb in both lines is identical: *thaut* 'to take off'.

The parallel between lines in the second section is best seen in the original Lao phrasing. Both include the identical verb *khao* 'to enter'. The parallel verbs are phrased so that they rhyme between lines:

             khao pai 'enter' and *khao kai* 'enter near'

Section Three is the conclusion of the first two sections. Little Crow has succeeded in entering the palace where he can observe unnoticed the activities of the servant girls and the princess.

The pattern can be described in the following chart:
1)   a1)
      a2)
2)   a1)
      a2)
3)   Conclusion

This pattern imitates an actual pattern in that it partially includes the attribute that is missing. The first two sections, if not parallel in meaning, are certainly parallel in structure, for each is composed of two parallel

281

statements. This type of parallel, however, is not enough to label the sections as A1 and A2.

3.4: Basic Characteristics of AAB Patterns

3.4.1: Tagging: Sections in an AAB pattern are frequently linked together by a device that will be referred to as 'tagging'. This involves the use of tag phrases or lines that are both parallel in meaning and similar or identical in phrasing. Tags are placed at the beginning or end of a) the initial two sections, A1 and A2, or b) less frequently, all three sections in a pattern. Although the individual sections may be distinct in their detail, they are bonded together by their parallel tags. The following example (Sections A1 and A2 of a larger pattern) is taken from a speech where the hero is asked about his intentions in journeying to another kingdom.

A1)
1   *meung ni*   *deun dung dan*   *ma phi het dai*
    "You have traveled here for what reason?
A2)
2   *an wa   dong luang kwang   himmaphan nyaw nyot*
The jungle is of great width, the forest is of long 'Yot'[15]
3   *phauy lao*   *deun dung dan*   *ma phi het dai*   *ni de*
    And still you have traveled here, for what reason?
(Inpong)

Sections A1 and A2 are linked together as parallels by the use of a tag. The sole line of Section A1 and the final line of Section A2 are identical except for their initial and/or final phrases which do not significantly alter their meaning.

3.4.2 Progressive Parallels: As the sequence develops in a pattern, the role of Section A2 is not merely to repeat the information stated in Section A1 but at the same time to progress it towards its conclusion in Section B. Some of the major types of progression between Sections A1 and A2 are:

1) Development of an Action or Idea: In this type of progression, in Section A2 the action or event originally stated in Section A1 is moved closer towards its conclusion. For example, in Section A1 a character is requested to perform an action whereas in Section A2 he performs it.

---

15 One *nyot* is a distance of approximately sixteen kilometers.

2) Progression in Narrative: In this type of progression, Section A1 introduces the action or event that is to be paralleled. Section A2, freed of the space-consuming burden of introduction, provides additional detail.

3) Progression in Perspective: In this type of progression, an idea, action, or event is initially narrated in the third person. Afterwards, the same idea, action, or event is repeated in the first person in the form of a speech of one of the characters. The effect is that the information appears closer both to the story's audience and to the character to whom the information is directed in the story itself.

4) The use of parallels to increase emphasis: Frequently the length of the second section of a pattern is greater than that of the first. The length is often increased not by the addition of new information but rather through the rephrasing of identical information in sets of parallels.

3.4.3 The Difference Between Sections A1/A2 And Section B: Whereas Sections A1 and A2 are linked together in structure, style, and meaning, at the same time they generally differ from the third part of the pattern. There are many ways in which Section B is distinguished from the preceding two sections. For example: a) Patterns where the conclusion in Section B is an action that is the opposite of the actions that occur in Sections A1 and A2; b) Patterns where Sections A1 and A2 describe the actions of one character whereas Section B describes the actions of another; c) Patterns where if Sections A1 and A2 are questions, Section B will be a statement, or the reverse; d) Patterns where Section B is distinguished from the preceding sections in the number of lines; e) Patterns where Section B is distinguished from the preceding sections in minor phrasing.

Section B is generally distinguished from Sections A1 and A2 in its use of language, even in minor details. When tag phrases occur in all three sections of a pattern, for example, the third and final tag commonly differs slightly from the preceding two. Although such phrasing may appear insignificant and does little to alter the meaning of the section, it consistently emphasizes Section B's uniqueness in the pattern as a whole.

3.5: Parallels Within Parallels
We have previously observed that once a parallel pair exists there is a tendency for it to replicate further into smaller and smaller parallels. We have seen, for example, doubled parallel pairs in which each individual pair consists of two parallel words, parallel hemistichs in which each

individual hemistich consists of two parallel words or phrases, etc. The phenomenon of reduplication occurs with great symmetry inside of AAB patterns and forms one of their most interesting aspects. There are two major categories of replication in patterns, parallel pairs and smaller patterns. Each type tends to occur in specific parts of the larger pattern:

3.5.1: The Placement of Parallel Pairs in a Pattern
The first type of parallel that occurs with frequency in a pattern is a parallel pair, i.e. the pairing together of two words, phrases, lines, or larger sections of analogous meaning. Parallel pairs are generally placed in the following manner:

3.5.1.1: Smaller parallel pairs have a tendency to occur inside of larger pairs. The largest parallel pair in an AAB pattern consists of Sections A1 and A2. One frequently observes that Sections A1 and A2 of a pattern each individually replicate into two smaller parallel halves:

$$
\begin{array}{ll}
\text{A1)} & \text{a1} \\
& \text{a2} \\
\text{A2)} & \text{a1} \\
& \text{a2} \\
\text{B)} &
\end{array}
$$

In the following example, the hero arrives in a foreign kingdom.

A1)
a1)   *khuan ku khao   pai nai ling lam   du thaun*
      "I should enter and have a look

a2)   *tang hai hu   meua na lam du*
      In order to know in the future; (I should) look"

A2)
a1)   *meua nan   bakhan thaw   thong ton ling lam*
      Then he looked

a2)   *lak laup li   khan khao beung du*
      He furtively crept in and looked

B)
1)   *kau jing   ken hau kaew   nang ngam du paseut   jing laew*
      Thus he saw the extraordinary palace of the beautiful woman

2)   *heuang heua jaeng   leuang leuam tae kham   jao heuy*
      Shiny and bright, completely of gold

(Inpong)

In the hero's speech in Section A1, he states in both lines that he should take a look. In Section A2, the narrator similarly states in each line that the hero took a look. In Section B, the conclusion, the hero is described as seeing the palace of the woman whom is to become his lover. Not only are the four lines in Section A1 and A2 parallel to one another, but each line concludes with a parallel word pair for 'look' in the second half of its second hemistich. The word pairs in the first lines of each section are identical: *ling lam* 'look at > look at'. The word pairs in the second lines, respectively *ling du* 'look at > look at' and *beung du* 'look at > look at', share similar second words.[16]

3.5.1.2: The second major tendency in the placement of pairs is that when a portion of narrative is divided into two sections (parallel or otherwise), smaller pairs are more likely to occur in the second half than in the first. For example, parallel pairs occur with more frequency in Section A2 than in Section A1. When parallel pairs do occur in both sections, the pair in the second section is usually of greater complexity than the pair in the first.

A1)

A2)   a1

a2

B)

(An example of the occurrence of smaller pairs in the second half of larger pairs can be seen in the following section.)

3.5.1.3: The 'itchy fingers' of a composer to replicate existing pairs rarely stops at a single layer. Following the same tendency as described in Section 3.5.1.2, when the second half of a pair divides into two parallel halves, its second half will frequently further divide into two even smaller parallel halves.

A1)

A2)   a1

a2   a1

a2

B)

---

[16] An additional example of a pattern in which Sections A1 and A2 each consist of a smaller parallel pair can be seen on page 8. It was initially used to illustrate how parallel verses within a quatrain can each be composed of a pair of parallel lines. The two verses are actually Sections A1 and A2 of a larger pattern.

The following example is a description of people running out in great confusion and uproar to see the hero as he is led in procession to become king.

A1)

a1)   *lang phaung*   *thao hua khaw*   *khaew laun kau pai*

Some groups of old people with white hair and fallen-out teeth went

a2)   *lang phaung*   *kha hak han*   *sak mai thao dao daet dao lom kau pai*

Some groups of people with broken legs, limping and clutching on canes, braved sun and braved wind, and went

A2)

a1)   *lang phaung faw ao*   *sin khaw mia phat ba laen pai*   *nam kon*

Some people in great hurry took their wife's white scarf,[17] placed it over their shoulders, and ran behind the others

a2)   a1:   *lang khon eun*   *phua to wa na baw*

Some people called their husbands their mother's younger brother

        a2:   *phua sam phat eun mia nan wa i a*   *kau mi*

Husbands in turn called their wives their father's younger sister

(Thaw Kam Ka Dam)

This pattern is organized as:

A1)

        a1) Some groups of old people went

        a2) Some groups of sick people, braving sun and wind, went

A2)

        a1) Some people in great hurry put on their wife's scarf and ran out

        a2)   a1) Some people called their husbands their mother's younger brother

             a2) Husbands in turn called their wives their father's younger sister

Sections A1 and A2 are parallel in that they are both humorous accounts of people who act contrary to their normal behavior due to their excitement to catch a glimpse of the hero.

---

[17] a white cloth worn on formal occasions.

In Section A1, the two lines are parallel in that they both describe people whom despite their disabilities go out to see the hero. Both end in the two syllable phrase *kau pai* 'to go.' A smaller pair occurs inside of the parallel pair which comprises Section A1, in the second half of its second parallel line. It consists of a doubled pair with identical initial words. This type of pair, with its unsubtle form of repetition, is not commonly present in Lao poetry. It is comprised of two phrases, each of two syllables, as follows: *daw daet / daw lom*, 'to brave the sun / to brave the wind'. It is interesting that an expression of four syllables was chosen for this position. While it is suitable for its replication, it completely destroys the poetic rhythm of the line, turning what should be a line of seven syllables into a line of ten.

The second section, A2, is divided into two parallel sections, lines one, and lines two and three. The sections are parallel to one another in that: a) each describes actions of husbands and/or wives in relationship to one another, and b) each describes silly actions that characters commit by mistake, not aware of what they are doing because of their excitement

The second parallel half inside of Section A2 further replicates into two yet smaller parallel halves:

a1) Some people (i.e. wives) call husbands   mother's   younger brother

a2) Husbands call wives   father's younger sister

These lines are parallels of one another in reverse. They are made up of the following three pairs of opposites:

A1 = Wives   B1 = Mothers   C1 = Younger Brother
A2 = Husbands   B2 = Fathers   C2 = Younger Sister

It is no coincidence that this replication of two, the most complex and symmetrical in the entire pattern, falls in the second half of a parallel pair which occurs in the second half of the larger parallel pair of Sections A1 and A2.

The position of the replications in the pattern can be summarized as:

A1) a1)
    a2) 1)   2) a1 > a2
A2) a1)
    a2)   a1) a1 a2   b1 c1
        a2) a2 a1   b2 c2

There are three layers of pairs in this example. It is also not uncommon to find further layers of parallel pairs that follow the same general rules of placement as AAB patterns break down into smaller and smaller parallel units.

3.5.2: The Placement of Smaller Patterns within a Pattern

The second type of replication that one commonly finds in an AAB pattern is a smaller pattern. The placement of smaller patterns is:

3.5.2.1: As replications of two occur with greatest frequency in the second section of a pattern, replications of three tend to occur in its third section, Section B. Section B frequently divides into three sections which share, on a smaller level, the identical structure of the pattern in which they occur. Generally, the smaller pattern in Section B serves to progress the events in the larger sequence towards their conclusion. The conclusion of the larger AAB pattern coincides with the third and final section of the smaller pattern.

A1)

A2)

B)   a1

       a2

       b   Conclusion

We described a pattern on pages 12-13 that can be summarized as:

Section A1: The king orders his servants to go and bring Little Crow before him.

Section A2: The king's servants go to Little Crow and tell him in parallel terms that the King wishes to have Little Crow brought before him.

Section B: Little Crow is brought before the king.

Section B of the pattern is comprised of the following smaller pattern:

a1)   *tae nan   khao kau   pha jaem jao   ba thaw su hong*
          Then they brought him to the palace

a2)   *khaw kau   uan ba kheun   hau luang nao nang*
          They led him up to the royal palace (where he) sat

b)   *khao kau   kom khap wai   thun jao su khon*
          Everyone prostrated and paid respect before the king

This three-line passage is a typical type of travel pattern in which the movement of the hero is described in the first two sections and his arrival at his destination is described in the third. Each line in the pattern begins with the identical initial phrase: *khao kau* 'He'. The verbs in the first two lines, *pha* and *uan* which have been translated respectively as 'to bring' and 'to lead', are interchangeable. The second word is a more literary term and thus serves as a stylistic progression that helps to make Sections a1 and a2 progressive parallels. Notice that the conclusion of the small pattern, the arrival of the hero before the king, is also the conclusion of the larger pattern as a whole. This pattern is a good example of the skillful way in which smaller replications are placed inside of larger ones so smoothly that they are hardly noticable.

3.5.2.2: There are also variations where smaller patterns lead up to Section B, which can be illustrated as:

1)
    A1)
    A2) a1 a2

      B)b Conclusion

2)
    A1)
    A2)
         a1
         a2
    B)   b Conclusion

In the first type of variation the initial two sections of the smaller pattern (a1 and a2) occur in Section A2 of the larger one. In the second type the initial two sections of the smaller pattern occur immediately after Section A2 and preceding Section B of the larger one. In both types of variation the third section of the smaller pattern coincides with the third section of the larger pattern.

To appreciate, in context, the role of smaller patterns that occur inside of or leading up to Section B, one must bear in mind the importance of the section in the pattern as a whole. Section B is the most important section of an AAB pattern. It is where a wish meets its fulfillment, or an idea reaches its fullest expression. The importance of the idea or event described in Section B is high-lighted by the fact that it occurs in the third and final position of a pattern of three. When a smaller pattern is placed inside of the larger one, it serves to further emphasize the importance of the final idea or event. The fact that the ultimate conclusion not only serves as the third and final part of the larger pattern, but also the third and final part of a smaller internal pattern, distinguishes it as being on a higher and more significant level than all that has preceded it.

3.5.2.3: We have previously observed in Section 3.5.1.3 that there are often several layers of parallel pairs placed symmetrically in the second halves of larger parallel pairs. In a similar fashion one frequently finds several layers of AAB patterns, each placed in the third section of the pattern that precedes it, as follows:

            A1)
            A2)
        B)   A1)
                A2)
            B)   A1)
                    A2)
                B)

In the following example there are five layers of patterns in a single passage. The chart on page 33 shows the overall pattern with the layers of smaller patterns that occur inside of it.

This is the largest pattern that we will discuss in this paper. It fits into the first category of progression where a wish is fulfilled through a sequence of actions. In Section A1 a group of young men invite the hero, Little Crow, to travel to the palace to play the khaen, a Lao wind-instrument, before the king. Little Crow agrees. In Section A2, Little Crow, together with the young men, travels to the palace grounds to play the khaen. In the concluding section, B, the king, upon hearing of Little Crow's arrival at the royal grounds, invites him into the palace where he plays the khaen. This will be referred to as the first-layer pattern.

If one looks at the chart, one will see that the first smaller pattern begins in Section A2 of the larger one and concludes in Section B. This pattern will be referred to as the second-layer pattern. In Section a1 of this smaller pattern the young men inform the townspeople that they are bringing Little Crow to play the khaen before the king. In Section a2 the townspeople repeat to the king what the young men have told them, that Little Crow is being brought to play the khaen. In Section b the king, upon hearing of Little Crow's arrival, initiates a series of orders that result in the final conclusion, the playing of the khaen by Little Crow before the king.

One will notice that Section b, the third section of the smaller second-layer pattern, which is simultaneously the third section of the larger first-

290

layer pattern, is also comprised of an AAB pattern. This pattern will be referred to as a third-layer pattern. It consists of three orders issued by the king, based initially upon the information that the king has received of Little Crow's presence outside his palace. His first order is for his servants to bring Little Crow inside of the palace. His second order is for his servants to identify him. His third and final order achieves his goal: He commands that Little Crow be given a khaen to play.

Now consider the fact that the passages describing each of the king's three orders consist of AAB patterns in and of themselves. There are, therefore, three fourth-layer patterns inside of the third-layer pattern. The first of these fourth-layer patterns, the king's first order, has been described on pages 11-12 and 25-26 of this paper. It has been used to illustrate the occurrence of smaller AAB patterns inside of Section B of a larger pattern. The three-line pattern in Section B of this smaller pattern is actually a fifth-layer pattern in the context of the larger pattern as a whole.

The following chart illustrates the placement of the different layers of parallels in this pattern. Notice that the conclusion of all three major layers of parallels occurs in the the third part of the third and final fourth layer pattern.

A1)				Beginning of the first-layer pattern
A2)				
	a1)			Beginning of the second-layer pattern
	a2)			
B) b)	a1)	a1)		Beginning of the third-layer pattern and
		a2)		the first of the fourth-layer patterns
		b)	a1)	Beginning of the fifth-layer pattern
			a2)	
			b)	
	a2)	a1)		Beginning of the second fourth-layer
		a2)		pattern
		b)		
	b)	a1)		Beginning of the third fourth-layer
		a2)		pattern
		b)	Conclusion	

For the pattern's relative complexity, it is only forty-five poetic lines or approximately two sides of a single palm leaf.

3.6: The Building of Plot through the Layering of AAB Patterns

To understand how plot is structured in Lao literature one must realize that AAB patterns, rather than occurring singly, tend to be organized in groups. Three small patterns join together to form larger patterns which in turn join together to form larger patterns, and so on. We have begun to observe this phenomenon in the previous example where five layers of parallels occur in a sequence of forty-five lines. There are countless more layers in the text of an entire story, which can stretch for hundreds of pages in length.

There are two frequent ways in which patterns join together to form a larger pattern, as illustrated in the following chart:

1)		2)		
A1) a1)		**A1)**		
a2)		a1)		
b)		a2) **A2)**		
A2) a1)		b) a1)		
a2)		a2)	**B)**	
b)		b)	a1)	
B) a1)			a2)	
a2)			b)	
b)				

In the first type of layering, (which we have observed in Section B of the example on pages 27-29), three AAB patterns join together to form the three sections of a larger pattern. In the second type, Section B of an initial pattern serves as the beginning of a second pattern. Section B of the second pattern then serves as the beginning of a third. Each of the three patterns forms a section of a larger pattern.

4) REPLICATION AND ITS ROLE IN THE EVOLUTION OF LAO LITERATURE

Lao manuscripts are continually recopied both for the purpose of circulation and to preserve the texts as the leaves that they are written on begin to deteriorate. When a transcriber copies a manuscript there is no restriction on the extent to which he can change and expand upon the existing text. This provides transcribers an occasion to display their individual talent, and explains why the Lao say that their stories are the collective work of many generations. From a comparative study of six manuscripts of a popular Lao story, *Thaw Kam Ka Dam*, it appears that in a story's evolution, the expansion of text, rather than depending merely upon the whims of individual transcribers, is strongly influenced by the conventions of parallelism described in this paper. A story evolves through a) the systematic grafting of new parallel patterns onto older patterns, b) the enlargement of existing patterns, and c) the strengthening of existing parallels between statements. As a story is continually recopied, therefore, one can expect to find more and more layers of repetition and stronger parallels. This sheds some light on the original formation of such patterns. Several writers in the past have suggested that the use of parallelism is a defining style of orally composed poetry. My study, however, would contradict this. It appears that whereas the AAB pattern is an important organizational device in the composition of Lao oral folk-tales, it is the continual copying and recopying of the written literature that is responsible for the incredible intricacy of its parallel layers.

One interesting aspect of the transcription of manuscripts that is revealed by a comparative study is that the ingrained tendency to compose in layers of parallels is so strong that it is not uncommon to find transcribers who sacrifice clarity or consistency of meaning in a passage purely in order to create a well-placed parallel. In the following example, a passage has been expanded through what might be considered an unskillful usage of replication. The enlarged sequence describes the hero dressing up to take part in a procession into the capital where he is to be coronated as king. It concludes that for all his dressing, the hero is still ugly and monkey-like in appearance:[18]

1   *meua nan   som salao thaw   ka dam nauy num*
Then the beautiful-figured youth, Black Crow

2   *thaw kau   e ot nyaung   theu maw seut kham*
He adorned himself, wearing an ornamental golden bracelet

3   *an wa   som hup hay   ba thaw kau hak yang*

---

[18] The two versions of this passage are taken from different manuscripts of the story 'Thaw Kam Ka dam'. The shorter version is from the Se village temple, Suwannakhet Province, Laos. The longer version is from Naung Um Temple, Kantharawichai District, Maha Sarakham Province, Thailand.

As for his figure, it still remained ugly.[19]

In another manuscript of the story the same passage has been expanded to create the following AAB pattern:

A1)

1 *meua nan   som salao thaw   ka dam nauy num*
   Then the beautiful-figured youth, Black Crow

2 *thaw kau   e ot nyaung   theu maw seut kham   thae laew*
   He adorned himself, wearing an ornamental golden bracelet

A2)

3 *nyang nyang leuam   kajom kham sup saut*
   He put on a radiant golden crown

4 *sup saut laew   theu maw seut kham*
   After he put it on, he wore an ornamental golden bracelet

B)

5 *maen wa   kham ti luan   thang to ao op   kau day laew*
   Even if his body were encircled with pure beaten gold

6 *an wa   som hup hay   ba thaw kau hak nyang   dauk na*
   As for his figure, it would still remain ugly

The chart that follows illustrates how the text has been expanded:

A1:

1) Beautiful Black Crow   1) Beautiful Black Crow

2) Dressed up; He wore a bracelet   2) Dressed up; **He wore a bracelet**

A2:

3) He put on a radiant golden crown

4) After it was on, **he wore a bracelet**

B:

5) Even if covered in gold

3) His figure remained ugly   6) His figure remained ugly

The expansion has only been accomplished at the expense of the passage's meaning. It does not make sense for the hero to put on an ornamental bracelet, put on a crown, and then put on the bracelet for a second time. It does, however, make perfect structural sense for the composer to create a

---

[19] It may appear contradictory that the hero is described in an epithet as 'beautifully-figured' in the first line of this passage. However the story's Lao audience would understand that the hero, as the Bodhisattva, is the most beautiful of beings and that his ugly outward appearance is only a costume that will inevitably be shed in the course of the story.

parallel counterpart to the second line of the original passage. In the expanded version, the phrase 'he wore a bracelet', identically worded, is placed as a tag in the second hemistichs of the second lines of the initial two sections, A1 and A2. This binds them together, making them a parallel pair, a necessary condition for the creation of an AAB pattern. The confusion in the story-line is caused precisely by this attempt to make the two sections parallel.

As with any art, the smoothness in the placement of parallels depends upon the skill of the composer.

CONCLUSION

The purpose of this paper has been to provide a general description of a system of parallelism that is a fundamental yet over-looked convention in the composition of Lao poetic literature. Traditionally, literary knowledge within Lao society was not learned through formal classroom training in versification, but rather through years of informal exposure to literary performances that were an integral part of every-day life. Therefore, Lao parallelism should not to be considered as a strict code of rules but rather as tendencies that exert a strong influence on Lao composition. Other aspects of versification regarding *Kaun An* that have been cited by previous scholars, such as the placement of words of low and falling tones in specific positions in a verse, and the designated length of lines, verse and quatrains, are similarly best understood as fairly flexible guide-lines rather than rigidly adhered to standards of composition.

Although my study is limited to *Kaun An*, there is evidence that an appreciation of parallelism would also increase the depth of our understanding of other types of Lao narrative, including Lao oral poetry (*Phanya*), prose literature, historical chronicles, and religious texts. It can also be speculated that our knowledge of the poetic forms of other Tai-speaking people such as the Yuan, Kheun, and Leu would similarly benefit from a consideration of the role that parallelism plays as an organizational device. A comparative study of parallelism would be likely to shed further light on the relationship between the various literatures within the larger Tai tradition.

Chart of the Pattern of Little Crow going to Play the Khaen
(described in section 3.5.2.3)

A1) A group of young men invite Little Crow to the palace to play the khaen before the king

A2) The young men together with Little Crow travel to the royal grounds.

    a1) The young men inform the townspeople that they are bringing Little Crow to play the khaen before the king

    a2) The townspeople inform the king that the young men are bringing Little Crow to play the khaen before the king

B) b)   A1) The King's First Order, to bring Little Crow into the palace

        a1) The king orders his servants to bring Little Crow to the palace

        a2) The servants travel to Little Crow and tell him the king's order

        b) a1)   They lead him to the palace

            a2)   They lead him up the palace

            b)   Little Crow pays respect before the king

    A2) The King's Second Order, to identify Little Crow

        a1) The king asks his servants: "Where is Little Crow?"

        a2) The king's question is repeated by his servants to Little Crow who identifies himself

        b) The king lights a candle, identifies Little Crow, and returns to his throne

    B) The King's Third Order, to give Little Crow a khaen to play

        a1) The king orders his servants to give Little Crow a khaen

        a2) The king's servants give Little Crow a khaen

        b) Little Crow takes the khaen

(Thaw Kam Ka Dam)

MANUSCRIPTS

Story: ***Thaw Kampha Kai Kaew***, Thatum Village Temple, Tum Tai Village, Sub-District Thathum, Meuang District, Maha Sarakham Province, Thailand.

Story: *Thaw Kam Ka Dam*, Naung Um Temple, Nasinuan, Kantharawichai District, Maha Sarakham Province, Thailand.
All examples of this story in this paper, unless otherwise noted, are taken from this manuscript.

Story: *Thaw Kam Ka Dam*, Se Village Temple, Se Village, Suwannakhet Province, Laos.

Story: *Thaw Kampha Phi Nauy*, Naung Lam Jan Temple, Naung Lam Jan Village, Suwannakhet Province, Laos

Story: *Thaw Bae*, Phukhao Kaew Temple, Khong island, Champhasak Province, Laos.

Story: *Inbong*, Naung Lam Jan Temple, Naung Lam Jan Village, Suwannakhet Province, Laos.

REFERENCES

Abhay, Thao Nhouy
  1959   "Versification". In *Kingdom Of Laos: The Land Of The Million Elephants And Of The White Parasol*. Rene De Berval (ed.), France-Asie Saigon.

Finnegan, Ruth
  1977   *Oral Poetry: Its Nature, Significance And Social Content*, Cambridge: Cambridge University Press.

Fox, James J.
  1977   "Roman Jakobson And The Comparative Study Of Parallelism". In *Roman Jakobson: Echoes Of His Scholarship*. Daniel Armstrong and C.H. Van Schooneveld (eds.), Lisse: The Peter De Ridder Press.

Jit Poumisak

    1981   *Ongkan Chaeng Nam Lae Ko'khit Mai Nai Prawattisat Thai Lum Nam Cao Phraya,* Bangkok: Mai Ngam.

Lord, Albert Bates

    1960   *The Singer Of Tales* . Cambridge: Harvard University Press.

Olrik, Axel

    1965   "Epic Laws Of Folk Narrative". In *The Study Of Folklore,* Alan Dundes (ed.) Englewood Cliffs: Prentice-Hall, Inc.

Prakong Nimmanahaeninda

    1981   "Mahakap Ru'ang Thao Ba Chueng: Kansu'ksa Choeng Wikhro'" (The Thao Ba Chueng Epic: An Analitical Study). Ph.D Thesis, Chulalongkorn University.

Printed by Chulalongkorn University Printing House
March 1995, 3804-75/1,000 (2)